WEST HAM IN THE SIXTIES

The JACK BURKETT Story

By Terry Roper

WEST HAM IN THE SIXTIES

The JACK BURKETT Story

By Terry Roper

FOOTBALLWORLD

First published in England in November 2009 by

FOOTBALLWORLD

Tel: 01708 744 333
www.footballworld.co.uk
www.ex-hammers.com

©Copyright Football World and Terry Roper

Printed in Great Britain by the MPG Books Group, Bodmin and King's Lynn

Distributed by Football World
103 Douglas Road, Hornchurch, Essex, RM11 1AW, England
Email: editorial@footballworld.co.uk

ISBN 978-0-9559340-4-9

For the Burkett family

Acknowledgements

FIRST and foremost, I would like to thank Jack Burkett because without his full and unconditional support, this book could never have been written. I am also hugely indebted to Jack for the integrity with which he allowed the project to be carried out. Although he took the opportunity to read and comment on every draft chapter, he only did so to guarantee that the book was as factually correct as possible. Never once did he try to influence my interpretation of the events relating to his remarkable life. I appreciate too his help with pictures from his own personal collection, a number of which have never previously been published.

I owe special thanks to Jack's charming and delightful wife, Ann, for the interviews that she accorded me and, also, for her caring manner and kind hospitality whenever I visited the Burkett household. In truth, I was very keen to meet her because I wanted to ascertain what it was like being a footballer's WAG in the 60s when compared to their modern day counterparts. Ann's contribution forms an extremely important component of this book because her honesty and forthright views were both refreshing and compelling.

I would particularly like to thank Tony McDonald, Susie Muir and all at Football World for their generous friendship, help and support. Without them, this project would not have been possible. Also, I am greatly indebted to Brian Allan, David Gerow, Mick Harris and Chris Hunt. Their co-operation is very much appreciated.

My publishers and I would also like to thank Dave Alexander, Tim Crane, Tony Hogg, Danny Francis, Jack McDonald, Anne Walker and Terry Connelly for their practical help.

Finally, a special thanks to my wife, Maria, and also my sons, Ian and Neil, for their unequivocal encouragement throughout the writing of this book.

Terry Roper
September, 2009

Contents

Jack Burkett with the biggest honour he won in the game – the European Cup Winners' Cup, in 1965.

Introduction

JACK Burkett once admitted that he was hugely flattered to be described as "A true football man." The description is entirely accurate because he spent nearly 50 years in the professional game.

As a player, he was a classic defender, a left-back, most notably with West Ham during the unforgettable Sixties. He was swift-tackling, athletic, stylish and comfortable on the ball. Jack was a player who particularly liked to attack down the left-flank, but there were no gimmicks in his style of play. He was modest and unspectacular, but he was also the ultimate team player.

During those halcyon days, he formed an impressive partnership with the iconic Bobby Moore on the left of Hammers' defensive formation. The hugely successful West Ham side of that golden era always looked a much better and more balanced team when Burkett was in their ranks. It was a fact acknowledged on more than one occasion by Ron Greenwood, the club's legendary manager from that period.

Jack played nearly 200 league and cup games for the club alongside the World Cup triumvirate of Bobby Moore, Geoff Hurst and Martin Peters. You have to be a good player to impress in such exalted company as that.

At one time, Jack was on the verge of international honours and, if he had played in another era, then he may well have been an England regular. It is somewhat ironic that the record books are littered with the names of full-backs who have been capped by England over the years, but who were hardly in the same class.

After his playing days were over, Jack became a highly respected trainer, coach, scout and manager with a number of clubs. He travelled all over the world and worked in various countries including such football outposts as Norway and oil-rich Saudi Arabia, where he witnessed a gruesome execution when a man was beheaded. His travels also took him to Ireland at the height of the religious troubles where some players, as members of the IRA, kept guns and balaclavas in their holdalls along with their playing kit.

He also worked as an employee of the Professional Footballers' Association during which time he became a mentor to some of the most famous present day Premier League players when they were just unknown youngsters trying to make their way up the ladder to stardom.

During his years in the game, Jack experienced life at both ends of the football spectrum, notably the glory of being a 'double' Wembley winner in major cup finals with West Ham, as well as having to overcome a career-threatening injury. He also faced the harsh economic realities that afflict so many clubs. Indeed, he later teamed up with Bobby Moore again when they formed a managerial and coaching partnership at unfashionable Southend United, who had no money whatsoever.

He was assistant manager at Fulham, who were so bankrupt that the players had to take their own toilet rolls into training! The endless hours and stress involved in helping to keep Fulham afloat during that difficult period almost had fatal consequences when he had a black-out on the M6 motorway in the Midlands late one night after a scouting mission.

It was a long way from those heady days at Wembley.

However, it was the 10 years that he spent as a player at West Ham United that were the most memorable of his career. Jack is now retired and lives near Southend-on-Sea in Essex. When he reflects on those great years at Upton Park, he says: "My time coincided with the most successful period in the club's history. We won the FA Cup in 1964 and European Cup Winners' Cup in 1965 with both finals being played at Wembley. Only seven players took part in both finals – Bobby Moore, Geoff Hurst, Jim Standen, Ken Brown, Ron Boyce, John Sissons and me. We were once dubbed 'The Magnificent Seven' and I feel very privileged to be one of such a select group of players who will forever remain an integral part of West Ham's history."

Naturally, Jack's story would not be complete without reference to his personal life, away from the world of professional football. He has experienced many of life's emotions – good and bad – and yet, by his own admission, he was totally unprepared for a single, devastating life-changing moment that lay ahead of him. It came in March 2005 when he was 62-years-old. It goes very quiet in Jack's house when he recalls that fateful day.

He says: "It was when I was told by a specialist that I had a virulent form of skin cancer; a full malignant melanoma. Perhaps it was at that moment when, subconsciously, I first harboured thoughts about documenting the events of my life. As I began my battle against cancer, those thoughts began to bear fruition. It has been almost a cathartic exercise to reflect upon everything that has happened to me.

"I have been fortunate enough to enjoy a marvellous life and a fantastic time in football. It was a privilege to wear the claret and blue of West Ham. I loved the club and I loved the fans. During those years, I was proud to play for the most successful team in its history. Whatever happens in the future, it is something that nobody can ever take away from me."

This is the story of that era – West Ham in the Sixties – and, also, one of the club's unsung heroes, Jack Burkett – a true football man.

1

Burkert or is it Burkett?

THE tracing of family ancestry has become a highly popular pastime in modern society. Indeed, a recent television series entitled *Who Do You Think You Are?* followed the fortunes of several well-known celebrities as they tracked back through the years to discover details of their genealogy. At times, it was unbearably moving as some astonishing discoveries were made by the subjects of the programme and it made compulsive viewing.

In truth, most individuals would like to learn more about their antecedents. It is a fascination that everyone holds about their family roots – their own unique, personal story. Fortunately, there is now a myriad of information available via the internet, censuses and the archives of both local and national newspapers. However, anyone setting out on this long and difficult road should tread with caution because, as the television programme so admirably demonstrated, it can often be a painful and emotional journey.

Jack Burkett began such a process in the summer of 2005, long before the conception of *Who Do You Think You Are?* He says: "It is something I had wanted to do for a long time, but perhaps it was being diagnosed with cancer a couple of months earlier that was the catalyst in getting me started on the project. Suddenly, you want to do all the things that, previously, you have only merely been thinking about. To say the least, it focuses the mind when you have been given news such as that.

"I suppose the history of my family had always been a bit of a mystery to me. What I didn't realise was that the research into my ancestry would lead me to France, Ireland and Germany. It is ironic because, in later years, I lived and worked in Ireland and it played a major part in my life, but it was the German connection that would ultimately throw up the greatest surprises.

"Obviously, I knew all about my parents' background, but I wanted to go further back than that – at least, to my great-grandparents. It became a very personal journey and ended with some discoveries that stunned and shocked me."

Jack's own story began on August 21, 1942 when he was born at the Royal Free Hospital in East London within the sound of the famous Bow Bells, which means he is a true Cockney. At the time that Jack was born, the Second World War had been raging for almost three years. It was the most destructive war in history and the German bombing raids had already taken a terrible toll on London. In the

Jack's Mum and Dad's wedding day in April 1938.

cushioned existence of the 21st century, it is almost impossible to imagine the conditions and hardship that afflicted the British people, particularly Londoners, during that period.

For example, during the 'Blitz', London was bombed on 57 consecutive nights by over 200 planes of the German Luftwaffe. In these raids, the Germans used high-explosive bombs and incendiary devices to create fires that would cause further damage. Over 30,000 Londoners were killed during the Blitz alone, with thousands more maimed and injured. Huge areas of the city were reduced to rubble.

Fortunately, the younger generations have never experienced a war so close to home, although, admittedly, we have subsequently lived through the anxieties of the Falklands, Bosnia, Iraq and Afghanistan. There have, of course, been terrorist campaigns by the IRA and, more recently, religious fanatics. However, we have endured nothing to compare with the Blitz when, night after night, whole streets turned into raging infernos. It was a scenario that Burkett's father would experience on many occasions.

Jack says: "The family home was at Islington, near the Arsenal football ground. I was christened Jack William Burkett after two of my uncles who had gone off to fight in the war. It was a sort of tribute to them in case they didn't come back. I am pleased to say that both survived and they came home unscathed at the end of hostilities. I always think it is a strange coincidence that although the family home was in North London, I was actually born in Bow in the East End which is just a few miles from Upton Park – the home of West Ham – where, in later years, I enjoyed success as a footballer.

"My Dad, James Alfred Burkett, was born at Islington in 1911. He was one of 15 children. There is no doubt that life was very tough in those days. After leaving school, he started work as a lorry driver for a local company in Islington. My Mum was born Lilian Georgina Cooper at Tottenham in 1917. She worked for a nearby cigarette company. They met at a dance and got married in 1938 by which time Dad was earning his living as a car washer. My parents lived in a house at Lofting Road in Islington, near the Angel underground station but the war broke out the following year in 1939.

"Dad didn't serve in the forces, but worked as a Fire Protection Officer throughout the war in the Tottenham area. It meant that when the bombs fell and buildings were ablaze, it was his job to raise the alarm and make sure that people could get out of their houses. There was a lot of devastation in the area. After the war ended, he got a job as a sheet-metal worker at a factory in Tottenham. Throughout his life, there was always a lot of unemployment in Britain but he always managed to hold down a job of some description.

"Because of the bombing, my parents moved from Islington to Lawrence Road in Tottenham during the early months of the war. My eldest sister, Doreen, was born in 1940 and, two years later, I came into the world. My other sister, Pat, and brother, Ron, came along much later. I'm not sure why our parents thought that Tottenham was a safer bet than Islington because, soon after I was born, a bomb exploded about 100 yards further along the road. It was a lucky escape, because our house was completely undamaged, although other houses had taken a direct hit.

"I can just about remember the end of the war in 1945 and all the celebrations that took place. There were street parties – one of which was in the road where we lived. My more vivid memories relate to the years immediately after the war when I was five or six-years-old. There were a lot of bomb sites around the area and through the eyes of a young boy like me, they were exciting and fascinating places. I suppose they were our adventure playgrounds. I appreciate it must be difficult for subsequent generations to fully comprehend the devastation of war.

"I vividly remember clambering into the bombed remains of a house in our street and there was debris everywhere. I found a small chair that, miraculously, was completely undamaged and yet, there was nothing left of the house itself – just crumbled bricks and charred remnants of everything that a family once possessed. It was quite possible that people had died in there. It was a surreal situation but I had the presence of mind to carry the chair all the way home and I proudly presented it to Mum and Dad.

"There was very little money around in those days and you had to make the most of every opportunity. When I look back, I have to say that Mum and Dad were wonderful parents and I know that my sisters and brother would agree with that statement. However, it wasn't until 2005 – long after our parents had passed away – that I discovered an astonishing secret had been kept from us. It was at the time when I began to trace the family history."

Initially, Jack was surprised to discover that his mother's family originated in France, but it was his father's ancestry that generated the biggest shocks for him.

He explains: "At the very outset, I discovered that Dad's surname on his birth certificate was spelt *'Burkert'* and, yet, the marriage certificate when he married my Mum in 1938 showed it as 'Burkett.' In other words, the penultimate letter in the second version had been changed. It completely altered the pronunciation as well as its spelling.

"It shocked me straightaway. I began the painstaking process of trying to discover this anomaly in the spelling of my family surname.

"My initial reaction was that the original name *Burkert* was German-sounding and my instincts proved to be absolutely correct. I was amazed to discover that I had German ancestry in me. It transpired that my great-grandfather, Karl Ernst *Burkert*, was born in 1862 in the village of Annaburg, near Leipzig in Germany. He was a baker by profession and in 1880, he moved to England when he was just 18-years-old. It must have been a huge step for him coming to a new country in those far off days.

"He set up a bakery shop in New Cross in South London and he married an Irish girl called Susan Ann Wignall, who had the wonderful nickname of 'Topsy.' My great-grandfather became quite successful and he eventually opened five more shops in the same area.

"Unfortunately, the First World War broke out in 1914 and I was shocked and dismayed to learn that he was interned throughout the war years. In other words, because of his German nationality, my great-grandfather was automatically regarded as a prisoner of war. As a result, he was arrested and sent to prison despite the fact he had done nothing wrong and had lived here for many years.

"It was appalling to think he had come to England to make a better life for himself and, yet through no fault of his own, the country where he had settled and worked so hard to make a honest living should have treated him like that.

"He was released at the end of the war but, by that time, he was nearly 60 years of age. It was a tragic situation and it was deeply upsetting to think that such a terrible injustice had been inflicted upon him.

"He had a son, Charles William *Burkert* – my grandfather – who was born in 1884 in South London. When he grew up, he worked in the London docks and later on, he was a cellar man which meant he used to unload barrels of beer into the cellars of the pubs in London. Like his father before him, he also married an Irish girl, called Fanny Elizabeth Rose, who had gipsy origins. Amazingly, they had 15 children, one of whom was my Dad.

"My grandfather liked his drink and he was a bit of a rogue. He was also a real hard-man and always getting into trouble with the police. When he worked in the docks, a lot of stuff used to get nicked and on one occasion, he turned up at home with a chimpanzee on a lead that he had mysteriously acquired! My poor, old granny nearly had a heart-attack, but he kept the chimp for some while and had it chained up to the banister-rail in the hall.

"One night, the police came knocking on the door looking for my grandfather and he set the chimp on them. The chimp didn't have any teeth and was quite harmless, although the police didn't know that. Another time, my grandfather kept a donkey in the back garden – again, it was something that had just happened to come into his possession in the docks. He was a real character.

"When the First World War broke out in 1914, he was called up to join the British Army. He was later awarded medals because of his bravery during the conflict. It is ironic that he went off to fight the Germans while, back in Britain, his own father – my great-grandfather – had been sent to jail as an entirely innocent prisoner of war. His only 'crime' was having been born in Germany. There doesn't seem to be a lot of justice in that.

"I continued to be intrigued by the fact that the surname on my Dad's birth certificate was spelt *Burkert* – the German variation – and, yet, by the time that he married my Mum, it had been changed to Burkett. I kept hoping there must have been some mistake but, inwardly, I knew it had been done for a specific reason."

The plot was thickening but Jack's investigations eventually unearthed the truth. It transpired that his grandfather – the lovable rogue, Charles William *Burkert* – had deliberately changed the spelling of the family surname to Burkett during the 1930s. His decision was determined by events that were taking place elsewhere in Europe at the time. During this decade, Adolf Hitler and the Nationalist Socialist (Nazi) Party had gained power in Germany.

Hitler had two ambitions: to conquer the lands that lay in close proximity to his own country and, also, the neutralisation of France, Germany's sworn enemy. Hitler believed that by achieving these initial objectives, his German 'Master Race' would be able to conquer the rest of Europe and, ultimately, the whole world.

The governments of Britain and France were prepared to do almost anything to avoid further conflict with Germany, bearing in mind that the atrocities of the First World War were still vivid in most people's minds. Hence, they adopted a policy of appeasement which proved to be a catastrophic decision.

One of the few people in Britain to express vociferous protest at Hitler's intentions was Winston Churchill, who was only an MP at the time, although he would later become Britain's greatest Prime Minister. Throughout the 30s, Churchill constantly warned his countrymen of the danger that Germany presented to Britain and Europe. In Churchill's view, the enemy was well defined and allowed a clear distinction between good and evil. Sadly, few people took heed of Churchill's words, but one of those who had the foresight to consider the possible consequences was Jack's grandfather, Charles William *Burkert*.

It was against this background of unease that he took the extraordinary decision to subtly change the spelling of the family name. He may have been a rogue, but he was also a very shrewd man. He realised that if the aggression posed by Hitler and the Nazis continued to gather momentum, then it was possible that Britain and Germany could resume hostilities in yet another war. He had good reason to be concerned because he was conscious of the dreadful jailing of his own German-born father during the First World War.

He was also aware that many people living and working in Britain during that

CERTIFIED COPY OF AN ENTRY OF BIRTH
(6 & 7 WM. IV., CAP. 86).

REGISTRATION DISTRICT					ISLIN

BIRTH in the Sub-District of **Tufn**

1911.

No.	When and Where Born. (1)	Name, if any. (2)	Sex. (3)	Name and Surname of Father. (4)	Name and Maiden Surname of Mother. (5)
476	Thirtieth April 1911 65 Vorley Road	James Alfred	Boy	Charles William Burkert	Fanny Elizabeth Burkert formerly Rose

---

CERTIFIED COPY of an EN
Pursuant to the Marriage Ac

The Statutory Fee for this Certificate is 2s. 7d. If required subsequently to registration a Search Fee is payable in addition.

Registration District _Edmonton._

1938. Marriage Solemnized at _Holy Trinity Church_ in the Cou
of _Tottenham._

Columns:— 1	2	3	4	5
N. When Married.	Name and Surname.	Age.	Condition.	Rank or Profession.
241 April 30th 1938	James Alfred Burkett		Bachelor	Car Washer
	Lilian Georgina Cooper	20.	Spinster	Packer

Married in the _Holy Trinity Church_ according to the Rites and Ceremonies of the _Chur_

This Marriage was solemnized between us, { James Alfred Burkett / Lilian Georgina Cooper } in the Presence of us, { Ellen Margaret / William George

The birth and marriage certificates of Jack's father denoting the mysterious change in the spelling of the family surname – the penultimate letter has been altered.

period endured appalling abuse purely because they had German origins. Hence, Jack's grandfather was not prepared to take any further chances with a German-sounding surname that had the stigma – albeit unfairly – of the Teutonic fatherland. Basically, he wanted to protect his family from any further injustices and vilification. So he officially changed the spelling of the family name to the more-English sounding Burkett. Admittedly, it was only the slightest of changes, but it prevented any potential insinuations or accusations of a connection with Hitler's despised German nation.

In doing so, he showed remarkable foresight because in September 1939, all of Churchill's unheeded warnings about Germany's obscene intentions proved to be correct. The Nazis invaded Poland in yet another act of aggression, and as a result of that invasion, Britain declared war against Germany. Within a matter of months, most of Europe had fallen into German occupation. Britain stood alone against the threat of the Nazis and it was only when Germany attempted to invade the Soviet Union and their ally, Japan, attacked America's Pacific Fleet at Pearl Harbour, that Britain suddenly had the two most powerful allies of all.

The British people's abhorrence to anything remotely connected with Germany knew no bounds and, once again, merciless retribution was administered on many individuals living in Britain purely because they had the remotest links with Germany. The decision by Jack's grandfather to alter the spelling of their German-sounding surname made remarkably good sense.

Nevertheless, it is easy to understand Jack's sadness and frustration in discovering such an amazing fact about the family name. He admits: "I was bitterly disappointed that Dad had never told me about my German ancestry and shocked to learn the family name had been altered. He was obviously aware of this fact.

"I accept there was a lot of anti-German feeling and it continued to exist long after the war had ended.

"However, I feel it is something that should have been made known to us. It seems that part of our family heritage had been deliberately airbrushed away and completely obliterated. Dad has long since passed on and all of this only became apparent after he had died, so it was not possible to ask him about it. It remains one of the biggest regrets of my life and, even now, I feel very upset."

Ironically, there is a German 'thread' that has subsequently run throughout Jack's life. He explains: "When I was with West Ham, we always used to play pre-season tour matches in Germany. Also, the greatest night of my career came at Wembley against a German team when we won the European Cup Winners' Cup.

"Later, I briefly coached in Germany and I could have worked there in the long-term. In recent times, I owned a German short-haired pointer dog.

"I accept that these could all be merely regarded as coincidences, but I would like to think there is something more to it than that. Perhaps my dear, old grandfather – Charles William *Burkert* – has been looking down on me over the years."

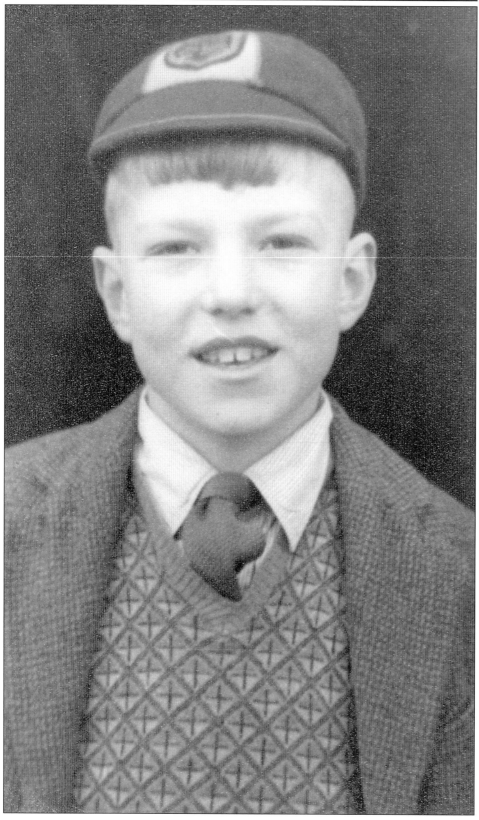

Jack aged nine, in 1951.

2

West Ham for me

INEVITABLY, as young Jack Burkett grew up in the austerity of the post-war period, he was blissfully unaware of the intrigues that existed regarding the family surname. It was an extremely happy and contented childhood despite the harsh economic conditions that prevailed in war-ravaged London.

He says: "I have great memories of family life in my early years. I think there was a great camaraderie amongst the British people at that time, basically because they had been through so much. There was food rationing and the whole country was still trying to recover from six years of war but people still seemed to be very happy. Most of them were relieved to have survived the war and they just made the best of things."

In Jack's early years, rationing was in force on such items as meat, bacon, cheese, sugar, tea and sweets. In fact, there was even less food around than during the war itself. There was no denying that times were brutally hard and this was compounded by the fact that nearly two million homes had been destroyed or severely damaged by German bombs. Britain's war debt was £3.5 billion, a staggering figure in those days, which merely added to the austerity of the nation as a whole.

Despite the hardship, Jack has clear memories about the way people set about rebuilding their lives in the aftermath of war. He says: "There were lots of parties in our family on Saturday nights and one of my uncles would always play the piano. It seemed that every house had a piano in those days. Everyone, including my own family, had grown used to facing disaster, but not giving in to it. All the kids were just immune to everything that had gone on. Basically, we didn't know any better.

"We used to play football and cricket in the street and that was my first experience of playing sport. It was a safe haven because there was so little traffic in those days. By this time, Dad had become a sheet-metal worker and he made a metal go-kart for me. I was the envy of all the other kids for miles around.

"I think kids in those days had a lot more respect for their elders and for people in authority such as schoolteachers and policemen. One of my abiding memories as a youngster was the local 'bobby' who used to walk along our street and, sometimes, he would join in our game of football. He was a big guy and as he walked away, he used to say: 'Remember, if there's any trouble, I know where you live.' It may just have been said for effect, but I don't recall any of the kids causing problems in the neighbourhood. We were all a bit fearful of him.

"Another of my childhood memories was that Dad used to keep about 40 birds in a shed in the garden. There were budgerigars, finches and canaries. One day, I decided to open the door and some of them got away. I kept quiet and my sister, Doreen, got the blame. Even today, I still have a complex about it.

"I was always very close to her – there were only two years between us and we had come through the war years together as youngsters. We got into a few scrapes and that brought us even closer.

"My other sister, Pat, was born in 1947 and my brother, Ron, didn't come along until 1957. The family home was a very happy place. I have a lot of marvellous memories of those years.

"I started school in 1947 at Downhills Infants and Juniors in Tottenham, which is where I played my first organised games of football. It is a natural progression. Suddenly, selection for the school football team becomes the first step in any young player's career. I played centre-half in those days and although I was only nine-years-old and a year younger than most of the other boys in the team, I was made captain. I became obsessed with football and on the way to school, I would even sprint between lamp-posts to improve my speed and jump up to head the leaves on trees to improve my heading ability.

"I played football at every opportunity, sometimes at Tottenham recreation ground and often against boys who were much older than me. It became a bit of a joke locally, because wherever a game of football was being played, there was a good chance that I would be involved. Even at that age, I was always looking to improve. I carried a tennis ball in my pocket and was first into the school playground each morning so that I could practice dribbling and shooting against the wall. It was an attitude that stood me in good stead during my years in the professional game.

"Like most boys, I was taken to watch football by my Dad. It was a magical time. We used to go to Arsenal with seven of my uncles and stand on the covered North Bank terracing, opposite the Clock End. We watched players like Arsenal's full-back Wally Barnes and goalkeeper Jack Kelsey, both Welsh internationals, who were big names in that era.

"There were always huge crowds in those days, most of them standing on the terraces. Young kids, including me, were often passed down over the heads of spectators, so that we would be able to get a better view from the front of the terracing. It was a frequent sight at games and, afterwards, I would meet up with my Dad and uncles.

"Despite the big crowds at Highbury, sometimes more than 60,000, there was never any trouble even though rival supporters used to stand together in the same parts of the ground. If Arsenal were playing away, Dad would often take me to White Hart Lane to watch Spurs and it was the same there – no trouble, but a fantastic atmosphere amongst the fans. Also, there was a lot of wit and humour in the crowd at that time. It is a sad fact, but I think it is something that is missing from the modern game.

"Football was in my blood because Dad's eldest brother, Charlie, was a decent

Jack (centre of the front row) as captain of Tottenham Schoolboys in June 1954.

player. When the Second World War broke out, he played a few games for Fulham in the war-time league, although he always used a pseudonym because he wasn't actually registered with them. He was in the Army but whenever he was on leave or stationed nearby, he would turn out for Fulham in the war-time league as a speedy right-winger. After the war, he played for the famous amateur side, Corinthian Casuals, so I really looked up to him.

"When I was about eight-years-old, he gave me a pair of his old boots and I suppose that was what first made me want to become a professional footballer. It is rather ironic that he should have played for Fulham, albeit during the war, because I also had a spell with the club on the coaching and management side more than 40 years later.

"I moved up into the junior school at Downhills in Tottenham and I did quite well academically, but football was my all-consuming passion. Gradually, I was beginning to make progress and got picked to play for the Tottenham Schools side. After a couple of games, I was made captain and by this time, my only ambition was to become a professional footballer.

"It is strange because it never occurred to me that I wouldn't make the grade. It was not conceit on my part, but merely naivety. At that age, you tend to think that anything is possible, although I have no idea what profession I would have gone into if I hadn't made it as a footballer.

"The teacher in charge of the Tottenham Schools team was the brother of Arthur Rowe who had been the manager of the famous Spurs 'push and run' side that won the first division championship in 1951, so he had some credibility in my eyes, if only by association with having a famous brother.

"The Tottenham Schools team was quite successful and we ended up playing in a cup final against Harrow boys at Wembley Town's ground. It was just up the road from Wembley Stadium and like all schoolboy footballers, I dreamed of playing there. We won the game 2-1 and were presented with a 'Certificate of Honour' which was signed by the former Tottenham and England wing-half Bill Nicholson, who later became the club's greatest manager. It was a strange coincidence because 10 years later, Bill tried to sign me from West Ham.

"Wherever I was playing during my schoolboy days, Dad always used to go and watch my games, usually making his way on his bike and arriving just in time for the kick-off. In later years, when I played for West Ham, he used to cycle to all the games at Upton Park and quite a few when we played away to other London teams. He liked to take his place on the terraces and never wanted a ticket in the stand.

"I passed my eleven-plus exam and went to Tottenham County High School but there were problems because it was a rugby school and they didn't play football. I was distraught. Despite my protests, I had to play rugby and ended up playing at scrum-half. But apart from the lack of football at the school, I also found I was beginning to struggle academically. All of these factors meant I was very unhappy and I became a bit of a rebel. I started refusing to join in the rugby training and I would take myself off to another part of the pitch and start kicking my tennis ball around. Ironically, I was quite good at rugby and I was picked to play in a trial match for the county side, but I refused to travel to the game. I just wasn't interested.

"In my view, it was quite simple. I wanted to play football and the more the school insisted I played rugby, the more I rebelled. Although I was attending a rugby school, I was still being picked for both Tottenham and Middlesex Schools teams at football, so I felt I had a good case in wanting to practice as much as possible. I really gave the sports teacher a hard time and he wasn't too sympathetic towards me, but that all changed one Wednesday afternoon.

"Spurs were playing in a FA Cup replay at White Hart Lane. It was the days before clubs had floodlights and games used to kick-off at 2.00pm, so that it would be finished before it got dark. I went into registration at school as normal at 1.30pm, but then I slipped away and ran down to White Hart Lane to see the game. I paid my money at the turnstile and as I was making my way into the ground, I walked straight into my sports teacher. I don't know who got the biggest shock – him or me. He stood there for a split second and said, 'I haven't seen you and you haven't seen me' and, with that, he walked away.

"He never mentioned the incident again, but his attitude towards me changed a lot after that and I felt he was a lot more understanding regarding my rebellious attitude about playing football instead of rugby.

"Fortunately, my outlet came at weekends when I sometimes managed to play three games of football. I would play for Tottenham or Middlesex Schools on a

Saturday morning and turn out for a men's team called Parkhurst FC at Wood Green in the afternoon. On a Sunday, I played for Parkhurst's youth team at Hackney Marshes, so at least I was playing plenty of football, even though it wasn't possible at school.

"In those games at Hackney Marshes, I played against some outstanding youngsters like David Webb, Rodney Marsh, Ron Harris and his brother Alan, who all went on to have successful careers in the professional game. It was a very high standard. By this time, I had switched to left-back and I felt very comfortable in that position. It also gave me the chance to attack down the left-wing and I was beginning to get some recognition in the local press.

"In fact, playing for Parkhurst's youth team gave me the first opportunity to play football on the continent. During the Easter period of 1957, we took part in a tournament in Amsterdam and one of the teams that we played against was Ajax who were the local side. At the time, nobody outside of Holland had heard of them but, in later years, they went on to become one of the greatest clubs in Europe. We reached the semi-final of that tournament and it was a good experience for me. It was another part of my football education.

"In the autumn of 1957, when I turned 15, I was spotted by Spurs whose scouts had been watching some of the Tottenham Schools games. The club contacted the teacher who was in charge of the district side and said they liked the look of me and a couple of other boys in the team. We were invited along to White Hart Lane for training with the other junior players on Tuesday and Thursday evenings. Unlike the modern game, clubs were not able to sign schoolboys in those days. It meant that youngsters could only sign for a club as they were about to leave school.

"In the meantime, clubs could ask promising schoolboys to go and train with them – as Spurs did with me – but no forms could be signed, although the youngsters were allowed to play in junior matches for the club. The training evenings and junior games gave clubs the opportunity to take a look at the young players with a view to possibly taking some of them on as ground-staff boys when they reached school-leaving age. I was excited at the prospect because Spurs were a great club and I felt my big opportunity had arrived.

"Unfortunately, my twice-weekly training sessions at White Hart Lane proved to be an unmitigated disaster. On the first night, all the youngsters got changed and we went out to the cinder track around the pitch. The Spurs' trainer,

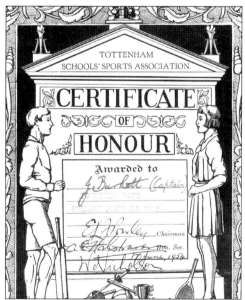

The certificate of honour that was presented to Jack when he captained Tottenham Schools at the age of 11. The last signature is that of Bill Nicholson who, 10 years later, tried to sign Jack for Spurs.

Cecil Poynton, was in charge of the session and he told us to start running laps around the track. We weren't allowed on the pitch and dear old Cecil stood there with a cigarette dangling from his mouth urging us on as we pounded out lap after lap. In the end, some of the boys got seriously fed up and started walking. We never saw a football and it was like that each evening I went to White Hart Lane.

"It was a ridiculous situation because Spurs had a wonderful tradition for playing good football and, yet, here they were denying themselves the opportunity of improving the skills and technique of some of the area's most promising schoolboys. After all, we were potentially the future lifeblood of the club, but it just went to prove that their youth policy was non-existent at the time. It was bitterly disappointing.

"Around this time, I played for Tottenham Schools in another game against Harrow. I was playing at left-back and marking their right-winger who had been making a bit of a name for himself. He was Derek Woodley who had already played for England Schoolboys. He was extremely quick and a real star.

"It transpired that West Ham's famous scout, Wally St Pier, was at the game to take another look at Derek. I had a really good game against him and, afterwards, Wally approached the teacher who was in charge of our side and asked if I would like to begin training at West Ham. When the teacher told me, I said I couldn't wait to start, but the only problem was that I had absolutely no idea where West Ham played. I knew they were based somewhere in London but that was about it.

"I didn't bother going back to Spurs and the following Tuesday evening, I managed to find out that West Ham played at Upton Park in East London. I made my way there by bus and tube train and reported for training."

At the time, Jack was not the only promising youngster who was training at West Ham. The club was in the process of discovering a whole host of young talent and it was entirely due to the foresight of manager Ted Fenton. In fact, Fenton almost had claret and blue blood coursing through his veins.

He had been born at Forest Gate in 1914. His birthplace was just a couple of miles from Upton Park and he was an outstanding schoolboy footballer. It was obvious he was good enough to make a career in the professional game and he joined Hammers as a young player in 1932. It was the year that the club had been relegated from the top sphere of English football into the old second division. Basically, the team of that period had grown old together and there were no ready-made replacements coming through the ranks. Relegation was a bitter experience, for West Ham would remain in the second division for the next 26 years.

Fenton served the club well as a player and amassed 163 league appearances scoring 27 goals, mainly from wing-half. After a spell away from West Ham during the war years and also as manager of Colchester United, he returned to Upton Park and became manager in 1950. He quickly realised that a similar situation existed to when he had first joined the club as a player all those years earlier – old players who were past their best performing in the first team with little quality in the reserves to bring comfort for the future. At the time, there were no youth or colts sections and money was scarce, so forays into the transfer market were few and far between.

PHONE: GRAngewood 0704

West Ham United Football Co., Limited

MANAGER
E. B. A. FENTON

SECRETARY
E. CHAPMAN

REGISTERED OFFICE
BOLEYN GROUND
GREEN STREET
UPTON PARK, E.13

Your Ref. ....

Our Ref. ....

21st May 1958.

J. Burkett Esq.,
27, Lawrence Road,
Tottenham. N. 15.

Dear Mr Burkett,

Thank you very much for your letter which I have received this morning.

I have spoken to Mr Fenton and Mr Robinson regarding Jack coming on the ground staff upon his leaving school, and we have decided that we will be pleased to have him with us.

Will you please let me know when Jack is leaving school.

Also, please convey to Jack, my very best wishes.

All the very best Mr Burkett.

Yours sincerely.

W St Pier

Chief Representative.

Letter from Wally St. Pier to Jack's Dad confirming that the club wanted Jack to join the ground-staff in the summer of 1958.

Above: West Ham's legendary scout Wally St. Pier who discovered a whole host of starlets, including Jack Burkett, plus Moore, Hurst and Peters.
Below: Malcolm Allison (left) and Noel Cantwell, senior pro's who did so much to nurture the youngsters through the ranks in the late-50s.

The astute Fenton decided to initiate the first ever youth policy at West Ham. His starting points were the playing fields of London and surrounding areas which were a rich and fertile breeding ground for outstanding schoolboy footballers. Arguably, Fenton's decision to instigate a youth policy at Upton Park was the most important ever taken by a West Ham manager. In the ensuing years, a whole host of young players joined the Hammers. Admittedly, some slipped through the net, most notably schoolboy starlets like Jimmy Greaves and Terry Venables from nearby Dagenham, both of whom went to Chelsea.

However, generally speaking, Fenton and his faithful chief scout, Wally St. Pier, were successfully pursuing some of London's most promising schoolboys, including 15-year-old Jack Burkett from Tottenham.

3

Early days at Upton Park

JACK reflects on the initial evenings training at West Ham: "We trained on the pitch and first team players such as Malcolm Allison and Noel Cantwell were in charge. Unlike my experience at Tottenham, there was no running. It was all ball work and I loved every minute of it.**

"Also, Ted Fenton and club secretary Eddie Chapman were there watching the training and, afterwards, they even introduced themselves to all of us. It proved to me just how much the club cared about their young players. It was a totally different environment to that which existed at Tottenham.

"Instinctively, I knew that I wanted to play for West Ham."

Burkett was instantly hooked by the training methods at Upton Park with Malcolm Allison at the helm. Without question, the charismatic Allison was the most influential player at West Ham during that period. Indeed, his impact on the club as a whole cannot be underestimated. In particular, his influence on the younger players coming through the ranks was immeasurable. Apart from Burkett, a whole host of youngsters benefited from Allison's perceptive coaching skills, especially a fair-haired defender called Bobby Moore.

Fenton had signed Allison from Charlton Athletic in 1950 and made him club captain. He was a tall, dominating centre-half and he went on to play over 250 league and cup games in the claret and blue. A master tactician and innovator, Allison was years ahead of his time in coaching and fitness routines, some of which were based on continental ideas. Initially, he was influenced by watching the Red Army team, Moscow Dynamo, training while he was doing his National Service in the army in the late-40s and then, most crucially, by the magical Hungarian team who decimated England 6-3 at Wembley in 1953. It was England's first-ever defeat on home soil by a foreign side and, for the likes of Allison, it changed his whole philosophy of football. It proved to him that football played in that manner was a game of art and beauty as well as muscular science.

Allison and his team-mate Noel Cantwell were widely regarded as the founders of the so-called West Ham Academy which originally consisted of fellow players such as Dave Sexton, John Bond, Frank O'Farrell, Malcolm Musgrove and Jimmy Andrews. They all later became highly respected managers and coaches in their own right and would acknowledge the huge influence that Allison and Cantwell exerted upon them in those formative years.

Sadly, Allison later contracted tuberculosis and had a lung removed during an operation at a London hospital when he was only 31-years-old. It brought a tragic end to his playing career but he later went on to become a high profile manager with such teams as Plymouth Argyle, Manchester City, Crystal Palace, Middlesbrough, Sporting Lisbon in Portugal and the Kuwait national side.

Noel Cantwell was born in Cork in the Republic of Ireland and joined West Ham as a 20-year-old in 1952. He had quickly established himself in Hammers' first team as a cultured left-back. Ironically, this was the position in which Burkett would succeed him in later years.

Cantwell was made captain of West Ham at the time of Allison's illness and he also captained his country. Astonishingly, Cantwell played cricket for the Republic of Ireland as well. Whilst he was less volatile than Allison on the football field, he was a player who commanded the utmost respect from team-mates and opponents alike.

Cantwell played 248 league games for West Ham and was later transferred to Manchester United in 1960 for £29,500 – a record fee for a full–back at the time. He was an extremely articulate man and, in later years, he became Chairman of the Professional Footballers' Association and also managed Coventry City and Peterborough United.

The grounding that Burkett and his contemporaries received from the likes of Allison and Cantwell during those early days was crucial to their overall development. In football terms, it would have been difficult to find two more influential and inspiring tutors, which is a fact acknowledged by Jack.

He says: "It was fantastic because it all took place on the Upton Park pitch. Malcolm was a commanding figure and the training routines that he set us were innovative and interesting. It immediately made me think about the game.

"Also, Noel was great to work with and he took a lot of interest in me. He had a unique running style with his elbows held out wide as he ran. He explained it was something he had purposely developed because it prevented opponents getting too close, thus making it more difficult to dispossess him. It was probably the best advice I was ever given and from that evening onwards, I tried to copy Noel's running style throughout my playing career. He was a fantastic player, one of the top left-backs of all time.

"I went back to Upton Park on the following Thursday evening and felt I did well. Within a couple of weeks, I played my first game for West Ham's junior side over at Wanstead in East London. One of my team-mates was a young midfielder called Ron Boyce. We formed a good friendship from that very first day and our development followed a similar pattern over the years culminating with us playing together in two Wembley cup finals.

"After I had been training with West Ham and playing in their junior side for three months, Tom Russell and Bill Robinson, who were in charge of the juniors, told my Dad they felt I had a good chance of being taken on as a ground-staff boy at the end of the season.

"West Ham were as good as their word and, in May 1958, Dad and I were told that Ted Fenton wanted to come to our house to see us. My heart was pounding as Ted

Ted Fenton got more than he bargained for on his first visit to the Burkett household.

arrived at the appointed time looking very smart in a new suit. He sat down and explained he had received good reports about me and the club were prepared to take me on as a ground-staff boy with a view to signing full professional forms when I reached the age of 17. It was the realisation of a dream – the chance to become a professional footballer – but at that precise moment, my young brother Ron, who was only a toddler at the time, managed to knock a cup of tea all over Ted's trousers. Ron's popularity was at an extremely low ebb that night!

"I couldn't wait to sign the forms but there was a problem because I still hadn't taken my 'O' levels at the time and the school tried to block my departure. Perhaps they were getting back at me for all the trouble I had caused during my rebellious years. We reached a bit of an *impasse*, but Ted wrote to the school saying he felt I had a good chance of making the grade and after some argument, the school relented.

"I signed for West Ham and officially became a ground-staff boy on July 1, 1958. It was a perfect time to join because the team had just been promoted back into the first division and there was a tremendous atmosphere around Upton Park as the club was gearing up to play in the big-time again."

If Burkett and the other new ground-staff boys had delusions that their introduction to the professional game was going to be a glamorous affair, then they were sadly mistaken.

Jack recalls: "I was told to report to Upton Park on my first day and I was also instructed to bring old clothes and a pair of boots with me – not football boots but rather like, say, walking boots. There were about 15 ground-staff boys there that morning and we all had to change into our old clothes and go onto the pitch. The groundsman was waiting and he gave each of us a garden spade.

"We discovered that our job was to dig up the whole pitch from one penalty-area to the other. We were told to keep out of the actual penalty-areas because that was his job. Also, some of the ground-staff boys had to climb up the floodlight pylons and start painting the steel girders. I managed to duck out of that one. I didn't fancy it at all. It sounds incredible to think about it now, but health and safety measures were non-existent in those days.

"I remember it well because it was the first time I met Bobby Moore who had already been on the ground-staff for a couple of years and who was about to sign

Young Hammers pay attention to trainer Albert Walker (holding ball), secretary Eddie Chapman and Wally St. Pier. The other players are (left to right): Brian Dear, John Charles, Mick Beesley, (Frank Caskey hidden), Eddie Presland, Ron Boyce, Dave Bickles (behind Presland), Derek Woodley, Roger Hugo, John Starkey, Martin Peters and Reggie Leséuf. Below: How the main West Stand looked in the early-60s after 'A' Wing had been added.

full professional forms. It was the start of a friendship that lasted for 35 years until Bobby's tragic death in 1993.

"At the time that I joined the club, Bobby was captain of West Ham's youth team and had already played for England Youth. It was obvious he had a great future in the game because, even at that age, he was very assured both on and off the field.

"Apart from Bobby, there were some other good players amongst that group of ground-staff boys, such as Geoff Hurst, Ron Boyce, Eddie Bovington, Andy Smillie, Mick Beesley, Tony Scott and Derek Woodley. I had played against Derek for Tottenham boys when Wally St Pier first spotted me. All of those players went on to play league football for West Ham which was a fantastic reflection on the club's youth policy.

"Bobby and Geoff later became World Cup winners along with Martin Peters who was a year younger than me and didn't join West Ham until the following season. Also, Eddie 'Bov' and 'Boycie' played in the 1964 FA Cup Final alongside Bobby, Geoff and me, so it was an incredibly successful group of young players.

"Amongst them was Bobby Keetch who had been a big mate of mine in the Tottenham boys' side. In the end, 'Keetchy' didn't make the grade at West Ham but he had a good career at Fulham and Queens Park Rangers.

"Arguably, the most outstanding youngster from the intake of ground-staff boys that summer was a midfield player called Micky Brooks. He had played with Keetchy and me in the Tottenham Schools team, although Micky had also played for England Schoolboys as well. If you had to put money on one player, apart from Bobby, who would have gone on to make the grade, it would have been Micky.

"He was fantastic and could do everything and, yet in the end, he was one of the few who didn't make the grade. It happens sometimes that a young player doesn't progress and his career just stalls. It is possible that Micky found the game too easy at schoolboy level because of his great skill, but you need more than that to make it in the professional game.

"Once we had dug up the pitch on that first morning, we were allowed to train on the forecourt in front of the main stand. Later that week, we had to paint the toilets in the various parts of the ground. It was a bit unpleasant because the gent's toilets were a definite health hazard.

"We also had to sweep out the old Chicken Run. It was a rickety wooden structure, a standing enclosure for the fans, which had been there since the ground was first built in the early 1900s. It is now the site of the East Stand. There used to be a lot of coins lying amongst the wooden steps where the supporters had dropped change out of their pockets. We made a few quid out of it but, looking back, it is amazing there was never a serious fire in the Chicken Run. There were hundreds of cigarette ends in there and, potentially, it was a huge fire hazard – a disaster waiting to happen.

"When one thinks back to the terrible fire at Bradford City's ground in 1985, then you have to say that West Ham were very fortunate indeed that a similar disaster hadn't occurred years earlier at Upton Park.

"Apart from the Chicken Run, I suppose Upton Park as a whole looked a bit

Ken Brown was one who had no trouble lifting heavy weights.

antiquated at the time that I joined the club. The North Bank – now the site of the Sir Trevor Brooking Stand – was an open terracing with no cover. Admittedly, the terracing on the South Bank – now the Bobby Moore Stand – was partly covered but those fans standing at the front always got a good soaking whenever it rained.

"I always thought that the Main Stand – now the imposing Dr. Martens Stand – looked a bit odd because it only stretched along two-thirds the length of the pitch. It seemed they had just stopped building it and the last third was missing. At least there was a standing enclosure under the main stand that did stretch the whole way along the touch-line. Later on, the North Bank was covered and the main stand extended but, apart from that, the ground remained unaltered throughout my time with the club.

"Obviously, it bears no resemblance to the modern stadium that exists today. The only thing that hasn't changed over the years is the position of the players' tunnel.

"The menial tasks that we had to do as ground-staff boys were all part of the process at the time. It is different now and the young Academy players in the modern game do not have to do any chores at all apart from looking after their playing kit. Obviously, they are a lot more cushioned and, while I don't think that is a bad thing, I believe the environment in which I grew up, along with the likes of Bobby Moore and Geoff Hurst, served us in good stead and definitely kept our feet on the ground.

"These days, promising young players who have only just started out in the game have diamond-studded ear-rings, nice cars and boot deals. I don't have a problem with that but I think it sometimes detracts from their hunger to succeed. Perhaps that is part of the reason, together with the influx of foreign players, why so few outstanding English-born youngsters are progressing through the ranks into the Premier League.

"During my early days at Upton Park, it took us a month or so to finish all the jobs around the ground. After that, we began full-time training, although we still had to get out all the training-kit for the entire playing staff and, afterwards, we had to pack it away again. We had to deliver it to the ladies who worked in the laundry at the ground, so it could be washed and dried in time for the following days training.

"In those days, ground-staff boys were paid £8 per week and we had to go to the office at Upton Park each Friday to collect our money. I suppose it wasn't too bad because I believe the average wage in British industry at the time was around £10 a week.

"On my first 'pay day', I opened up the envelope and discovered that after paying tax and national insurance, I was still £1 short of what I should have received. So were all the other new ground-staff boys. When we queried it, we were told the club was holding back £1 per week as savings for us. Although I wasn't too happy about it at the time, it did instil a good discipline in terms of saving for the future. Later on, after signing professional forms and progressing through the ranks, I always added to the money that the club held back as savings for me. In fact, that 'pot' of money ended up being the deposit on my first house when I got married."

Clearly, it was a good arrangement for Burkett and the other young players at West Ham knowing that they would have a small 'nest-egg' even if they did not ultimately make the grade. The person behind the players' savings arrangement was Jack Turner whose unofficial title was 'Property Manager', although he was not directly employed by the club. Admittedly, he had a small office at Upton Park and he did a good job in giving the players invaluable advice about various financial matters such as pensions, savings and mortgages. In effect, he was one of British football's first agents – albeit on an unofficial and part-time basis – although, in due course, he formally acted on behalf of Bobby Moore. If he had lived in the modern era acting for the multi-millionaire Premier League players, it is likely that the shrewd Jack Turner would have ended up a very wealthy man indeed.

Despite the inspired coaching from the likes of Allison and Cantwell, there were other aspects of West Ham's training that, perhaps, should have been disregarded in terms of influences upon the young players. Jack smiles as he recalls those days saying: "Some of the youngsters like Andy Smillie, Eddie Bovington, Mick Beesley and myself were good athletes and we were always up front in the pre-season road runs.

"We used to train at a place called Grange Farm at Chigwell, in the Essex countryside. Ted Fenton would send us off on these runs around the leafy lanes and it would be a tough six-mile run taking in some steep hills. It was great for stamina-building. Andy, Eddie, Mick and me would be really bombing along and we would get back to Grange Farm dripping with sweat.

"What we couldn't understand was that some of the first team players, like John Bond and John Dick, had always beaten us back to the finish. They would be standing there waiting for us to appear and when everyone had completed the run, Ted would say 'well done' to those players who were first home. We felt really upset with ourselves because we were young and enthusiastic and wanted to make a good impression.

"In fairness, 'Bondy' and John were not exactly the greatest athletes in the world and we just couldn't fathom out how they kept beating us. We were so naïve at the time and it was only later that we discovered they used to take massive short cuts, often knocking three or four miles off their own runs. Sometimes, they would even catch a bus! Apparently, when the bus used to pass the rest of us, Bondy and John would duck down behind the seats, so that we couldn't see them.

"They were real characters and, despite their hatred of running, they were great players for West Ham."

Burkett acknowledges it was a good time to have joined West Ham because, under Fenton's management, they had become one of the most forward-thinking and innovative clubs in English football. He recalls: "Ted had introduced weight-training which was very new in those days. West Ham were the pioneers of using weights in football and Ted brought in Bill Watson, a former weight-lifting champion, to oversee the training. Some of the older, bigger built players like Ken Brown or Noel Cantwell, would often perform 30 squat jumps while holding two 15lb dumb-bells. That took a huge amount of stamina. On the other hand,

Johnny Dick thunders a shot towards the Arsenal goal, watched by Tony Scott. Dick wasn't the best trainer but he is among the all-time great West Ham goalscorers.

youngsters like myself would have to lift lighter weights but, on a pro-rata basis, the effect on the body was the same.

"At the time, weight training was good for the younger players because it did give us more bulk and strength. However, with the benefit of hindsight, I now wonder if it was such a good idea because in later years, quite a few of the young players such as Geoff Hurst, Martin Peters, Ron Boyce and myself, all had trouble with lower back injuries.

"I got a serious back injury playing in a game against Birmingham City in 1965. It nearly ended my career and still causes me problems to this day. I have often thought there may have been a connection with the lifting of heavy weights at such an early stage of our development.

"Even so, Ted was an often under-rated manager because he always wanted to bring new ideas to the club. There was one occasion when he brought a trampoline into the gymnasium at Upton Park. His basic thinking was that it would help develop leg muscles and balance. We did a lot of strength work in the gym in those days and, sometimes, we would have to work in pairs and throw medicine balls to each other. These were very heavy and it would be OK for a big guy like Ken Brown, but when he threw the ball at a youngster like me and I had to catch it and throw it back at him, well, that took a bit of doing.

"However, Ted's routines obviously worked because, under his management, West Ham's players were super-fit and it was a very successful period in the club's history.

"Also, until that time, teams had always worn baggy shirts and long shorts. It is a

WEST HAM UNITED

1958-59

Jack Burkett's first season as a Hammer

This picture was taken at West Ham's training ground at Grange Farm, Chigwell in Essex just prior to the 1958-59 season – just a month after Jack Burkett had signed as a ground-staff boy.
Back row, left to right: Fred Cooper, Vic Keeble, John Dick, Brian Rhodes, Ernie Gregory, Stephen Earl, Malcolm Pyke, Joe Kirkup, Bobby Moore.
Second row: Mick Newman, Andy Malcolm, John Lyall, John Cartwright, Harry Obeney, Harry Cripps, Doug Wragg, Malcolm Allison.
Third row: Albert Walker (trainer), Bill Robinson (trainer), John Bond, Noel Cantwell, Andy Nelson, A.N. Other, Mick Beesley, Tony Scott, Geoff Hurst, Pat O'Mahoney, Andy Smillie, Mike Grice, Ken Brown, Bill Lansdowne, Bob Curry, A.N. Other, Harry Butler, Ted Fenton (manager).
Front row: Jack Burkett, Derek Woodley, Micky Brooks, Bobby Keetch, John Smith, Billy Dare, Malcolm Musgrove.

style which, admittedly, has come back into fashion but Ted changed all of that in the late-50s. He introduced a more athletic strip at West Ham with a tight-fitting V-necked shirt and abbreviated shorts.

"Despite this, it seemed to me that he never really got involved with a 'hands-on' approach in terms of coaching. That was left to the likes of Malcolm Allison, Noel Cantwell and, to a lesser extent, John Bond. Perhaps Ted realised that he was lucky to have so many aspiring coaches amongst his playing-staff and he just let them get on with it.

"All the ground-staff boys treated the first team players with a lot of respect. I suppose we were slightly in awe of them, but they usually treated us well. We weren't allowed in the first team dressing-room unless we knocked on the door and someone said 'come in.' There was always the usual banter, but it was never malicious and I think Ted had instilled a good discipline within the club.

"He was very strict, particularly with the young players. I would never step out of line with him. During the war years, he had been an army PT instructor in Africa and Burma and this was reflected in the way he handled himself as manager of West Ham. I was a bit frightened of him. One or two of the young lads had to go to his office because they had been messing around during training and got a dressing-down, but it never happened to me.

"The ground-staff boys were each 'given' four first team players to look after throughout the season. Basically, we had to attend to them in terms of laying out their training kit each morning and collecting it up afterwards. We had to take their dirty kit to the laundry room, so that it could be washed overnight and then we would repeat the process the following morning. We had to clean their boots each day and also in readiness for Saturday's game.

"In my first season, I had to look after Noel Cantwell, Malcolm Musgrove, Bill Lansdowne and Fred Cooper. It was good because you began to build up relationships with the first team players and, sometimes, they would give you a pair of boots as a way of saying 'thank you.' If you forgot something, though, they would certainly let you know all about it.

"As ground-staff boys, we had to attend first team matches at Upton Park unless, of course, we were still travelling back from one of our games in the colts' side which were usually played on a Saturday morning. The reasons were two-fold. Firstly, it was regarded as part of our football education to watch the first-team and, secondly, it was our job to clear up the dressing-rooms after everyone had gone home and wash the baths out. Again, it was a great learning curve for all the young players and it was another way of getting integrated into the club."

The first six weeks of Jack Burkett's career at West Ham as a ground-staff boy had been enlightening but now the season was about to start in earnest. It would mark the beginning of an extraordinary journey for him.

4

The winds of change

JACK began his West Ham career in the colts' side playing alongside the other ground-staff boys such as Geoff Hurst, Ron Boyce, Eddie Bovington, Derek Woodley, Micky Brooks and Bobby Keetch. However, he admits those early games put a doubt in his mind about making the grade in the tough world of professional football.

He recalls: "Straightaway, I found myself playing against youngsters at clubs like Arsenal and Chelsea who were invariably a year older and who appeared so much stronger and fitter than me. I wondered if I would have the necessary strength and stamina. I was riddled with self doubt but, once again, it was Noel Cantwell who set my mind at rest. He always remained one of my greatest mentors.

"He was aware of my concerns and one day after training, Noel took me to one side and said: 'Don't worry. These opponents are at least 12 months older than you and that is a huge amount of time at this stage of your development. I guarantee you will get stronger with each day's training, not necessarily in your build, but in terms of your stamina, which will let you cope more easily with bigger and stronger teams.

"He added: 'At the age of 16, you don't have the physical presence to impose yourself on other players but you must have patience because that is exactly what will happen in due course.'

"Noel was absolutely spot-on because, as the weeks and months progressed, I found I was getting fitter and stronger. Clearly, the intense training on a daily basis plus the use of weights meant I was beginning to impose myself on opponents and I felt more confident as a player because of it."

Fenton took a keen interest in the physical development of his young players and he seemingly encouraged Burkett to take supplements in order to build himself up.

Jack explains: "Ted said he had 'some little white powder' that he wanted me to take home to my Mum. She had to sprinkle it on my food over the course of several weeks. It was like a calcium powder which, supposedly, would give me more strength. I don't know if there was anything dodgy in the powder, but the taste of it was absolutely disgusting. I have no idea if it had any effect or not, but perhaps it was just as well that there were no drug tests in that era!"

Irrespective of Fenton's secret potions, one outstanding aspect of young Burkett's play as left-back in the colts side was his ability to advance down the left flank and add support to his team's attacking options. In modern times, it has become a necessity for wing-backs to get forward from deep positions, but in the late-50s, this was something new in the British game.

Jack says: "For years, full-backs were very static and rarely ventured over the half-way line. Their job was purely defensive and all they had to do was nullify the threat of the winger who they were marking. It was great full-backs such as Manchester United's Roger Byrne, who died in the Munich air crash in 1958, and the Brazilian World Cup winner Nilton Santos, who completely changed the thinking about full-back play.

"West Ham were very instrumental in this revolution because it would have been difficult to find two more attack-minded full-backs than John Bond and Noel Cantwell from that era. This change to a more attacking style of full-back suited me down to the ground and it was a perfect time to break into the professional game."

Burkett could easily monitor the way the club viewed his progress in his first six months as a ground-staff boy because West Ham issued a report on December 31, 1958 – rather like a school-report – which was sent directly to his parents at home. All the parents of Hammers' young players received a similar document and it was indicative of Fenton's forward-thinking when it came to youngsters coming through the ranks.

Interestingly, Burkett's attitude to the game was described as 'conscientious' while it was also noted he needed to 'get stronger in the tackle.' Jack now looks back on that report and says with a smile: "It must have been issued before Ted's white powder began to take effect!"

It was shortly afterwards that all the heavy work with weights and medicine balls began to pay off. Just as Cantwell had predicted, Burkett was indeed becoming more aggressive and assured. He says: "It was just after Christmas 1958, which was half-way through my first season with the club. The West Ham youth team got involved in a good run in the FA Youth Cup and, suddenly, I was playing at famous grounds such as Villa Park and Highbury in front of relatively large attendances.

"In those days, youth team football was always well supported. I was beginning to feel part of a big club. I thought my form was good and, at the end of the season, we reached the FA Youth Cup final against Blackburn Rovers which was played over two-legs.

"They had some outstanding players, such as Mike England who later went on to have a great career with Spurs and Wales. Also, Keith Newton and Fred Pickering played for Blackburn in that final and later in their careers, they were both capped by England with Keith playing in the 1970 World Cup in Mexico.

"We drew the first leg 1-1 at Upton Park but we should have won it on the night because Andy Smillie was unlucky to miss a penalty. Unfortunately, that miss proved to be crucial because they beat us 1-0 in the second leg to take the trophy 2-1 on aggregate.

"We felt really sick at the end and Bobby Moore was particularly upset about the result. At the end of the season, we took part in an international youth tournament in Switzerland and finished in third-place against such teams as local side FC Zurich and Verona from Italy. Again, it proved to be a good experience, but my over-riding memory of that tournament was the form of Bobby.

"At the time, he was playing centre-half, but he always seemed to have so much time on the ball and his distribution was immaculate. He never wasted a pass and, although he was only 17-years-old, he still had an imposing presence.

"Bobby was fairly quiet as a youngster and tended to keep himself to himself but he was a prodigious trainer. It was also noticeable that when we were training with the senior players, he was always listening and picking up on things, particularly from Malcolm Allison and Noel Cantwell.

"He could see and interpret everything that was happening on the pitch in front of him. Bobby was always looking for space so that he could make a pass into it for a team-mate. He was also a great interceptor, one of the best of all time and that was an outstanding facet of his play, even in those early years."

When the West Ham youngsters returned home from their trip to Switzerland, Fenton told Jack that if he continued to make progress and worked on his strength and fitness, there was every chance that he would be taken on as a full professional the following season. Jack went off for the close season break in a good frame of mind. He has clear recollections of that summer of 1959 because he took a temporary job outside of football in order to supplement his meagre earnings. It was standard procedure for many professional footballers in those days and it was synonymous with the austerity of that period.

Some Hammers' players worked at the local City of London cemetery at Manor Park, digging graves and tending to the gardens. Others, like Jack together with Bobby Moore, Eddie Bovington, Andy Smillie and Tony Scott, worked at a company called William Warne Ltd who had business premises in Barking.

Jack recalls: "Bobby's mum used to work there or, at least, she had some connections with the company and she got us the summer work. It was a rubber factory and it was very close to Bobby's home in Waverley Gardens. We would go back to Bobby's place after we had finished work. His mum and dad were lovely people and they never changed, even when he became captain of England."

As Burkett's second season with the club – the 1959-60 campaign – got under way, he celebrated his 17th birthday and awaited the opportunity to become a fully fledged professional. It was at this time that several of the older ground boys, including Moore and Smillie, had subsequently been taken on as full professionals, thus leaving room for a new set of recruits to join the ground-staff. Amongst the newcomers were two local youngsters who had played together in the England Schools side the previous season. One was a robust winger-cum-striker called Brian Dear, from East Ham, and the other was a tall, lean midfielder from Dagenham who had a delightful elegance about him even at that tender age. His name was Martin Peters.

Jack reflects on his first sighting of the gifted Peters: "In many ways, Martin was a bit like me a year earlier because he looked a bit weaker than the rest of the ground-staff boys. It was obvious he was going to have to work on his strength and stamina but what set him apart from the others was his fantastic touch. It was clear from the outset that he had a superb football brain.

"I always think Martin was the player who typified everything about West Ham's style of football. In my opinion, he was the most technically gifted of the three World Cup heroes.

"There is no doubt that Bobby and Geoff had to work on their games before they became great players. It only happened when they changed positions because Bobby was originally a centre-half and then a wing-half. It was only later in his career when Ron Greenwood, who succeeded Ted Fenton as West Ham's manager, switched him to a slightly deeper role, playing alongside the centre-half, that he achieved greatness for West Ham and England.

"Similarly, Geoff was also a wing-half and while he was good going forward, I think even he would say that he didn't know how to defend properly. When the ball was behind him, he just didn't seem to know where it was. Again, it was only when Ron switched him to a front-running role that he developed into a world class striker."

When all of the ground-staff boys had finished our jobs on the first day back, we linked up for training with the rest of the playing staff. It meant that day in July 1959 was the first time the trio of Moore, Hurst and Peters had met up and trained together. I don't suppose that even in their wildest dreams, they could have envisaged that they would be World Cup winners within seven years. It puts into perspective the fantastic scouting regime that Ted Fenton had installed at the club.

Burkett was suitably buoyant regarding Fenton's earlier comments about being taken on as a full professional. His start to the new season was impressive as he performed well in the third team that participated in the highly competitive Metropolitan League. Soon afterwards, he made his reserve team debut and more than justified his inclusion with a series of good displays.

In West Ham's match day programme against Leeds United at Upton Park on September 5, 1959, there was a brief report on the previous reserve match against Leicester City which stated: 'Jack Burkett fought hard to keep out the Blues.' It was only a brief mention but it proved that his career was moving in the right direction and his progress was being well monitored from within the club.

He had become a fiercely determined defender and had adopted a tactic early in his career which stood him in good stead.

Jack explains: "As a left-back, it was part of my job to stop the opposing outside-right from playing. I don't say it was necessary to use unfair means but it was me against him and in the first few minutes of any game, I always made sure that I got in a good, solid challenge. In other words, he knew I was going to be breathing down his neck throughout the game.

"In those days, referees used to give defenders the benefit of the doubt if you happened to misjudge a tackle in the opening minutes, so there was always a margin for error."

In the early weeks of the 1959-60 season, Burkett's excellent displays brought the ultimate reward when he signed full professional forms. Again, the subsequent West

Ham match-day programme against Blackpool at Upton Park on October 24, 1959 marked the occasion with the words: 'We take this opportunity of welcoming Jack Burkett to our professional staff . . . Jack has played in our Combination side several times this season and we expect him to have a promising future.'

In the modern era of extortionate wages being paid by Premier League clubs, even to young players, it is worth noting that Burkett's income at West Ham when he signed as a full professional was increased to a miserly £10 a week less tax and National Insurance as well, as the £1 that the club deducted for their players as 'savings for a rainy day.' Nearly 50 years later, Ashley Cole was famously quoted in his autobiography as saying Arsenal, his club at the time, were 'taking the piss' by offering him the derisory amount of £55,000 per week. So he left Arsenal and joined Chelsea for a wage that, presumably, was more to his liking.

Admittedly, Cole was an established England international at the time but it does make one wonder if modern day players have any sense of reality.

Despite Jack's obvious potential in the autumn of 1959, it should be said that first division football was still a distant dream. There was still a long way to go before he could be considered for first team action and there were some considerably more experienced players all vying for selection in the league side.

Nevertheless, his continued progress was confirmed with a call-up for training with the England youth team at Lilleshall. Amongst his team-mates at those training sessions were the ebullient Terry Venables of Chelsea and cultured Chris Lawler of Liverpool. In the end, Burkett missed out on an England youth cap.

He explains: "I played in a couple of representative games for England Youth but they weren't against countries and they couldn't be classified as proper internationals. It was disappointing to get so close to winning a cap but not the end of the world."

However, his career was about to take a big step in terms of progress at West Ham. There was a chain of events that occurred at the club around this time that would slowly and, inextricably, lead him to making the breakthrough into the first team. Burkett had no control over those events and it was still necessary for him to demonstrate that he possessed the requisite ability to succeed.

Meanwhile, the winds of change were about to blow through Upton Park and it would result in sweeping changes at a club where, in the past, such dramatic events were almost unknown. The Hammers were about to experience their very own *annus horribilis*.

The spectacular fall-out that followed would ultimately play a major part in Jack's progression to becoming a first team regular. It forms an integral part of his story and, hence, it is necessary to briefly reflect on the events that took place at Upton Park during that period.

Jack recalls: "I knew it was going to be very difficult to get into the league side because the players in front of me for the left-back position were club captain Noel Cantwell and also, playing regularly in the reserves, was another youngster called John Lyall. He was a couple of years older than me. John was a good player who was very hard and had a great left-foot."

WEST HAM UNITED FOOTBALL CLUB

YOUTH REPORT FORM

SEASON 19*58*/*59*.

REPORT ON *J. BURNETT* Date *DEC 31*

AGE *16* years *4* months

ATTENDANCE AT TRAINING SESSIONS *Groundstaff*. Out of possible

APPEARANCES: RESERVES "A" TEAM *3* COLTS *16* JUNIORS

ATTITUDE TO TRAINING:

Very Keen

Signed:

ATTITUDE TO THE GAME:

Conscientious.

Signed: *Stan Wilcockson*

PROGRESS IN (a) Skills: *Ball control. Style. Accuracy*

(b) The Game

Steady

WEAKNESSES IN (a) Skills: *Recovery. Aggression.*

(b) The Game

Too placid.

PHYSICAL DEVELOPMENT:

Weight on *Aug* : *9* st. *7* lbs. Height on *Aug* : *5* ft. *8¾* ins.

Weight on *Dec* : *9* st. *11* lbs. Height on *Dec* : *5* ft. *9* ins.

REMARKS:

Jack has made very good improvement this season. Progress — Skill is good. Must get stronger — try tackle

Youth Section Manager

ADDITIONAL REMARKS: John has made the right sort of progress for his first year. Now he must not rest on his laurels, and must now work hard on all his weaknesses so there will be no doubt when it comes to the important time of professional football.

G. Fenton
Club Manager

The report sent by West Ham to Jack's parents on December 31, 1958. Ted Fenton's comments are shown under the heading 'Additional Remarks'.

In the early months of the 1959-60 season and led by the inspirational Cantwell, West Ham were playing like champions-elect. By mid-November, they were top of the league. However, a shattering 7-0 defeat at Sheffield Wednesday in late November sent Hammers into freefall. An appalling run of results followed including a 6-2 reverse at Blackburn Rovers, a 5-2 home defeat at the hands of the eventual champions Burnley and, worst of all, a shocking 5-1 defeat to second division Huddersfield Town in a third round FA Cup replay at Upton Park.

This was no mid-season 'wobble' – it was an earthquake. West Ham plummeted down the table and, at one time, they were in severe danger of being dragged into a relegation battle.

It was an astonishing downturn in their fortunes considering their earlier lofty position. It would be churlish to suggest that Fenton was panicking but he made a staggering nine changes in one game which was still lost. In another, he played full-backs Bond and Cantwell in attack. Inevitably, another morale sapping defeat duly followed and Hammers' first team squad were becoming seriously disillusioned, not only by their poor form, but also by the tactics that they were being asked to play by their manager. It seemed that overnight, they had become tactically naïve and anachronistic. However, if it were possible, things were about to get considerably worse for all concerned.

West Ham lost yet another game, this time to Newcastle United at Upton Park on February 20, 1960. It became one of the most infamous games in the club's history. Hammers quickly found themselves 3-0 down with two of the goals being of a notoriously 'soft' variety. Despite the score-line and roared on by their remarkably loyal fans, West Ham fought back to level at 3-3 early in the second-half, only for Newcastle to be allowed to score two more soft goals and run out 5-3 winners.

Within a few days, dark rumours began to circulate about match-fixing and the Fleet Street press-boys smelt blood. Unfortunately, some of it was the claret and blue variety. In fact, two games played on February 20 were coming under scrutiny – West Ham United v Newcastle United and Brentford v Grimsby Town. The bookmakers were complaining bitterly that large amounts of the 'smart money' had been placed on both Newcastle and Grimsby just prior to their respective kick-offs.

The inference was clear and in the case of Newcastle's win at Upton Park, there were serious questions being asked about the nature of the visitor's goals.

West Ham closed ranks and there was a wall of silence from the club. A curt 'no comment' was the best that the hovering press hordes could obtain. Ted Fenton later said: "The board of directors and myself decided to take no steps about the whole disgusting affair. We decided to let it blow over as quickly as possible and when the bookies stopped squealing at their losses and paid out, we thought that we were right."

Fenton's comments were fair enough in retrospect but the silence at the time was the whole essence of the problem and merely added fuel to the flames that were getting dangerously out of control. If West Ham had immediately rebuffed the allegations with a firm denial, then the rumours may have been quashed forever.

However, it seemed the club merely wanted to defuse the situation and hope that the problem would 'go away', but the match-fixing rumours continued for many years thereafter. It was a stigma that West Ham and some of their players could well have done without. It is a fact that there was match-fixing in that era. Indeed, three Sheffield Wednesday players – Peter Swan, Tony Kay and David 'Bronco' Layne – were later found guilty of such a crime in a game involving their own club and were sent to prison for their misdemeanours.

Sadly, it ultimately transpired that the rumours surrounding West Ham's game against Newcastle were not without foundation. In later years, it was confirmed by a player who was with the club at the time that the 'sting' did take place and that more than one player profited from the fix. Their 'windfall' for throwing the game amounted to £100 each. It was hardly a fortune even when compared to their legitimate earnings which were limited to £20 a week at the time, due to the restrictions of the maximum wage. It was a dark day in West Ham's history.

Jack recalls: "There were definitely some rumours going around the club at the time and one player, in particular, had been mentioned. I had only managed a few games in the reserves by this point and I was still a young player. Therefore, I certainly didn't have the audacity to discuss the matter with any of the senior players. The youngsters talked about it amongst ourselves but we tended to disregard it because we didn't think anything 'dodgy' could have happened. Obviously, we now know that was not the case."

Unfortunately, it is a sad fact that football has been tainted a number of times over the years by the stigma of match-fixing. Apart from the West Ham v Newcastle travesty and the demise of Swan, Kay and Layne at Sheffield Wednesday – all, admittedly, nearly half-a-century ago – the game continues to be similarly affected, even in the modern era. There have been football corruption investigations in more than a dozen countries including Austria, Greece, Czech Republic, Slovakia, Portugal, South Africa, Vietnam, Finland and China. Even Brazil – the greatest football nation of all – has been similarly tainted with such scandals. Also, the reputation of Italy's *Serie A* was seriously dented when Italian police implicated giants Juventus, AC Milan, Fiorentina and Lazio in a ring of deception where 'sympathetic' referees were assigned to certain matches.

Even so, it is reassuring to hear Jack's comments when he says: "Clearly, these things do go on but, generally speaking, I believe the majority of people who work in football are basically honest. I spent nearly 50 years in the game working in various parts of the world and, apart from West Ham's match against Newcastle in 1960, I personally never heard of any individual being involved in such a thing."

As confirmed by Jack during his recollection of events surrounding the Newcastle game, all rumours at the time were purely speculative. Nevertheless, it should be acknowledged that the effect on West Ham's morale as a whole was considerable. Fortunately, they managed to scramble to safety and finished in 14th position but two of their saviours were youngsters Bobby Moore and Joe Kirkup who had established themselves in the team during this bleak period. Whilst their outstanding form was crucial in halting the immediate slide, it could not prevent irreparable damage to the team's form in the longer term.

To say the least, confidence amongst the players was at an all-time low and this was confirmed by the astonishing fact that they went 11 months without gaining a single away point. It was an appalling run of results by any standards. At least their form at Upton Park was reasonable, which was their saving grace.

By now, there were a number of seriously disgruntled players at the club and this, coupled with the team's poor form, meant that the sand was shifting ominously beneath the feet of manager Ted Fenton. One of the repercussions that came about as a result of the growing unrest was the notable and surprising departure of club captain Noel Cantwell. After eight years loyal service, the Irishman felt he had gone as far as he could with West Ham and was duly transferred to the somewhat more glamorous Manchester United. Hence, the biggest single barrier to Jack's potential progress to the first-team had suddenly left the club.

The natural successor to Cantwell for the left-back position was 20-year-old John Lyall who had shown some good form when he first got into the side in February 1960. Unfortunately, Lyall had already begun to suffer a series of knee injuries, which ultimately restricted him to just 30 league appearances. Sadly, he would be forced to quit the game due to the recurring knee problems that continued to plague him throughout his all-too-brief career. No doubt, in later years, the immensely likeable Lyall found solace in the fact that he became one of West Ham's greatest managers.

Jack vividly recalls the night when Lyall sustained his very first knee injury and which, arguably, was the catalyst for all the problems that followed culminating in his premature retirement. He says: "West Ham were playing Arsenal in a meaningless Southern Floodlit Cup tie at Upton Park and Tommy Docherty, who was playing at wing-half for them, caught him with a really late tackle. John stayed on the field but he spent the rest of the game limping on the left-wing. There were no substitutes in those days. It was the beginning of the end of his career."

Burkett's path to the first team was beginning to open up before him, ostensibly due to Cantwell's departure and the misfortune which had befallen Lyall, plus his own good form in the reserves. However, there was another major event that was about to take place at Upton Park. Not only did it change the status of the club forever, but it also had a profound effect on Burkett's career. Manager Fenton was sacked in March 1961 after 11 years in charge.

Jack admits: "It was a huge shock. Admittedly, the first team were struggling in the lower half of the table but I don't think any of the players saw it coming."

West Ham dispensing with the services of their manager was big news. At the time, Fenton was only the third manager in the club's 61-year history, so it was inevitable that it would create many headlines in both the national and local press. To this day, Fenton's departure has never been satisfactorily explained. It is most likely that he paid the ultimate price for his team's failure to recover from their spectacular collapse the previous season, which had not been helped by the furore concerning the on-going rumours about the players' match-fixing scandal against Newcastle.

The board of directors felt a change at the top was necessary but it is doubtful if anyone connected with the club – players, officials and fans alike – could ever have envisaged the dramatic improvement that was about to take place in Hammers' fortunes with the appointment of Fenton's successor.

His name was Ron Greenwood.

WEST HAM IN THE SIXTIES

Above: West Ham's youth team in 1958-59. Back row, left to right: Eddie Bovington, Micky Brooks, Jack Burkett, Frank Caskey, Harry Cripps, Bobby Moore. Front: Derek Woodley, Andy Smillie, Mick Beesley, John Cartwright, Tony Scott. Geoff Hurst replaced Brooks in the FA Youth Cup final against Blackburn Rovers. Below: Some famous names of the future on the team-sheet for the first leg of that final, on April 27, 1959.

WEST HAM UNITED Colts

Colours: Claret Jerseys with Light Blue Sleeves and Collars, White Shorts

1
F. CASKEY

2
H. CRIPPS

3
J. BURKETT

4
E. BOVINGTON

5
R. MOORE

6
G. HURST

7
D. WOODLEY

8
J. CARTWRIGHT

9
M. BEESLEY

10
A. SMILLIE

11
T. SCOTT

Referee: Mr. W. CLEMENTS (West Bromwich)

Linesmen: Mr. A. J. STURGEON (Red Flag) and Mr. A. J. STEWART (Yellow Flag)

11
P. MULVEY

10
P. DALY

9
J. JERVIS

8
A. BRADSHAW

7
B. RATCLIFFE

6
V. LEACH

5
K. NEWTON

4
M. ENGLAND

3
F. PICKERING

2
D. WELLS

1
B. GRIFFITHS

BLACKBURN ROVERS Colts

Colours: Blue and White Halves, White Shorts

ANY ALTERATIONS IN PUBLISHED TEAMS WILL BE ANNOUNCED THROUGH THE PUBLIC ADDRESS SYSTEM

5

Under the Greenwood tree

NEARLY 50 years after the event, Jack admits to being saddened at the departure of Ted Fenton: "It was a big blow to me and a lot of other players as well because it was Ted who had brought us all to the club. I never got close to him as a person because I was still only a youngster at the time, but he did a lot for me.

"To be honest, I thought Ted leaving West Ham might be the end of my career at Upton Park and quite a few of the other lads were of the same opinion in terms of their own futures. When a manager leaves a football club, it creates a great deal of uncertainty. It is the same in all walks of life because it is inevitable that a new manager in any industry will always impose his own ideas on the organisation and some of the employees will not form part of those plans.

"Initially there was a lot of talk that Welsh international Phil Woosnam might get the job. Phil had joined us from Leyton Orient three years earlier for £30,000, which was a big fee. He was a classy midfielder and, after Noel Cantwell had gone to Manchester United, it was Phil who had eventually taken over the captaincy at West Ham.

The influential Phil Woosnam in action at Leyton Orient, the club who sold him to West Ham.

"Phil had become a major influence at the club. He was a deep-thinker about the game and always coming up with new moves and tactics on the training ground, although they always seemed to involve him. Phil didn't get the job in the end, although the role of player-manager, which is what he would have become, had not really been invented in those days."

Behind the scenes, West Ham had already begun the process to replace Fenton. The club's chairman, Reg Pratt, made an approach to Arsenal about their chief coach, Ron Greenwood, taking over the managerial reins at Upton Park. Greenwood had an impressive record in terms of coaching and he would become the first West Ham manager who did not have a prior connection with the club.

Greenwood was born at Burnley in Lancashire on November 11, 1921 and, during a distinguished playing career, he amassed nearly 200 league appearances as a cultured centre-half for Bradford Park Avenue, Brentford, Chelsea and Fulham. He gained a League championship medal with Chelsea in 1955 which, at the time, was their only honour.

While still a player, Greenwood became a qualified FA coach and after retiring from playing at the age of 35, he became manager of non-league Eastbourne United. He also successfully managed the England youth team and became chief coach at Arsenal where his coaching capabilities really began to flourish. By 1960, he had proceeded to combine that job with being manager of the England under-23 side who had a certain West Ham youngster called Bobby Moore in their ranks.

During his meeting with Pratt, Greenwood stated that if he accepted the job, then he wanted full control of all matters at Upton Park. Pratt confirmed that was not an issue and Greenwood duly became Hammers' manager on April 11, 1961. Amazingly, he did not want a contract because he felt the board of directors were entirely trustworthy and, even more importantly, he had an innate confidence in his own coaching and managerial capabilities. It was an extraordinary situation and one that would be impossible to contemplate in the modern game.

At the time, Greenwood was earning £1,500 at Highbury but his salary when taking over at West Ham was £2,000. It was a substantial increase but the move was not about money. Greenwood was acutely aware of the wealth of talent at Upton Park and it excited him.

Amongst the senior professionals were accomplished players like John Bond, Ken Brown, John Dick, Andy Malcolm, Phil Woosnam and Malcolm Musgrove but Greenwood must have felt like Lawrence of Arabia catching his first sight of Damascus when he cast his eyes on the list of young players at the club. These included Jack Burkett, Bobby Moore, Geoff Hurst, Martin Peters, Joe Kirkup, Eddie Bovington, Ron Boyce, Tony Scott, Derek Woodley, John Charles and Brian Dear. The legacy of Ted Fenton's youth policy was immeasurable and now Greenwood had the opportunity to nurture and embellish it.

Jack recalls Greenwood's first morning in charge: "Ron had a meeting with all the playing staff on the pitch at Upton Park. He said everyone had a chance of playing in the first team, even the youngest kids. I thought that was great because it meant he was going to take a good look at all of us.

Above: Jack, 17, in action for the Reserves against Bristol City at Upton Park in 1959-60.

"I was impressed that he seemed to know all the players' names and he certainly knew mine. He said he liked players with 'good habits' on the field of play. In other words, he meant that players who consistently did the right things automatically. They duly developed good habits and became good players. Those with bad habits, he said, were inconsistent. He also stressed the need to improvise and surprise the opposition.

"The biggest difference in Ron's training sessions was the fact that he quickly introduced more technical work, including 'phase play.' This meant we would play three men against three in tight areas or even two against one. On other occasions, it would be four against three and, sometimes, eight against two. If you were one of the 'pair', then you really had to work hard in a session like that.

"He also liked five-a-side games where five attacking players faced five defenders. Ron maintained the team of defenders would always win because they knew how to organise themselves in their half of the field which gave them a sound basis on which to mount their own attacks.

"There was a lot of one-touch or two-touch football during practice matches. It was all about encouraging us to get our technique right.

"West Ham were a forward-looking club when Ted Fenton was manager and he deserves a great deal of credit for all that he achieved. However, when Ron took over, there was a complete change of training methods and philosophy. He placed less emphasis on the use of heavy weights and instead of going on long cross-country runs, he got us running shorter distances, but at a much more intense pace.

"He introduced interval training, which meant we would jog or run easily for, say, 50 yards and then we had to sprint for the next 100 yards. The sprinting distances would be varied and the 'recovery' run would get less and less, so the sessions were very hard.

"It was all done in front of Ron and the coaching staff, so there was no chance of anyone taking short-cuts as John Bond and John Dick had done during those long runs in the Essex countryside in Ted's days. Also, a lot of sprinting was done with a ball at our feet to improve our skill."

Greenwood's tactical awareness was much in evidence within a few days of joining the club. Jack recalls: "Ron had only watched a couple of first team games and he immediately made the point that some of our defenders were too conscious of marking their opponents on a rigid man-to-man basis. At times, they were forgetting about the ball. Ron stressed the need for flexibility. It was simple, but instantly effective.

"He felt that there was not enough talking during matches. In other words, he wanted more communication. Again, it was something a good coach would immediately pick up on and attempt to correct.

"It was obvious right from the start that Ron liked us to have our say on tactics. He encouraged us to discuss things that happened on the pitch and he wanted us to put over our own ideas in training. If it worked well, he would introduce those ideas into games. Ron's coaching revolved around his players having the ability to pass and hold the ball, as well as creating space and moving off the ball. Ron's emphasis was always on the technical side of the game.

"In the confines of a football club, it is usual for players to moan about a new manager as he looks to shake them up from established routines and impose his personality but I don't think that there were too many complaints about the arrival of Ron Greenwood. Right from the start, he insisted that we called him Ron – not 'Boss' – because it created respect from both perspectives.

"In terms of the game itself, he was like a man talking a different language. He had this amazing ability to make things sound blatantly obvious. These were things that we should have known for ourselves but, for some reason, they had always been overlooked.

"Ron opened our eyes when it came to the subject of making the best use of space.

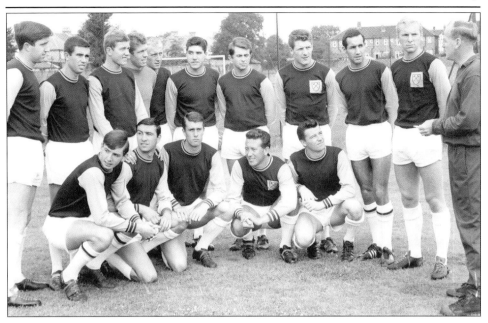

The master and his pupils . . . Ron Greenwood and (standing, left to right): John Bond, Ron Boyce, Jack Burkett, Lawrie Leslie, Joe Kirkup, Alan Sealey, Tony Scott, John Lyall, Eddie Bovington, Bobby Moore. Front: Martin Peters, Peter Brabrook, Geoff Hurst, Ken Brown, Johnny Byrne.

He said that space didn't just happen of its own accord. We needed to create it ourselves. Instead of waiting for a gap to arise, we had to make that gap appear by some of our attacking players making diversionary runs and taking opposing defenders with them even though our forwards knew that they wouldn't receive the ball. He explained that the runs some of our players made were really laying decoys for our opponents because of the gaps they created for others.

"Ron told us that space only remained space as long as we didn't run into it. If there was a gap in the opposition's penalty-area, then most attacking players have a natural instinct to run into it, but if an opposing defender ran with him, then the space no longer existed. Ron wanted our players to stay out of that space until we were ready to make the best use of it. In other words, it was necessary to wait until the team-mate with the ball was ready to make a pass, so that we could see how the move could be further developed to our benefit.

"He always maintained that good football stemmed from good habits, particularly from the mastery of the basics of the game. In doing so, it meant that players did the correct things by instinct. He used to say to us: 'You must leave the ball playable.' He meant that when we made a pass to a team-mate, it had to be at the right pace and angle so that it could be played off first time by our colleague.

"Ron constantly drilled into us the underlying principles of football such as the value of making intelligent runs into space, the importance of taking up good positions and the need to be constantly thinking about the game as a whole. He would never criticise any of his players for attempting something that didn't come off, so long as we had not forgotten the underlying principles.

"He also recognised the value of the near-post cross which he described as 'the soft underbelly of opposing defences.' It was a tactic that brought West Ham dozens of goals over the years.

"Some of the training techniques that Ron introduced into the game in the early-60s are still being used by clubs today. Those techniques may be subject to different interpretations but the principles will always remain the same.

"Ron was a wonderful visionary and that is his great legacy. He never watched games from the dug-out like the modern day managers. He would always sit motionless in the front row of the main stand, just level with the half-way line. Ron felt that overlooking the pitch from a higher elevation gave him a better perspective of the overall play – and it made a lot of sense."

Clearly, the deep-thinking Greenwood had made a huge impression on the West Ham players. He insisted that as many of them as possible went on FA coaching courses at Lilleshall, so that they could understand and grasp the principles to which he referred. It also ensured his players were able to talk about the game, confidently and with a degree of authority. It was a clever ploy by Greenwood because it also meant that he was able to transmit his own ideas to his players more easily.

On one occasion, Greenwood arranged for the entire West Ham playing staff to take over Lilleshall for a whole week – the first time a league club had made such an arrangement. The players worked throughout the week – mornings, afternoons and evenings – with a view to giving them a clearer insight into all aspects of coaching. At the end of the week, several players passed their preliminary coaching badges.

Given this grounding, it is little wonder that numerous Hammers' players from the Greenwood era went on to become first class managers and coaches.

In the 1961-62 campaign, Greenwood's first full season in charge, West Ham consistently maintained a position in the top half of the table and eventually finished in eighth place. They played constructive, intelligent football but, unfortunately, the good progress in the league was somewhat tempered by a disappointing 3-0 defeat in the third round of the FA Cup at lowly Plymouth Argyle.

Greenwood had strengthened his team that season with two spectacular signings. The first came when Scotland's goalkeeper Lawrie Leslie was transferred from Airdrieonians for £15,000. Leslie was brave, courageous and charismatic. The historic warrior William Wallace has always famously been described as Scotland's 'Braveheart' but so far as West Ham's fans were concerned, Leslie was the 20th century equivalent.

He was voted Hammer-of-the-Year at the end of the season after a series of breathtaking and spectacular displays.

Even more importantly, Greenwood signed centre-forward Johnny Byrne from Crystal Palace for £65,000 – a then British record transfer fee. West Ham had never been known for making big splashes in the transfer market and the fact that Greenwood had paid such a big fee for Byrne confirmed his intentions of taking the club to a new level. The 23-year-old Byrne had already been capped by England and Greenwood likened his style to the legendary Alfredo Di Stefano of Real Madrid. Praise did not come any higher than that.

*Greenwood with Lawrie Leslie and Ian Crawford – his first two signings in 1961 – and (below) the chatterbox
'Budgie' Byrne, who never had any difficulty making himself heard!*

Byrne was a constant chatterbox and he quickly earned the immortal nickname of 'Budgie.' He was only 5ft 7ins tall but he was solidly built and able to withstand the physical assaults that came from many of the cumbersome centre-halves of that punishing era. Byrne was perfectly balanced and had a low centre of gravity. His control of the ball was sublime and, with a short stride and nimble brain, he was invariably able to outwit his opponents with sheer skill and artistry.

It was also during that season, in a game against Leicester City, that Greenwood switched Bobby Moore to the position of sweeper alongside Ken Brown. Thanks to the perception of the manager, Moore had found his true niche in a role that would ultimately make him immortal for both club and country. In later years, notably 1966, England would owe Greenwood a huge debt of gratitude for the way that he had moulded Bobby Moore, Geoff Hurst and Martin Peters.

West Ham's last game of the 1961-62 campaign came on the evening of April 30, against Fulham at Upton Park. It had been postponed from earlier in the season and the rest of the league programme had already been completed 48 hours earlier. It was the game in which 19-year-old Jack Burkett was selected to make his league debut. The boy from Tottenham was about to realise his dream.

He has an instant recall of the events of the day: "We had to report for training at the ground that morning. There had been a mention in the previous day's newspaper that I might be playing against Fulham but Ron didn't say anything to me until after the training session. It was then that he told me that I would be making my debut that evening.

"The problem was that there wasn't enough time for me to make my way home to Tottenham by public transport and then get back to Upton Park in time for the game, so I just decided to hang around all afternoon. I had some lunch at Cassettari's Café in the Barking Road and then I went to the pictures.

"I managed to leave a telephone message for Dad with a neighbour – we didn't have a phone of our own. He left work early and cycled all the way to Upton Park from Tottenham. He got to the ground just in time for the kick-off and stood on the terraces.

"I didn't feel nervous during the afternoon but as I walked to the ground past the Boleyn pub and saw all the fans starting to gather for the game, then the nerves really kicked in. I passed virtually unnoticed amongst the supporters who were milling around in Green Street. Nobody wished me luck or said a word to me because no-one recognised me."

It would be unthinkable now for a Premier League player to walk through the surrounding streets on his way to the ground but back in 1962, footballers were not pursued by hordes of admirers and well-wishers.

"Ron had picked a fairly young side that night. Lawrie Leslie was injured and Alan Dickie, who was a year younger than me, was playing in goal in only his second league game. Martin Peters was in the side, although he had only made his league debut a couple of weeks earlier.

"In the dressing-room, Ron told me I would be marking Fulham's Scottish international winger Graham Leggat and I should play my normal game. But he pointed out that Leggat was quick and I had to deny him space."

Despite Burkett's detailed recollections of the build-up, it is ironic that he can remember very little about the game itself. Fulham had only just escaped relegation that season, which was surprising since they had such household names as Johnny Haynes, George Cohen and Alan Mullery in their ranks.

At Upton Park that night, Fulham played their part in a six-goal thriller with West Ham running out deserving 4-2 victors. Jack says: "I remember thinking afterwards that I hadn't let anyone down. We had won and Leggat hadn't scored, so I felt quite satisfied."

In fact, he had made a highly impressive debut and because of his assured performance, Greenwood decided he should be included in the first team's forthcoming close-season tour to Africa. As Burkett sat in the bath after the Fulham game, the manager told him of his inclusion and stressed that he needed to go to the Hospital for Tropical Diseases in London the following day and get the necessary inoculations that were required for a trip to the African continent.

Jack admits: "I was a bit stunned at first and blurted out to Ron that I was due to

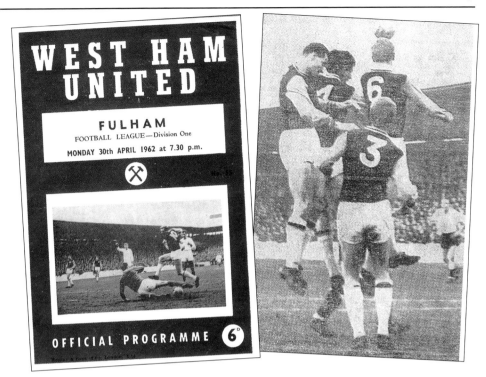

The match programme for Jack's league debut and the only picture of Jack from that game against Fulham. Bill Lansdowne (left), Martin Peters (4) and Bobby Moore (6) all get ready to head clear as Jack (3) watches.

go on holiday to Italy with Ann, my girlfriend. He was very good about it and said that I could return home from the African tour a few days early, so I wouldn't miss my holiday.

"But getting various injections in one go for the likes of typhoid and yellow fever caused a real problem. Apart from making me feel really ill, my arm swelled up and I had to slit the sleeves of my shirts. Obviously, all the other lads had received their injections over the course of the previous few weeks and there were no problems for them – but when we flew out from Heathrow a few days later, I certainly didn't feel at my best."

West Ham's tour to Africa in the summer of 1962 was a gruelling trip. There were two absentees since Bobby Moore had gone off to make his debut for England in the World Cup in Chile and Joe Kirkup was given special dispensation to remain at home because he was getting married.

The tour consisted of six matches in three countries plus eight flights and two lengthy train journeys. From a football perspective, the tour was a success because five games were won and one was drawn, with Hammers scoring 20 goals and conceding only two.

In terms of events off the field, the part of the tour in Nyasaland (now Malawi) and Rhodesia (Zimbabwe) did not present any problems for the West Ham party but their time in Ghana proved to be a nightmare. The army had taken over the running of the country following a military coup and Ghana was in complete chaos. Hammers' hotel in Accra was little more than a doss-house with bugs infesting the

Martin Peters challenging Fulham's Alan Mullery with Johnny Byrne waiting to pounce.

beds on a nightly basis. Jack shared a room with Ron Boyce and admits the sight of small lizards scurrying up and down the bedroom walls was not conducive to a good night's sleep!

More seriously, it was a trip that had sinister repercussions for him in later years.

He explains: "Obviously, there is always quite a bit of free time on close-season tours and we were in our element. It was blisteringly hot and we did as much sun-bathing as we could possibly manage. Unfortunately, most of us got badly burnt and although there were sun creams in those days, they were not nearly as effective as they are today.

"There were no warnings about the effects of exposing the body to the rays of the sun and, like everybody else from that era, we were blissfully unaware of the dangers. We played one game where we all had to take the field covered in Calamine lotion to try and soothe the sunburn. Ron was not too pleased with us.

"I'm convinced that trip was when I first contracted skin cancer. Obviously, it didn't manifest itself for more than 40 years but it can lay dormant for that sort of period. With the benefit of hindsight, I know that was when the damage was done."

6

In search of the Promised Land

ALTHOUGH Jack had made his league debut the previous April and performed creditably on West Ham's African tour, he found himself back in the reserves as the 1962-63 season got under way. However, he was only a few days away from becoming a first team regular and it came about because Hammers made a catastrophic start to the new campaign.

In their first league match, they travelled to Aston Villa where they were 2-0 down after just two minutes. The nightmare continued throughout the game as Villa's rangy striker Derek Dougan gave Hammers' defence a torrid afternoon. In the end, they were thankful to get away with only a 3-1 defeat after Villa hit the woodwork three times in the second-half.

On the following Monday evening, Wolverhampton Wanderers were the visitors to Upton Park and they promptly handed Hammers a severe 4-1 beating. Three of Wolves' goals were fired in from 25 yards and most of the danger came from their tricky right-winger Terry Wharton, who scored their second goal. West Ham's left-back John Lyall was given a hard time by the impressive Wharton.

Things went from bad to worse five days later when Spurs beat West Ham 6-1 at Upton Park. It was a massacre in the sun as Jimmy Greaves and his Tottenham team-mates ran riot. It was only wasteful second-half finishing by the visitors plus some outstanding saves by Lawrie Leslie that kept the score down. Lyall was unfortunate to score an own-goal that started the rout when he inadvertently turned a low cross into the net after just 10 minutes.

Three games and three heavy defeats meant that it was the worst opening to a season in living memory. It seemed that West Ham could not score enough goals, nor stop conceding them.

In the modern game, such a start would have instantly sent a lethal strain through the media bloodstream via irate phone-ins and forums calling for the head of the manager. However, in that era, fans were considerably more patient and, anyway, Greenwood was still enjoying a honeymoon period with the Upton Park faithful. Nevertheless, the omens were not good because Hammers' next match was the daunting return fixture against high-flying Wolves at Molineux. The Midlands side were top of the table having won all three of their opening games and scoring a staggering 14 goals in the process. Conversely, Hammers were pointless, bottom of the table, bereft of confidence and had conceded 13 goals. West Ham's enfeeblement meant, in football parlance, that this was a 'home-banker' if ever there was one.

Greenwood made two changes by leaving out the unlucky Lyall and, also, injured left-winger Malcolm Musgrove. Their replacements were Jack Burkett and Brian Dear, who was making his league debut. Jack's pre-match instructions were to 'get tight' on the highly potent Wharton who had caused so much damage at Upton Park the previous week.

The partnership of Burkett and Moore on the left side of Hammers' defence worked perfectly that night at Molineux and was hugely instrumental in gaining a 0-0 draw. It was a highly impressive result given the defensive carnage that had occurred in the preceding three games.

It was the game in which Burkett established himself as a regular in West Ham's first team.

There was another team change made by the perceptive Greenwood in the early weeks of that season. Jack looks back on those events which changed the course of England's football history: "It was around this time that John Dick was sold to Brentford. He was a Scottish international and had been a prolific scorer for West Ham for 10 years but he was coming to the end of his career. We all knew that he would be sorely missed and wondered who would take his place. What we didn't realise was that Ron was about to make one of the most important footballing decisions of all time.

"We were due to play Liverpool on a Monday night at Upton Park early in September and when the team was announced, Geoff Hurst was wearing the number 10 shirt as John's replacement. Until that time, Geoff had always played at wing-half but he had never been able to establish himself. Obviously, Bobby's place in the side at left-half was already assured and both Martin and Eddie Bovington were beginning to push for the right-half spot, so Geoff's opportunities were becoming limited.

"A few months earlier, there had been some talk that Geoff might be transferred to Crystal Palace as part of the deal that brought Budgie Byrne to West Ham. But, for whatever reason, that part of the transfer didn't materialise. In the end, it was Ron Brett who ended up as being the 'make-weight' in the deal and Geoff stayed at Upton Park.

"It is strange how things can sometimes work out in football. If Geoff had gone to Crystal Palace, then it is most likely that without his goals, England would not have won the World Cup in 1966. Geoff later explained that on the morning of the Liverpool game, Ron called him into the office. Geoff had played poorly in the reserves at Shrewsbury Town a couple of days earlier and he was expecting some criticism. Instead, Ron said he wanted Geoff to play up front in the first team against Liverpool that night. He said he wanted someone who was big and strong and not afraid to work.

"It was typical of Ron that he also told Geoff that if it didn't work out, then it wouldn't be held against him. Obviously, Ron had seen something in his style of

Above: A team group from early in the 1962-63 season. Standing, left to right: Ken Brown, John Bond, Lawrie Leslie, Martin Peters, Jack Burkett, Bobby Moore. Seated: Tony Scott, Johnny Byrne, Phil Woosnam, Geoff Hurst, Malcolm Musgrove. Below: Johnny Byrne with his children. Budgie was more used to making the news rather than typing it.

play that he had not even seen in himself.

"In the game against Liverpool, Geoff's running off the ball and his changes of direction were phenomenal. He dragged their defenders all over the place and, in doing so, created space for other players. We ended up winning 1-0 thanks to a goal from Tony Scott – but it was Geoff who did the damage.

"It was an amazing decision on Ron's part. He turned Geoff from being an average wing-half, who didn't appear to have a future at West Ham, into one of the greatest strikers in world football.

"Even so, I don't suppose Ron ever envisaged that Geoff and Budgie would form such a fantastic partnership. Once they adapted to each other's style of play, they were brilliant together and their pairing made things a lot easier for the rest of us. We knew that if we cleared the ball anywhere in the vicinity of the centre-circle, then Budgie would be able to kill it instantly with his majestic first touch or on his chest before volleying it to one of our wingers.

"He was one of the greatest volleyers of a football of all time with either foot. His technique was sublime. Budgie used to pull away from his marker and make himself available and it didn't matter if we fired the ball at him with pace because he had such wonderful control. He had a superb football brain and, as a finisher, he was deadly.

"We also knew if we were under pressure, then the other option was to clear the ball to the left of the centre-circle and Geoff had the strength and physical presence to challenge for it. He would often make a bad pass look like a good one because of his ability to win possession deep in opposition territory."

As the 1962-63 season progressed, Greenwood's influence at the club was beginning to have a considerable effect. His new and exciting young team was starting to take shape. So far as the Upton Park faithful were concerned, it was just feasible that here was a manager who could take their team to the 'Promised Land' after so many years of disappointment.

Leslie was performing well in goal and there was a settled back-four consisting of Kirkup, Brown, Moore and Burkett. The hugely gifted Peters was excelling in midfield alongside the industrious Boyce who was now a first team regular.

On the strength of Boyce's blossoming talent, Greenwood had allowed club captain Phil Woosnam to be transferred to Aston Villa. It was a surprise decision but Greenwood felt Woosnam's better days were behind him and it was difficult to argue against that decision. The skilful Woosnam had always imprinted his personality on the team but the quiet and unassuming Boyce had settled into a midfield role which was personified with indefatigable grafting that went both unnoticed and unheralded. Boyce was a vital cog in Greenwood's emerging team.

Bobby Moore was named as West Ham's new captain following the departure of Woosnam. In the meantime, Greenwood signed England international winger Peter Brabrook from Chelsea for £30,000 to give more penetration down the right-flank. Meanwhile, Byrne and Hurst were cementing their formidable striking partnership up front.

In the youth team, a scintillating youngster called John Sissons was making his way through the ranks and he would make his debut before the end of the season. With his instinctive play, close control and lethal left foot, Sissons was an exciting player to watch.

Despite such a wealth of talent, it was inevitable that an inglorious cup exit would mar some impressive results in the league. It appears to be part of the make-up of

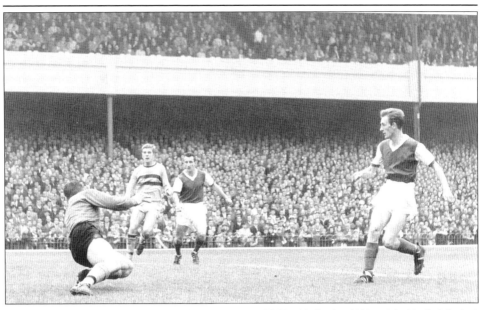

Above: Lawrie Leslie saves from Arsenal's George Eastham at Highbury in October 1962, watched by Jack Burkett.
Below: A disconsolate Jack looks on as Jim Standen, the man who replaced Leslie, picks the ball out of the net after Ray Crawford had scored Ipswich Town's third goal on Good Friday in April 1963.

Above: Snow men – Bobby Moore, Johnny Byrne, Alan Sealey and Tony Scott lead the way as the players brave the snow and ice to keep fit jogging round the Boleyn pitch during the big freeze. Below: One of the few games played during that winter – Jim Standen tips a header onto the bar as Jack Burkett covers and Ken Brown watches during the thrilling 4-3 victory at Nottingham Forest in December 1962.

any West Ham team from any era. This time it was unglamorous Rotherham United who tipped Hammers out of the second round of the League Cup by 3-1 in mid-October. Sadly, an even bigger catastrophe struck in the first division game against Bolton Wanderers at Upton Park on November 3.

Jack recalls the incident: "It was the day that Lawrie Leslie broke his leg – I will never forget it. In the first-half, Bolton's Francis Lee went in a bit late for the ball and could have injured Lawrie. There was a bit of pushing and shoving and a few harsh words exchanged but we just got on with the game. The same thing happened in the second-half.

"It was always noticeable that whenever the opposing team were attacking at Upton Park, then our crowd would go quiet. This time, it was Warwick Rimmer who went in late for the ball and he caught Lawrie's leg. Because our crowd were so silent, I heard the crack of Lawrie's shin breaking. It was a sickening sound.

"Although Lawrie was in a lot of pain, he tried to get to his feet because he wanted to have a go at the Bolton player. Ken Brown leant over Lawrie and gave him a crack on the chin and virtually laid him out. It was the only way Ken could prevent Lawrie from doing any more damage to his leg.

"It was a terrible sight as Lawrie was carried off on a stretcher. There were no substitutes and Martin took over in goal. In the end, we lost 2-1 but the score hardly mattered because we were so concerned about Lawrie."

Leslie was out of the game for nearly six months, although he made a good recovery from an extremely serious injury. Unfortunately, he never regained his first-team place on a permanent basis because Greenwood signed a perfect replacement. He bought 27-year-old Jim Standen, who he had known from earlier days at Arsenal, from Luton Town for a knock-down price of £6,000. The unlucky Leslie was transferred to Stoke City the following season.

Jack was immediately impressed by Standen: "Jim was an excellent goalkeeper with a lot of experience. He wasn't as spectacular as Lawrie but Jim had a safe pair of hands and great reflexes. He also had fantastic positional sense. I played in front of Jim for the next five years and we always had a good understanding.

"When you consider what Ron paid for him and the fact that Jim went on to play in two Wembley cup finals for the club, you have to say that his signing was one of the bargains of the century. The signing of Jim meant that Ron now had all the players on his books who would go on to win the FA Cup and European Cup Winners' Cup within the next three years."

As Christmas approached, a quirk of nature brought football – and, indeed the entire country – to a standstill. The winter of 1962-63 was the coldest since 1740. Christmas Day was frosty with temperatures falling to minus nine degrees and by Boxing Day morning, thick snow had fallen over most of the country. Incredibly, snow covered much of Britain for the next two months. At one point, the temperature plunged still further to a numbing minus 16 degrees.

Supplies of food and fuel ran low and about 50 people died during that period, many trapped inside their cars. On January 18, a blizzard completely cut off Scotland from England. By this time, Britain was strewn with abandoned vehicles.

It was not until February 14, St Valentine's Day, that there were the first signs of a thaw – admittedly, only in the West Country – which created even more problems with serious flooding occurring in Devon. The terrible winter also dealt a harsh blow to the economy with output dropping by nearly £400 million.

A handful of football matches were actually played during the 'big freeze', albeit in atrocious conditions that only the intrepid Antarctic explorer Captain Scott would have found acceptable. One club, Blackpool, even used a flame-thrower on their pitch in an endeavour to beat the snow and ice. Despite such initiative, nearly 500 league and cup matches were postponed. The season had to be extended by nearly four weeks to allow the back-log to be cleared.

West Ham's last match before the snow came was a thrilling 4-4 draw at Tottenham on December 22, with Burkett subduing Spurs' dangerous Welsh international winger Terry Medwin. Hammers did not play regularly again until February 16, when they won 2-0 at Sheffield United on a pitch that resembled an ice-rink. In fairness, the enforced mid-winter break did Hammers no harm at all because once football resumed, they were quickly back into their rhythm. They overcame Fulham and Swansea in the third and fourth rounds of the FA Cup before being drawn at home to Everton on March 16.

It was a niggling and ill-tempered affair with West Ham winning 1-0 thanks to a coolly taken 60th minute penalty from Budgie Byrne. It was a decision hotly disputed by the Everton players because Dennis Stevens appeared to merely obstruct Bobby Moore and the referee, Jim Finney, surprised everyone by awarding a penalty. Everton's vociferous protests did little to help the mood of antagonism that was beginning to surface from within certain sections of the crowd. Four Everton fans climbed over the barrier and attempted to remonstrate with Finney before being hauled away by the local constabulary. One policeman was injured in the fracas and he was helped to the touchline by an ambulance man before order was eventually restored.

It was the game that saw one of the first major outbreaks of hooliganism at Upton Park. In those days, opposing fans were invariably massed together with no segregation on the primitive, urine-soaked terraces. It was the way that the majority of people watched football in an era when all-seater stadiums were just a fanciful dream. After Byrne side-footed home his penalty-kick, trouble quickly flared on the South Bank. A running battle broke out between West Ham and Everton fans in the central area of the terracing.

Hammers were defending that end of the ground and it was a sad sight as scores of uniformed policemen raced behind Standen's goal and climbed over the barrier to fight their way – literally – to reach the main protagonists. The spectre of hooliganism would cast a long shadow over football for virtually the next 25 years with tragic circumstances on a number of occasions. At least, Upton Park was never tainted with such tragedy and, for that at least, we should all be eternally grateful.

The star of Hammers' team in the cup-tie against Everton was Jack Burkett who completely marked their Irish international right-winger Billy Bingham out of the game. In later years, Bingham would become a highly respected manager of

Everton and the Northern Ireland international team. In the following morning's newspapers, one soccer scribe wrote: 'England's new manager Alf Ramsey could do a lot worse than take a look at West Ham's Jack Burkett who may well be the answer to the troublesome left-back spot. He will be in his prime for the 1966 World Cup.'

Sadly for Jack, it didn't quite work out like that but it was considerable recognition for a young player who had made his league debut less than a year earlier.

Apart from Burkett's excellent form, the mercurial Budgie Byrne was fast becoming West Ham's talisman. Whenever he was in possession of the ball, it seemed that the Upton Park fans were instantly expecting something magical to happen. In recent times, perhaps only the hugely talented Paolo Di Canio had the same mesmerising effect.

Jack remains convinced about the value of Byrne to West Ham during that period and pays a remarkable tribute to him by saying: "He brought a whole new dimension to the entire club and completely transformed us. In my opinion, Budgie was the greatest West Ham player of all time – and I include Bobby Moore in that statement."

In the quarter-final of the FA Cup, West Ham were given the worst possible draw – an away tie against Liverpool who were on their way to creating the magnificent Anfield dynasty under the management of legendary Bill Shankly. The irrepressible 'Shanks' was regarded as a Messiah on Merseyside and he was building a formidable team that included such famous names as Ron Yeats, Ian Callaghan, Ian St John and Roger Hunt. Despite the tough task that awaited them at Anfield, Jack had no doubts about West Ham's ability to deal with Shankly's 'Red Army.' He recalls his confidence by saying: "I was convinced we were going to win the FA Cup that season. To be honest, I couldn't see anything stopping us. We were playing so well at the time."

Jack Burkett tackles Ian St. John, while Joe Kirkup looks on, during the FA Cup quarter-final at Anfield.

More action from the agonising Anfield cup-tie defeat in March 1963, as Liverpool's Roger Hunt bursts between Burkett and Ken Brown, with Ian Callaghan on the left.

If there had been any justice at Anfield, then Jack's prediction may well have come true. Admittedly, miscarriages of justice occur all the time in football, although seldom more scandalously than the 1-0 defeat that Liverpool handed to West Ham that day.

From the start, Hammers dominated the proceedings. The majestic Moore marshalled his defence as only he could, while Burkett constantly forced the lively Callaghan inside and away from the touch-line, thus nullifying any potential danger from the Liverpool winger. In midfield, the excellent Boyce caught the eye with his probing and perceptive passing, whilst up-front, the magical Byrne was a force of nature, linking, switching, quickening and slowing the play to establish rhythm.

The Kop, for once, was silenced as it seemed their team could be facing a FA Cup exit at their own Anfield fortress. At times, West Ham completely outplayed Liverpool but their only failing in an otherwise superb display was, most crucially, their finishing. It was their Achilles Heel.

In the first-half, Sealey, Scott and Brabrook all missed golden chances which would have effectively finished the game as a contest before half-time. However, the most crucial miss came 10 minutes from the end with the score still locked at 0-0. Once again, the unfortunate Sealey was the culprit but, this time, the miss proved costly in the extreme.

With just seven minutes left on the clock and Hammers looking as if they had gained a replay – the very least their performance deserved, Moore proved that he was human after all. The West Ham captain hesitated when attempting to clear a cross from the left and Roger Hunt slid in Jimmy Melia's pass from a tight angle. Despite their supremacy, West Ham were out of the FA Cup. It was a sickening blow.

Ian St. John smiles in disbelief that Liverpool have scraped through to the semi-finals – Jack Burkett and Tony Scott can't believe it either.

Jack was distraught: "I sat in the dressing room and couldn't believe that we had lost. At the time, it was the biggest disappointment of my career and I thought that we had blown our best-ever chance of getting to Wembley. There was a picture taken as we were coming off the pitch at the end of the game. Ian St. John is smiling but there is almost a look of disbelief on his face that they had got through to the semi-final at our expense."

Despite Burkett's intense disappointment at Hammers' FA Cup defeat at Liverpool, it had been an excellent season for him. He had established himself as West Ham's first-choice left-back and played a total of 45 league and cup games. In fact, the team as a whole had made considerable progress under Greenwood who had now been in charge for two years.

Clearly, Hammers were undergoing some kind of Greenwood-inspired rebirth. He was encouraging his players to aspire to higher levels of technical expertise and tactical nous. Although the West Ham players did not realise it at the time, they were about to embark on the greatest period in the club's history.

7

An American tale

THE early-60s was a good time to be a professional footballer. In January 1961, Jimmy Hill – who was chairman of the PFA and, also, a Fulham player at the time – led his members to victory in their bid to secure the abolition of the Football League's maximum wage structure.

The previous archaic regime, in which stars like Stanley Matthews and Tom Finney could only earn the same £20 a week maximum wage as the lowliest fourth division player, was dead and buried. Protecting the rights of workers in any profession is a noble struggle and Hill had achieved it brilliantly for the footballers of that era.

Jack has no doubt about the importance of Hill's endeavours: "Professional footballers owed Jimmy a huge debt of gratitude because we all benefited."

Almost immediately, the Fulham and England captain Johnny Haynes became the first £100-a-week player. Admittedly, most of them didn't get anything like Haynes was earning but it did mean that, on a pro-rata basis, their wages were increased considerably when contracts came to be renewed.

"Within a couple of years, my money had gone up to £40 a week but there were no such things as agents acting for players," says Jack. "At the end of a season, Ron would meet with each player individually and say: 'I've managed to get an increase for you' and confirm the amount.

"In later years, Bobby had a few contract problems with West Ham but he was the captain of England and he had some bargaining power. So far as the rest of us were concerned, we basically took what we were given."

At the end of the 1962-63 season, West Ham jetted off to America to take part in an International Soccer Tournament. As a drive to popularise football, the United States Soccer Authority had invited various club sides, including the Hammers, to take part in the tournament. Burkett is in no doubt about the importance of that trip in the context of Hammers' history and his own development as a player.

He says: "It was a great learning curve for us and Ron felt that it would be a huge benefit, both individually and collectively, to play against teams from Brazil, Italy, Mexico, West Germany, France and Scotland. Most of us were still very young at the time but playing against club sides from different countries gave us a confidence and belief in ourselves.

"The tournament consisted of two groups of seven teams with the winners of each group meeting in a two-legged championship play-off. I believe we grew up and matured as players that summer. It was the catalyst for the success that followed in the next couple of years.

"We flew from Heathrow and landed briefly at Prestwick Airport in Scotland before flying to New York. It took about 13 hours – it was a horrendous journey. The plane was an old propeller job and there wasn't much room in the seats. Bobby and Budgie weren't with us because they were on a European tour with England but the plan was that they would fly out and join us later.

"We stayed at superb apartments in Manhattan, just one block from Fifth Avenue and right by Central Park. I shared with Alan Sealey. He was nicknamed 'Sammy' around the club and I got on very well with him. He was a good lad. Alan loved the horses and when we were in America, he was always on the telephone back home to England finding out the latest racing results and laying bets. He knew what he was talking about and gave me some winners. Alan was a real joker and he had a very dry sense of humour.

"All of our training sessions were held in Central Park. They were just loosening-up sessions really, particularly after a hard season and because we would be playing games so regularly out there. A few people used to watch us training, including some New York cops, but basically they just let us get on with it.

"We drew the opening game 3-3 against Kilmarnock at Randalls Stadium in New York. They were a decent side having just finished runners-up in the Scottish first division."

The West Ham party flew to Chicago for the second match, against Mantova of Italy, but the 'Windy City' did not live up to its reputation as the temperature soared to almost 90 degrees. Hammers – still without Moore and Byrne – lost 4-2 and were well beaten by the highly talented Italians. This game proved that life-long friendships can be forged in football even in the most unlikely circumstances.

Jack explains: "I was marking a player called Luigi Simone. He was very skilful and afterwards, we shook hands and got chatting. We got on really well and kept in touch by letter for years afterwards. Luigi spoke good English, better than my Italian, and whenever he came to London, we would meet up for lunch.

"Later on, he played for AC Milan and I was very sad when he died in 2003. Luigi had a son who followed in his footsteps and also played for Mantova, AC Milan and the Italian under-23 side. It was a great friendship.

"By this time, we were bottom of the table and we flew back to New York that night where we met up with Bobby and Budgie who had just arrived after the England tour. It was on that trip that Bobby had captained England for the first time, so he was a bit of a celebrity. The tournament was getting quite a bit of publicity and in one interview, Bobby told the press: 'Turn the table upside down and you might see the winners of the competition.' As things turned out, he was absolutely right."

West Ham's next game at Randalls Stadium kicked-off within 24 hours of Moore and Byrne's arrival in New York. Remarkably, neither player showed any signs of jet-lag or fatigue and Hammers emphatically won their first game of the tournament against Oro of Mexico by 3-1. The temperature in The Big Apple was also hovering around the 90 degrees mark.

Jack recalls: "It was very hot and humid throughout the whole trip, particularly in New York. We played a couple of matches when it was really sweltering and even during the evening games, the humidity really got to us. We didn't drink as much water as the players do now. In modern football, you see them coming out of the tunnel before a game taking drinks out of water bottles but in our day, it just wasn't done. We merely used to take salt tablets to offset the effects of the heat.

"In between games, we did all the usual sight-seeing trips in New York including the Empire State Building and Times Square. We took a boat trip along the Hudson River past the Statue of Liberty. We went on the New York subway and did all the shops like Macy's on Fifth Avenue and Bloomingdales. The club gave us six dollars each day spending money. It wasn't a great deal but it was enough.

"It was amazing being in New York. In those days, the world – metaphorically speaking – was a much bigger place. Nowadays, everyone jets off on holiday to the most exotic locations but at that time, we had only seen pictures of New York on television or in the newspapers. It was the trip of a lifetime for most of us."

Hammers flew to Detroit for their next game, to play the German side Presseun Munster under the floodlights of the University Stadium. Detroit had a large German population and before the game the local press had somewhat hyped-up the occasion by billing it as 'England v West Germany.' The Germans were duly beaten 2-0 with Hammers' goals coming from Geoff Hurst and Martin Peters. To a certain extent, history would repeat itself three years later when the same players scored England's goals in the World Cup final at Wembley. Perhaps the press boys of Detroit knew something after all.

Jack continues: "We flew back to New York again and beat Valenciennes of France by 3-1. It was our best performance of the tournament and Geoff got the first hat-trick of his career.

"The next day was free with no training, so Bobby, Budgie, Ken Brown and me went to a coastal town called Coney Island near New York. We were on the sidewalk and because it was so hot, we all took our shirts off. All of a sudden, a policeman appeared and told us in no uncertain terms to put our shirts back on, otherwise he would arrest us. There was a law that said you couldn't walk on the sidewalk without wearing a shirt. It was unbelievable.

"They had gun crime and New York was the murder capital of the world at the time and yet, you could be arrested for not wearing a shirt! The next day, it was reported in the newspapers under the heading: 'English soccer players nearly arrested.' It seems ridiculous now but that's how it was in Coney Island in 1963."

With the German team Presseun Munster blowing their chances of topping the table by losing their last match, West Ham knew that a draw against the talented Recife from Brazil would be enough to end the tournament as group winners. It was another hot and humid night in New York and Byrne gave Hammers an early lead.

Things were hotting up on the field as well and the game became a bad-tempered affair with West Ham proving that they were more than capable of looking after themselves as a series of bad and reckless challenges initially went unpunished by the remarkably lenient referee.

Jack recalls: "It was a real kick-up and Alan Sealey and Guimares, who was a terrific player, were sent off after a strange incident. Guimares had committed two bad fouls on Alan and, after the second challenge, Alan needed some treatment. The referee sent Guimares off – but he refused to go and held the ball behind his back while making wild gestures with his other arm. The game was held up for some minutes and, amazingly, the referee then sent off Alan as well.

"We had a reputation of being a bit of a soft touch at times but we could mix it with the best of them and really got stuck in after that. Actually, we lost our concentration for a few minutes and Recife equalised just before half-time.

"As we were coming off for the break, their manager threw some West Ham badges in Ron Greenwood's face. They had been exchanged for some Brazilian badges as part of the pre-match pleasantries – but Ron wouldn't get involved in anything like that. He just smiled and walked into the dressing room with us.

"During the break, I decided to take off my shin-pads for the second-half. It was very hot again and I was getting a bit of cramp. Early in the second-half, I went into a tackle with their right-winger Canario and, instinctively, you know when an opponent is going to 'do' you. He came right over the top of the ball and sliced my shin open with his studs. It was potentially a leg-breaking tackle. I had some treatment and got on with the game but I was limping quite badly for some minutes. It ended in a 1-1 draw – enough to make us winners of our group.

"Afterwards, I went to hospital and a doctor stapled the skin back together again. It was the only time in my career I didn't wear shin-pads and it was a painful lesson.

"I got my own back on Canario a couple of years later, though. He had been transferred to Real Zaragoza in Spain and we beat them in the semi-final of the European Cup Winners' Cup. He was a good player and later played for Real Madrid and Spain. I will always remember him for that tackle in New York. I still have the scar on my shin to this day."

Bobby Moore's words had been remarkably prophetic and Hammers had indeed ended as group winners. The West Ham party flew home the following day for a two-week break whilst the second group matches were played on the same basis in New York, Chicago and Detroit. Thereafter, the Hammers' party were due to fly back to America to play the winners in the two-legged championship final.

During the period back home, the club announced that the players' wives and girlfriends could accompany the team on the return trip. Needless to say, it was a decision greeted with much delight – particularly by the ladies.

DAILY EXPRESS TUESDAY JUNE 25 1963

SKYLINE VIEW OF THE BRITISH SOCCER BOYS WHO ARE TOPS IN AMERICA

SPORT STARTS HERE

WEST HAM CAN WIN IT

WEST HAM, the happy Soccer boys from London's East End, feel on top of the world.

They look out over Manhattan from the sun roof of their New York hotel and dream of winning yet another title for Britain.

They have stormed to the top of New York's International Soccer League.

One more victory, against Recife of Brazil, tomorrow and they win their section.

WEST HAM, FROM THE RIGHT, LAWRIE LESLIE, KEN BROWN, JACK BURKETT. JOHNNY BYRNE, JOHN SISSONS, BOBBY MOORE AND MANAGER RON GREENWOOD

Above: A cutting from the Daily Express, dated June 25, 1963, and a picture of some of the West Ham party looking out over Manhattan from the sun roof of their New York hotel.
Below: West Ham line up before facing Kilmarnock in the opening game of the tournament. Back row, left to right: John Lyall, Jim Standen, Ken Brown, Alan Sealey, Lawrie Leslie, Joe Kirkup, Dave Bickles, John Sissons, Ron Greenwood. Front: Jack Burkett, Ron Boyce, Martin Peters, Geoff Hurst, Tony Scott, Peter Brabrook.

The front covers of the programmes for West Ham's American tour games against Gornik (left) and Dukla played at Randalls Island.

Jack Burkett clears from Dukla Prague's Jan Brumovsky while Bobby Moore looks on during the first leg of the American Challenge Cup game played at Randalls Island Stadium in New York.

8

A West Ham WAG

IN modern football, one of the most nauseating aspects has been the emergence of the WAGS – the millionaire players' wives and girlfriends with their Gucci bags, designer wardrobes, hair-extensions, shopping and sheer vanity. Generally speaking, their demeanour is usually about as fake as their boobs and sun tans.

They adorn the pages of the celebrity magazines and tabloid dailies with monotonous regularity. In effect, they have become the personification of the grotesque cult of celebrity and the majority are living proof that money cannot buy class.

The WAG culture reached a sickening crescendo in the 2006 World Cup in Germany when the antics of some of the England players' wives and girlfriends became more newsworthy than the appalling under-achievements of their men folk on the pitch. At times, their antics caused extreme embarrassment. The word 'crass' does not even begin to describe the champagne-fuelled table-dancing of one individual on a particularly 'memorable' night during the tournament.

The modern-day WAGS are material lottery winners whose stories delude young girls into making 'WAGdom' their greatest ambition in life. The hugely reserved and unpretentious Neil Armstrong – the first man to walk on the surface of the moon and the ultimate celebrity if he chose to be so – was once famously quoted as saying: 'People should be recognised for their achievements in life and the value it adds to society. Celebrity shouldn't supersede the things they've accomplished.'

Clearly, the eloquent Armstrong was not talking about the loathsome football WAGS when he uttered those profound words.

Nevertheless, it should be stressed that the West Ham WAGS of 1963 were a somewhat different breed when compared to their modern day counterparts. They were distinctly less pretentious and, in most cases, considerably more intelligent. At the time, Ann Rivers was 19-years-old. She was blonde haired, pretty and she was also Jack Burkett's fiancée.

Ann was born at Harringay in North London in 1944. Her mother – Sarah Molony – originated from County Kildare in Ireland. Sarah came to England at the age of 24 to seek work as a nurse. She met Ipswich-born Alfred Rivers who lived and worked in London as a chef. They duly married and set up home in a small rented house in Primrose Hill. They later bought a modest flat in Harringay and it was there that Ann and her sister, Mary, grew up. One of their near neighbours was a budding young actress called Barbara Windsor. Ann is a devout Roman Catholic and had a strict upbringing during her time at a convent school, St Mary's Priory, in Harringay.

She left there at 15 and began work as an office junior with a publishing company based in St. James's Square in London. At the age of 18, she went to work in the West End offices of a company in fashionable Bond Street which produced handbags and suitcases for stars such as Shirley Bassey, who was a frequent visitor to the premises. Ann thoroughly enjoyed working in the bustling environment of London all those years ago and, at the time, admits to having absolutely no interest in football. It could have been a bit of a problem because she was about to meet a promising young player from West Ham.

To the inhabitants of North London, the Tottenham Royal will forever remain the ultimate 'Palais-de-Dance.' It was there, in the bleak mid-winter of 1960, that a classic love story was about to unfold . . . girl meets boy . . . boy meets girl . . . fall in love . . . get married . . . have children . . . live happily ever after. It was at the 'glitzy' Tottenham Royal that Ann and her girlfriends would usually congregate on a Friday night with their fashionable bee-hive hair-styles and excruciatingly pointed-toe shoes with stiletto heels that crippled the feet, but looked good on the dance floor. Friday was the only evening of the week that they met up because their relatively meagre earnings did not allow too many other social nights out.

Ann recalls: "On this particular Friday night, I was standing outside waiting for my friends to arrive. I turned round and saw this blond-haired, incredibly handsome young guy standing there. But when I looked again, he was gone. When my friends arrived and we went inside, I looked out for him, but there was no sign.

"A couple of weeks later, I went to a New Year's Eve party at my friend's house and he was there. I couldn't believe it. We started talking and he told me that his name was Jack Burkett and he played football for West Ham. I have to be honest and say that being a footballer meant nothing to me but so far as I was concerned, it was love at first sight from that night outside the Tottenham Royal.

"I know people say that such a thing isn't possible but I can categorically state that it happened to me. When the clock struck midnight to herald the New Year, I kissed him and we have been together ever since. It was as simple as that, although the first time that Jack came to my house, I still had rollers in my hair and I was trying to glue the heel back on my stiletto shoe! Fortunately, such a sight didn't seem to put him off.

"We started courting but neither of us earned much money. Jack was still playing in the reserves and hadn't got into the first team at that point. We didn't go out much apart from an occasional visit to the pictures – that was about as much as we could afford. Sometimes, Jack would walk from his house in Tottenham to my place in Harringay just to save the bus fare.

"We got engaged in 1962 after he came back from West Ham's tour of Africa. He had made his league debut by then but he was still only earning about £10 a week.

"By that time, I had started going to Upton Park to watch Jack when he was

*Left: Early courting days for Jack and Ann in January 1961. According to Ann, it was love at first sight.
(Right): The engaged couple on holiday in Italy in June 1962.*

playing. I used to travel to the games on my own by bus and tube. I can't imagine Victoria Beckham or Coleen Rooney doing the same these days.

"I never professed to understand the technicalities of the game – not many footballers' wives do – but, obviously, I began to take a big interest in the team and how they were playing. It was Jack's profession and I wanted them to do well.

"I remember that Ron Greenwood said he liked his players to settle down and get married at an early age because it offered stability and it was good for their careers. He maintained marriage matured his players as people. Also, he wanted to create a family atmosphere at the club and that is why he decided to take all the wives and girlfriends on the trip to America.

"I recall many years later, during the 1974 World Cup, there was a lot of press coverage because the Dutch players were allowed to have their partners with them throughout the tournament. It was regarded as being very revolutionary but Ron had already instigated that on West Ham's trip to America in 1963.

"I suppose the West Ham party was split into two groups of players and their partners so far as socialising was concerned. Both groups got on well and I can't say I was ever aware of any problems. Our group consisted of Joe Kirkup and Jill, Geoff Hurst and Judith, Martin Peters and Kathy, Ron Boyce and Dawn, together with Alan Sealey and Janice.

"Joe and Jill were the only couple who were married at the time and the rest of us were engaged. Looking back, I suppose they were all the younger players in the team who had come through the ranks together, so it was inevitable that they would be close to one another.

"The other group consisted of Bobby Moore, Budgie Byrne, Ken Brown,

Hammers New York Bound For Finals

New York-bound – Hammers set for lift-off to the States in 1963. From right: Ann Rivers (Jack Burkett's fiancee), Joe Kirkup, Ron Boyce, Jill Kirkup, Jim Standen, Elisa Standen, Peter Brabrook, Doreen Brabrook, Alan Sealey and his fiancee Janice Gilbert.

John Bond, John Lyall, Peter Brabrook, Eddie Bovington, Jim Standen and their wives. Generally speaking, they tended to be the older and more senior players at the club.

"Obviously, Bobby and Budgie moved in higher social circles than the rest of us because they were England internationals and West Ham's star players. I liked Bobby's wife Tina very much but I can't say I ever got to know Bobby very well. He was always very polite and the perfect gentleman but I felt he was always on his guard and remained a bit aloof.

"I loved Ken Brown, though. He was warm and friendly to everybody. In all the years at West Ham, I don't think I ever heard anyone say a bad word about Ken.

"I had only ever been abroad once before and that was the previous summer when Jack and I had gone away on holiday to Italy. I had to ask for time off work for the trip to America. It was fantastic. Before we left, my Mum had expressed concern about the proposed sleeping arrangements in New York! It seems stupid now, but all the single players 'paired off' and shared rooms and so did all the girls. I shared an apartment with Alan Sealey's fiancée, Janice, and Jack shared a room with Alan. There was no sleeping together for any of the unmarried couples.

"When you look back, it was just ludicrous, but that's how things were at the time. The 'Swinging Sixties' were still a long way off for most of us.

"We went on a couple of shopping expeditions to Macy's and Tiffany's but most of the girls had gone to America on a shoe-string budget. The single girls, in particular, didn't have much money and I ended up buying some towels for when Jack and I got married the following year. I can't imagine many of the current WAGS going to New York and spending their money on towels and nothing else."

It transpired that West Ham's opponents in the championship final would be the formidable Gornik of Poland, who were the winners of the second group matches. They were a quality side and had previously gained considerable experience of playing in European football. The two legged-final would be a severe test for West Ham and it would give them a clear indication of the progress they were making under Greenwood's astute management.

Jack says: "Before we left for the return trip to New York, Ron told us that if we won the two-legged final against Gornik, we would be required to stay on for an extra week. The organisers had arranged for the winners to play a Challenge Cup match, again over two legs, against the previous year's winners, Dukla Prague from Czechoslovakia.

"Both games against Gornik were played at the Randalls Island stadium in New York which was becoming almost like a second home to us. The first leg was a dour affair and we drew 1-1 with a goal from Budgie. There were a lot of Polish immigrants in the crowd and when the referee turned down a late penalty appeal for Gornik, their fans started throwing beer cans on to the pitch.

"In the second leg, things got even more volatile and some of their fans ran on to the pitch waving Polish banners and flags after the referee disallowed two Gornik goals for offside. A fan threw a punch at one of the linesmen and the referee was manhandled as he tried to take the players off the field.

"We thought it was going to be abandoned but the game eventually restarted after half-an-hour. The referee was so badly shaken that he was unable to continue and one of the linesmen took over from him. I have no idea where they got a substitute linesman from but, soon afterwards, Geoff scored the only goal of the game and we won 2-1 on aggregate.

"Bobby was presented with the trophy, which was good practice for him bearing in mind the other trophies that he would pick up in the next three years. Because of the delay, the game against Gornik had actually taken two-and-a-half hours to complete but we had played well and kept our heads. We were the better side and well pleased with ourselves in the dressing room afterwards.

"It meant that we would stay on for the extra week and play the two-legged Challenge Cup final against Dukla. We knew that this would be a big test because the previous year, Czechoslovakia had lost 3-1 to Brazil in the World Cup final and six members of that side played for Dukla, including Josef Masopust. He was one of Europe's greatest-ever players, the captain of both Czechoslovakia and Dukla.

He had been voted European Footballer-of-the-Year in 1962 and was immensely gifted.

"The first leg was played in Chicago and, again, the temperature was in the high 80s. We lost 1-0 but were very unlucky. They had a Czech international goalkeeper called Pavel Kouba and he was fantastic. We created enough chances to have won comfortably but Kouba was the difference between the two teams.

Bobby and Tina Moore.

Jack Burkett and fiancee Ann Rivers (centre) celebrate West Ham's victory over Gornik together with Joe and Jill Kirkup (left) and Ron Boyce and fiancee Dawn Ames (right) at an official club function in New York.

It was one of the best goalkeeping performances I have ever seen.

"The second leg was played back in New York on another blisteringly hot day. Peter Brabrook had one of his best games for us and, together with Joe Kirkup, he set up the chance for Tony Scott who scored to put us level on aggregate. In the end, Dukla's overall class eventually told and Masopust began to take control in midfield. He scored an equaliser when he played a one-two on the edge of our penalty-area and shot past Jim Standen.

"The game ended in a 1-1 draw, which meant we lost 2-1 on aggregate, but Masopust was very complimentary about us after the game. He said we would be a top class side within the next two years and considering what we achieved in that time, you have to say that he wasn't a bad judge."

On August 13, the West Ham party flew back to England in readiness for the new season which was only 11 days away. There had been some criticism of Ron Greenwood for subjecting his team to a summer of competitive football plus a considerable amount of travelling. The fear was that West Ham would be tired and stale before a ball had been kicked in the new season.

Greenwood was entirely upbeat about the whole affair and was quick to point out that the tournament had opened up his players to international football and their performances against Dukla had been the most technically perfect displays he had seen from any team with whom he had been associated. It was praise indeed from a man who was not generally noted for such gushing compliments.

Greenwood had read the situation perfectly. That tournament in the summer of 1963 signalled the coming of age for the young players of West Ham. It is ironic that it should have occurred 3,000 miles away across the Atlantic Ocean in New York – 'the city that never sleeps' – as immortalised in Frank Sinatra's song. Although they were unaware of it at the time, they were about to reach the Promised Land . . .

9

Home truths

AS the 1963-64 season got under way, Ron Greenwood had developed a regular routine for his players in preparation for a Saturday game. Jack explains: "After training on a Friday, we would have a team meeting and Ron would go through our opponents in terms of individual players, their strengths and weaknesses and formations they were likely to adopt.

"He always surprised me with his depth of knowledge about other teams, particularly later on when we played in Europe. Sometimes, he would send a couple of the lads to go and spy on future opponents and, if necessary, he would prepare dossiers for us to read.

"After our team-meeting on the Friday, he didn't say anything else until we were in the dressing room on the Saturday afternoon getting ready for the game. He would quietly go round the room talking to each player in turn, reminding us about a certain aspect of our immediate opponent's play and what was expected from us. Sometimes, the opposition may have made a late change, so it would be necessary to have another brief team meeting in case we had to slightly alter our tactics.

"The West Ham match-day dressing-room in that era was a relatively calm place. We had done all our work on the training ground during the week, so it was not necessary to be hectic or noisy. Players like Budgie and Peter Brabrook would be talking a lot but most of the lads preferred to be quiet. I think that particularly applied to the likes of Bobby, Martin, Boycie, Eddie Bov, Sisso and me. It was usually quiet at half-time as well.

"Even if things were not going to plan, Ron wouldn't shout or scream. In those days, the half-time period was just 10 minutes – and that was from the moment when the referee blew his whistle to signal the end of the first-half to the beginning of the second period. So Ron had only about six minutes to talk to us and explain any tactical changes he wanted to make. The half-time break is often the greatest test of a manager's competency.

"It was strange, but Ron never believed in discussing things immediately after a game. He might mention one or two things as we were getting out of the bath or getting dressed but, after that, he would just say: 'See you all at training on Monday' and that is when we would talk about the game.

"Basically, he wanted us to think about it and also our respective performances. He felt by waiting until Monday, it gave us time to collect our thoughts. It was then that he would have his say about Saturday's performance, both collectively and individually. The players would also be encouraged to have their say as well but, generally speaking, it was very civilised – and, perhaps, that was part of West Ham's problem."

Burkett is correct in his summary of Greenwood's way of handling things. There was no ranting or raving from the manager even after a bad defeat. The infamous 'hair dryer' treatment administered by Sir Alex Ferguson to his Manchester United players in recent times would have been an anathema to Greenwood. Perhaps that is why Ferguson has enjoyed 20 years of trophy-winning glory, while Greenwood's team only sustained it for two years.

As a possible consequence of this perceived lack of motivation, one or two established players in Hammers' first team had definitely drifted into a comfort zone, knowing their places in the side were relatively assured. The team's position in the league during the opening months of the 1963-64 season supported this theory because, despite the immense talent in the team and the manager's undoubted coaching acumen, the fact remained that they were becalmed in the middle of the first division table.

Their results were an irritating mixture of good and plain awful. As examples, the 'good' included an emphatic 4-2 defeat of League champions Everton at Upton Park and a 1-0 victory over FA Cup holders Manchester United at Old Trafford – even though Hammers were reduced to 10 men after Alan Sealey had been carried off. The use of substitutes in Football League matches was still two years away.

Amongst the performances that came into the 'plain awful' category were two abysmal defeats at relegation-threatened Birmingham City and Ipswich Town, by 2-1 and 3-2 respectively – the latter occurring even though West Ham were two goals up after an hour's play and, seemingly, coasting to victory on an ice-bound Portman Road pitch.

The team was not playing as well as the previous season. They were starting to play a 'cavalier' type of football and, somewhat worryingly for their more discerning fans, it was possible to detect a degree of arrogance afflicting their game. Most crucially of all, the players were forgetting about the basic principles they had so assiduously worked on since Greenwood had joined the club. It was almost inevitable that a catastrophic defeat was on the horizon and, in many ways, it was a turning point – not just in West Ham's season, but in the club's entire history.

Jack takes up the story: "We were due to play Blackburn Rovers, both home and away, over the Christmas holiday period. The home game was played on Boxing Day with the return match at Ewood Park being held 48 hours later. At the time, Blackburn were top of the league, although it was generally assumed that either Manchester United or Liverpool would overhaul them before the season's end. However, they were a good side and had some outstanding players in their ranks such as Mike England, Keith Newton and Fred Pickering – all internationals – who had played against Bobby Moore and myself in the FA Youth Cup final five years

Burkett heads clear from Trevor Hockey as Moore watches in the 2-0 home defeat by Nottingham Forest in September 1963.

earlier. They were captained by Ronnie Clayton, who had previously skippered England, but the man who made them 'tick' was their little midfield general Bryan Douglas, another former England international.

"The pitch was very heavy and they annihilated us. To this day, it makes me shudder to think about it because we lost 8-2 on our home ground. It was West Ham's heaviest home defeat in their history and I was part of it.

"It was Bryan Douglas who did most of the damage – he tore us apart. I can remember sitting in the dressing room afterwards and looking round at the other players. It was like a morgue. We were totally shell-shocked. My over-riding memory of the game itself was that, amazingly, the West Ham fans didn't give us any stick whatsoever. Perhaps they were as shocked as we were but they still gave the Blackburn players a fantastic ovation as they walked off the pitch at the end.

"Ron came into the dressing-room. His face was ashen but there was still no shouting. He told us that we would be travelling north the next day and staying overnight at a hotel near Blackburn for the return game on the Saturday. It was there that we were to hold the 'inquest' into the debacle that had just occurred on the pitch at Upton Park.

"I later learnt that he went up to his office and wrote out the team for the return game. First of all, he made nine changes. Then he wrote down another team and there were eight changes. Then he altered it again, this time with seven changes. Then another with six and so on . . . until, in the end, he decided to retain the same side with only one change. The unlucky player was Martin Peters, who was replaced by Eddie Bov in midfield. Ron's thinking was that Eddie's more aggressive style of play would counteract the threat of Bryan Douglas.

"It was a long journey to Lancashire the following day and hardly anyone spoke. Never let it be said that footballers don't care, because we were mortally wounded.

This picture was taken in November 1963. Back row, left to right: Ken Brown, Martin Peters, Jack Burkett, Joe Kirkup, Jim Standen, John Bond, Eddie Bovington, Bobby Moore. Front: Alan Sealey, Martin Britt, Ron Boyce, Johnny Byrne, Geoff Hurst, Peter Brabrook, Tony Scott.
Below: It's January 1964 and Hurst, Standen, Sissons and Burkett observe the sign that says
'Please Keep Off This Pitch'.

We had no idea of Ron's plans in terms of team changes when we met up in the hotel that evening. He began by asking what we thought of our performance. Initially, there was a highly embarrassed silence before Ken Brown stood up and spoke. He was – and still is – one of the most genial and easy-going people you could ever wish to meet. He is always smiling and has a wonderful outlook on life. But we suddenly saw a different side to him. Ken let us have it with both barrels.

"He said: 'I've been with this club for 10 years and it's the worst thing that has ever happened. We were a disgrace yesterday and all of us need to take a long, hard look at ourselves. We have all become too cocksure. I don't know how many years I've got left in the game but I tell you now, nothing like that is ever going to happen to me again and you lot had better start thinking the same way.'

"That is only a very brief description of Ken's 'call to arms', which included a number of extremely colourful expletives, but it was exactly what was needed. One of the senior and most respected players at the club telling us a few home truths."

Jack continues: "After that, we all had our say and, for the first time I could recall in a team meeting, the gloves were off and we didn't pull any punches. Nobody escaped criticism irrespective of their reputation. Previously, there had never been any criticism of either Bobby or Budgie. After all, they were England internationals and our best players but on this night, someone started by having a real go at Bobby, saying he was our captain and should have taken more responsibility in terms of talking to us.

"We all accepted that Bobby wasn't a great talker on the pitch and he led by example. But the point was, when we were getting turned over to that extent on our own pitch, then we needed something more from our captain.

"As defenders, some of us were critical of Budgie and Geoff because we felt that as Blackburn started to over-run us, we couldn't find them with our clearances – the ball kept coming straight back at us all the time.

"Our wingers Peter Brabrook and, in particular, Sisso were criticised for going into hiding. In other words, they didn't seem to want the ball.

"Bondy and myself were criticised for giving our opposing wingers too much room and allowing them to run at us. Someone said that Jim Standen was not commanding his area as he should have done. Someone else said Martin and Boycie kept getting caught in possession in midfield, which was putting us in trouble.

"We were also critical of Ron Greenwood because we weren't happy about his decision to not allow things to be discussed immediately after games and having to wait until the next training session. We felt that if things needed to be said in the dressing room when players were fired up, then so be it. We said to him: 'What's the point in waiting for nearly 48 hours to discuss things that have gone wrong?'

"There was a lot of swearing but it wasn't malicious. It was the ultimate 'clear the air' meeting. It started around 7.30pm and didn't finish until midnight.

"In many ways, that meeting changed things for a lot of us. I took a long, hard look at myself and it made me even more determined as a player. I think Bobby became a better captain because he did start to become more vocal on the pitch. Also, I think it had an effect on Ron because no manager likes to be criticised by his own players and it seemed to make him harder as a person.

"In fairness, he accepted the criticism, but after that, I felt he was distinctly cooler towards most of us. That certainly applied to the relationship that I had with him. Perhaps that wasn't a bad thing because a manager shouldn't get too close to his players.

"I think that as individuals, we became more accountable and, perhaps, a bit more wary of each other. Most of us had come through the ranks together and we were all big mates. Possibly, some of us were too close and the outcome of that meeting was that it made us more professional in our outlook. After that, I definitely think there was an extra edge and added bite amongst us during training sessions, particularly practice matches.

"On the coach journey to Blackburn's ground the following day, Ron announced the team with only one change – Eddie Bov replacing Martin at right-half. We felt sorry for Martin because we knew that Ron could so easily have dropped all of us. Typically, Martin accepted the decision with good grace but he was a close friend and I knew how much the decision had hurt him."

It has since become an integral part of the club's folklore that, miraculously, the players of West Ham exacted the ultimate revenge upon Blackburn Rovers. On a brutally cold, wet afternoon, they won 3-1 thanks to two goals from Budgie Byrne and another from Geoff Hurst. It was a majestic performance in the Ewood Park mud but even more incredulously, Greenwood had suddenly found the 11 players – and the formation – that, in just over four months, would take West Ham to Wembley and win the FA Cup for the first time in the club's history.

For older West Ham fans, the names of the 1964 FA Cup-winning side roll easily off the tongue: Standen, Bond, Burkett, Bovington, Brown, Moore, Brabrook, Boyce, Byrne, Hurst and Sissons. They are immortalised because, in effect, they were the players who won Hammers' first major trophy since the club's formation at the beginning of the century. For the Upton Park faithful, it had been a long wait.

They were also the 11 players that turned the season around with that shock 3-1 win at Blackburn Rovers within 48 hours of the Boxing Day debacle at Upton Park. Apart from the odd injury or occasional resting of players, the team remained unchanged throughout the remainder of the season.

Jack reflects on the astonishing turn-around in Hammers' fortunes by saying: "Basically, it came about because we all acted on what had been said during that meeting. From that moment onwards, we never looked back. We got involved in another good run in the FA Cup, although the draw was kind to us in the early stages."

In the third round, Hammers beat second division Charlton Athletic 3-0 at Upton Park without too much difficulty. Next, they accounted for Leyton Orient, again by 3-0 at home, after drawing 1-1 at Brisbane Road. In the fifth round, West Ham won 3-1 at third division Swindon Town, which could have been a tricky tie, but the visitors were well in control. Suddenly, they were in the quarter-finals again and were drawn at home against Burnley, one of the best sides in the country at the time. They had a team brimming with internationals, including Willie Morgan,

Above: Standen collects on a frosty Upton Park top as Burkett covers and Liverpool's Roger Hunt moves in during Hammers' 1-0 win in January 1964. Below: A few weeks later, in February '64 . . . Standen saves from Jimmy Greaves, watched by Bobby Smith, Burkett and Moore during the 4-0 home slaughter of Spurs.

Ray Pointer and John Connelly, so they knew it would be a tough game. It was Connelly who gave Burnley the lead in the first-half but Hammers staged a tremendous fight-back and ran out 3-2 winners, with Byrne scoring twice and Sissons getting the other.

"The star of our team that day was Budgie," says Jack. "He was tremendous and just seemed to skip over the clinging mud that epitomised the Upton Park playing

West Ham looking relaxed at their hotel before the FA Cup fifth round victory at Swindon in February 1964. Ron Greenwood is seated on the far right of picture, with the injured John Lyall next to him. Although Lyall's career had just been ended by injury, the manager insisted he remained part of the group throughout the Cup run.

*The players laughing at a joke from Tony Scott (far right) are (left to right): John Sissons,
Eddie Bovington, Geoff Hurst, Jack Burkett, Johnny Byrne, John Bond, Peter Brabrook, Joe Kirkup, Ken Brown,
Ron Boyce, Bobby Moore and 12th man Martin Peters (partly hidden).*

Above: Swindon defenders look suitably despondent as John Sissons congratulates goalscorer Geoff Hurst.
Below: It's Johnny Byrne's turn to celebrate on the way to our sixth round victory over Burnley.

In training at Forest Gate roller skating rink prior to the 1964 FA Cup quarter-final win against Burnley. From top:
Johnny Byrne, John Sissons, Geoff Hurst, Jack Burkett, Eddie Bovington, Ron Boyce.

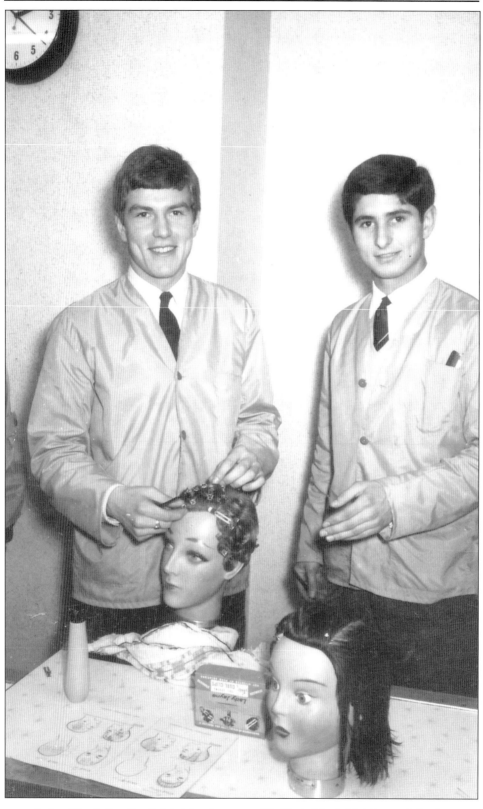

Jack and Dennis Burnett on their hairdressing course at the Morris School of Hairdressers in London.

surface in those days. His first goal was a gem – a first-time volley from the edge of the penalty area following a good run and cross from Peter Brabrook."

As West Ham's FA Cup run gathered momentum, Jack's good looks, fair hair and coltish running style were beginning to gain a whole host of admirers amongst Hammers' growing legions of female fans. Every time he touched the ball, a barrage of Beatle-type screams rose up from the terraces as numerous girls on the North and South Banks gave passable impressions of Meg Ryan's famous restaurant scene in the film *When Harry Met Sally*.

Jack gives a rueful smile when he remembers their reaction: "At first, I didn't realise what was happening. I didn't feel embarrassed, although I took a bit of stick from the lads. It was quite amusing really and it certainly didn't bother Ann.

"I was lucky because I had a great relationship with the West Ham fans throughout my years with the club. I think, generally speaking, they always had a 'soft spot' for youngsters who had come through the ranks. In the Chicken Run, they liked players who could tackle and were enthusiastic, so I never had any problems. They treated me well and, even now, I look back on them with a huge amount of gratitude."

Ann has an infectious laugh and a tremendous sense of fun which is epitomised by her recollections of the female attention that Jack received during those matches.

She says: "I wasn't jealous – far from it. I used to sit in the stand listening to the girls and think to myself, 'They're screaming for this good looking guy and he's mine and I'm engaged to him.' I thought it was great."

Despite the fact that Jack was enjoying such popularity from a certain section of the fans and the team was just one game away from Wembley, it didn't stop him considering preparing for the day when his playing career might come to an end. Earlier that season, Jack – together with young reserve full-back Dennis Burnett – had decided to take a ladies hairdressing course with the Morris School of Hairdressing in London.

He says: "Dennis and I went along together. We were doing OK and, as the course progressed, there were a few articles about us in the *London Evening News*. It seemed like a good idea at the time but, soon afterwards, West Ham got involved in the FA Cup run and I suppose my interest waned a bit. The hairdressing course became too time consuming, so I just packed it in.

"Dennis did well and finished the course but as far as my absenteeism was concerned, there was an amusing quote in the newspaper a few weeks later from Kenneth Morris, one of the school's directors, who said: 'We haven't seen much of Jack lately'."

In truth, Burkett had more important things on his mind. The semi-final draw paired West Ham and Manchester United with the game due to be played at Hillsborough, the home of Sheffield Wednesday. The other semi-final was an all-second division affair between Preston North End and Swansea Town (it was only in later years that they changed their title to 'City.') It was the draw that most Hammers' fans feared.

At the time of the semi-final, Manchester United, managed by the legendary Matt Busby, were on course for a unique treble – First Division championship, FA Cup

Above: Jim Standen and Jack Burkett on their way to the FA Cup semi-final as their train leaves Kings Cross.
Below: The teams with a mention for the Dagenham Girl Pipers, who unwittingly may have had a hand in the
outcome of the match, plus the programme cover and match ticket.

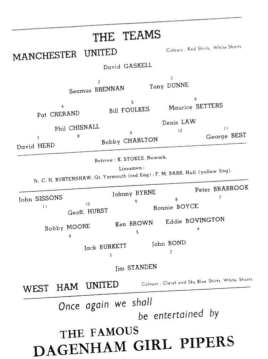

THE TEAMS

MANCHESTER UNITED   Colours : Red Shirts, White Shorts

David GASKELL

2   3
Seamus BRENNAN   Tony DUNNE

4   5   6
Pat CRERAND   Bill FOULKES   Maurice SETTERS

Phil CHISNALL   Denis LAW
7   8   9   10   11
David HERD   Bobby CHARLTON   George BEST

Referee : K. STOKES, Newark.
Linesmen :
N. C. H. BURTENSHAW, Gt. Yarmouth (red flag) ; F. M. BARR, Hull (yellow flag).

John SISSONS   Johnny BYRNE   Peter BRABROOK
11   10   9   8   7
Geoff. HURST   Ronnie BOYCE

Bobby MOORE   Ken BROWN   Eddie BOVINGTON
6   5   4

Jack BURKETT   John BOND
3   2

Jim STANDEN

WEST HAM UNITED   Colours : Claret and Sky Blue Shirts, White Shorts

Once again we shall
be entertained by

THE FAMOUS
DAGENHAM GIRL PIPERS
also the popular
DANNEMORA STEEL WORKS BAND

SATURDAY
MARCH 14th 1964
KICK-OFF 3.0 p.m.

1/-
OFFICIAL PROGRAMME

Semi-Final

MANCHESTER UNITED
VERSUS
WEST HAM UNITED

SHEFFIELD WEDNESDAY F.C. LTD.
HILLSBOROUGH, SHEFFIELD

FOOTBALL ASSOCIATION CHALLENGE CUP
SEMI-FINAL

Saturday, 14th March
KICK-OFF 3 o'clock

RES. SEAT 20/-

Issued subject to the Rules, Regulations and
Bye-Laws of the Football Association
No Ticket exchanged nor money refunded

General Manager and Secretary
THIS PORTION TO BE RETAINED

NORTH STAND
LEPPINGS LANE
ENTRANCE
A
GANGWAY
F
To the RIGHT
ROW   SEAT
40   4

YOU ARE REQUESTED TO
TAKE UP YOUR SEAT THIRTY
MINUTES BEFORE KICK-OFF

and the European Cup Winners' Cup. They were the FA Cup holders and with the likes of Denis Law, Bobby Charlton, Pat Crerand, Maurice Setters and Tony Dunne in their ranks, it meant that Busby's team were hot favourites to overcome West Ham and appear in the FA Cup final at Wembley for a second year in succession.

Six months earlier, Busby had introduced a 17-year-old winger called George Best into his team and, already, it was abundantly clear that the young Irishman had a brilliant future.

Jack says: "The week before the semi-final, we played Manchester United in a league game at Upton Park. We had our full team out but Matt Busby rested some of his players in readiness for the semi-final and included some of their reserves. They beat us 2-0 without breaking sweat.

"I think we had the semi-final on our minds. We were awful and as we walked off the pitch at the end, their goalkeeper David Gaskell was insanely cocky. He shouted across at us: 'Don't bother turning up next week.'

"After that, there was no need for Ron to give us a talk before the semi-final. Gaskell had already done his job for him."

As the teams arrived at Hillsborough for the semi-final on that memorable Saturday afternoon, the conditions were, quite simply, deplorable. The whole country had been deluged for the previous 48 hours and the city of Sheffield had taken more than its fair share of rain during that period. An hour before kick-off and with the rain still pouring down, the Hillsborough pitch resembled a paddy-field in the heartland of China. There were huge pools of water covering the playing area and the valiant Hillsborough ground-staff appeared to be fighting a futile battle as they plunged garden forks into the waterlogged ground to try to drain away some of the water.

Many of the 65,000 all-ticket crowd – a large proportion of whom were already soaked to the skin as they stood on Hillsborough's huge uncovered terracing – were of the opinion that the game would kick-off as scheduled, but would be abandoned after just a few minutes. This would allow both clubs, plus hosts Sheffield Wednesday, to take their respective 'cuts' from the considerable gate receipts with the attraction of the game being played again the following Wednesday evening with another big pay day. It was, perhaps, a rather cynical view but given the conditions, not an entirely unreasonable train of thought.

However, the fact remains that the game was played to its conclusion and West Ham produced one of the greatest performances in the club's history.

In a strange way, the eventual outcome of the match may have been partly decided by an incident which took place 40 minutes before the kick-off. The pre-match entertainment was a marching display by the Dagenham Girl Pipers. Clearly, football fans in those days were somewhat easier to please than those in the modern era. The girl troupe stood in the players' tunnel bravely waiting for the signal to march out on to the pitch and face the monsoon. They were resplendent in their Royal Stuart tartan kilts, socks, velvet jackets and Tam o'Shanters with bag pipes at the ready.

At that precise moment, the West Ham players were already in their dressing room

John Bond (left) and Jim Standen are helpless as Jack just manages to block David Herd's early effort.

diligently preparing for the most important match of their careers.

Jack recalls that Ron Greenwood walked in with a beaming smile on his face. He says: "Ron could barely contain himself. He said that he had just seen some of the United lads nonchalantly chatting to the Dagenham Girl Pipers in the tunnel. They were all apparently laughing and joking. Ron said: 'They think this is going to be easy. We've got a fantastic chance to win this game.'

"I honestly believe that innocent chain of events affected the final result. We knew that we were ready but, even more importantly, we knew that the Manchester United players were not."

Jack describes the tense early minutes: "It was very even as both teams tried to adapt to the atrocious conditions. It was so bad that Eddie Bov tried to find Boycie with a short pass in midfield, only for the ball to get stuck in one of the puddles in the centre-circle.

"The first chance fell to Manchester United when the ball was played into our penalty-area and dropped at the feet of their Scottish international David Herd who I was marking. I just managed to block his shot and the ball hit my foot and was deflected over the bar. I still think it was a crucial moment because a goal then may have brought about a completely different outcome.

"On the other flank, Bondy was marking George Best who gained possession wide on the left touchline and cut in and fired in a shot from the edge of our penalty-area. The ball clipped the top of the cross-bar and bounced over. Apart from that, they didn't cause us too many problems."

It says much for Hammers' thorough pre-match planning that the threat of Best was virtually nullified as they set about restricting the service to him from his Manchester United colleagues. This tactic, together with the fact that Bond got much tighter on his man, meant that Best saw little of the ball thereafter.

So far as Burkett was concerned, he was described in one post-match report as having 'A quite brilliant day.' He hardly allowed the dangerous Herd a touch of the ball throughout the entire game with a series of perfectly timed challenges and classic sliding tackles, which were well suited to the Hillsborough mud. Indeed, such was Burkett's superiority over his opponent that the unfortunate Herd suffered some serious verbal abuse from the Manchester United fans. If this personal duel had been a boxing match, it would have been stopped long before the end.

At the heart of West Ham's defence, Brown marked his old adversary, the irrepressible Denis Law, with tremendous strength and fortitude. Alongside him, the majestic Moore performed the sweeper role with absolute perfection. There was no immediate opponent for him to mark – just endless interceptions, blockings and challenges – whilst, at the same time, setting up his own team's attacks with a series of immaculate and probing passes from deep inside his own half.

Boyce worked tirelessly in the midfield morass as his perception and anticipation blunted the forays of the immensely talented Pat Crerand. Elsewhere in midfield, iron-man Bovington completely marked the legendary Bobby Charlton out of the game.

Gradually, Hammers began to impose their authority on the proceedings. Hurst went close when keeper Gaskell was almost caught out by his clever and wickedly-aimed in-swinger from the left-wing, but Gaskell managed to palm the ball away. Byrne was beginning to find space and starting to cause United problems with his clever footwork and lightning turns, despite the quagmire.

At half-time, there was still no score but, if anything, West Ham had just edged the first period and, surprisingly, they had adapted to the conditions somewhat better than their more illustrious opponents.

"At half-time, we sat in the dressing room and knew that we were playing well," says Jack. "There was no need to make any tactical changes. Ron just impressed on us the need to keep playing as we were and we could go on and win it. In fact, he was spot-on because we took the lead early in the second-half through Boycie.

"He won possession in their half and looked up before hitting a 25-yarder past Gaskell into the top left-hand corner of the net. About 10 minutes later, we scored again. I won a corner-kick after playing a one-two with Sisso. As I was running back into my position in defence, I realised that their defenders were expecting an orthodox corner and they had lined up in their penalty-area to deal with it.

"I raced back upfield and called for a short corner from Sisso. He played the ball to me and I crossed it first time, left-footed, straight on to Boycie's head. His header flew past Gaskell. We were two goals up and we could almost see the Twin Towers of Wembley.

"As the minutes started to tick away, they started to get a bit desperate. Law was giving it everything, by fair means or foul, knowing that time was running out. In fairness, you had to admire his tenacity. With 10 minutes left, Denis went in hard on

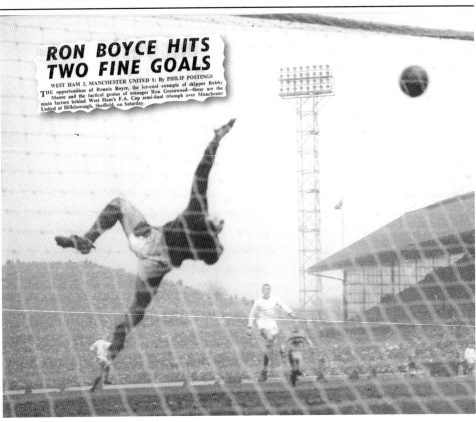

RON BOYCE HITS TWO FINE GOALS

WEST HAM 3, MANCHESTER UNITED 1: By PHILIP POSTINGS

THE opportunitism of Ronnie Boyce, the ice-cool example of skipper Bobby Moore and the tactical genius of manager Ron Greenwood—these are the main factors behind West Ham's F.A. Cup semi-final triumph over Manchester United at Hillsborough, Sheffield, on Saturday.

Ronnie's double delight – the flying David Gaskell was clutching thin air (above) as Boycie's shot puts Hammers ahead at Hillsborough . . . and the United keeper was made to eat his words again (below) when Ron made it 2-0 with a header from Jack Burkett's cross.

BOYCE—THE MUD-LARK
Bobby's boys whip holders—

Geoff Hurst (far left) watches his shot enter the net to clinch a mammoth victory in the mud.

Jim Standen. We got the ball away but Jim was hurt and it took a few minutes of treatment before he could continue.

"Suddenly, we were in trouble. Jim was still struggling when a cross came into our penalty-area and Denis climbed above Bondy to head home. It was 2-1 and I thought we would have a real fight on our hands. But straight from the kick-off, we scored again. Bobby won possession deep inside our half and went racing away with the ball down the left wing, past Crerand and Chisnall. He just managed to keep the ball in play before hitting a perfect through-ball to Geoff, who shot past Gaskell from the edge of the penalty-area to put us 3-1 ahead.

"It was pandemonium. We knew Manchester United were finished and they wouldn't come back again. It was a fantastic feeling to walk off the pitch knowing we were at Wembley. I shook hands with Gaskell. I wondered if he remembered his words from the previous week.

"At the end of the season, United finished up with nothing because they missed out on the League championship and the European Cup Winners' Cup as well."

It is a fact that Moore played a huge part in the goal that clinched victory on that historic day at Hillsborough. However, in later years, Hurst was slightly critical of the post-match reports because they entirely overlooked the superb run he had made into space, thus creating the opportunity for Moore to find him with his majestic through-ball. It was a good point because Hurst's run was timed to absolute perfection.

FABULOUS HILLSBOROU

HAMMER

Boyce goal magic then Moore genius

By BOB PENNINGTON   West Ham 3 Man. U. 1

MAGNIFICENTLY marshalled by Bobby Moore in the finest performance of his career, inspired by two uncharacteristic goals in seven minutes of magic by Ron Boyce, West Ham surged through to their first Final for 41 years with a superlative show.

WEST HA ARE IN CUP FIN

Discipline defeats swamp and genius

WEST HAM UTD. 3 MANCHESTER UTD. 1

THE Hillsborough heroes you can call them! Eleven gutsy, grafting Hammers whose

No sign of Ron Greenwood . . . but Moore, Brown, Hurst, Kirkup, Boyce (almost hidden), Byrne and Brabrook were blowing bubbles after the semi-final victory that sent Hammers to Wembley. Inset: Budgie Byrne and a fan.

HEROES !

Jack reflects on the celebrations: "After our semi-final win, there was a strange incident on the train journey back to London that evening. We were celebrating big-time. After all, we were entitled to do so because West Ham had just reached the FA Cup final.

"A lot of people were crowding into our carriage and the atmosphere was great but I noticed that Ron Greenwood was sitting at the far end on his own. He looked less than impressed. Bobby went over and spoke to him and, afterwards, Bobby told me that Ron was unhappy at all the hangers-on who were surrounding us. Bobby said to him that the so-called 'hangers-on' meant, at last, we were successful and he hoped they would be with us for a long time.

"It was odd but Ron was very unhappy about it."

Greenwood's unhappy demeanour was subsequently confirmed by a later quote from the West Ham manager who emphatically proclaimed: "This is the greatest day of their lives. I will let nothing and nobody spoil it before Wembley. I have been proud to be associated with them. Now the world and his friend will claim them. I accept that this must happen but I will not let the leeches, the hangers-on, the glad-handers destroy what they have built for themselves. I will do everything I can to protect them from the wrong sort of reaction to this success."

It was an astonishing outburst by the normally reserved Greenwood and it proved that, apart from being a fantastic coach and tactician, he could also be something of a complex individual.

The next day, the Fleet Street press boys, who had virtually written off West Ham's chances before the game, were unanimous in their praise for the performance of Greenwood's team. The headlines were ecstatic saying: 'Hammers – they were majestic' and 'Fabulous Hammers are Wembley bound'. Another said: 'Hail London's Pride'.

However, bearing in mind the conditions that had prevailed on the day, perhaps the most succinct and apt headline simply called them: 'Moore's Muddy Marvels'.

In the other semi-final played on the same afternoon, Preston beat Swansea by 2-1 at an equally drenched Villa Park. So second division Preston were now endeavouring to become the first team outside the top sphere to win the FA Cup since West Bromwich Albion had achieved the feat in 1931. It meant that West Ham were immediately installed as red-hot 5-2 on-favourites to win the FA Cup final at Wembley on May 2, 1964. If only things were that simple . . .

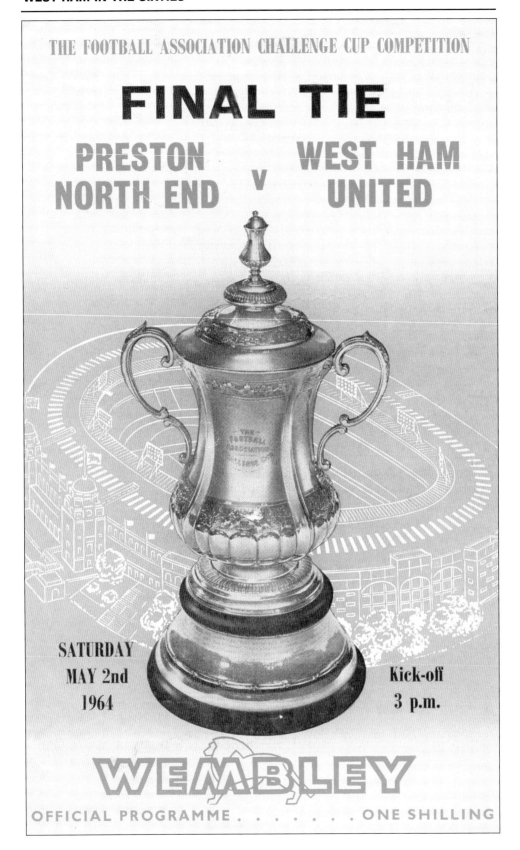

10

Davie Wilson's kneecaps

THERE was a seven-week gap between the semi-final and the FA Cup final itself. Jack recalls the build-up: "I suppose the main priority was not to get injured and miss the big day but at the same time, it was necessary to maintain form because the thought of getting dropped from the team for Wembley was too awful to contemplate.

"We were in mid-table, so there was no danger of having to battle against relegation. Four days after the semi-final win over Manchester United, we returned to league action with a re-arranged game against Leicester City at Filbert Street. We drew 2-2 and Roger Hugo and myself scored the goals. It was Roger's league debut and it was my first-ever league goal. The opposition goalkeeper was no less than Gordon Banks.

"In those days, it was customary for the two cup final teams to set up players' pools which was a legitimate way of making some extra cash in the weeks leading up to Wembley. Earlier in the season, John Lyall had been forced to announce his retirement from the game at the age of just 24 due to injury. He was a married man with a young son and his retirement was a great personal tragedy. Ron had kept John involved with the squad, particularly as our cup run to Wembley got under way. He sent John on some scouting missions to look at future cup opponents.

"We asked Ron if John could run the players' pool for us and he readily agreed. John set up an office in the club's press room. At the time, I don't suppose that even in his wildest dreams John could ever have envisaged that he would eventually succeed Ron as manager at West Ham and lead out the team in two FA Cup finals at Wembley in later years.

"Through the pool, we produced a cup final brochure and a special commemorative tie, which were sold to the fans. Also, getting to Wembley meant there were a few advertising and marketing opportunities for some of the players, plus some perks from newspapers and promotions. All the pool did was ensure that the whole squad got the benefit of the money and not just the 'star' players like Bobby and Budgie.

"Basically, everything earned from these spin-offs went into the pool which was shared equally amongst us. There were 15 players in the pool and, in the end, I made about £150. The club were due to pay us a bonus if we won the cup at Wembley and this amounted to £25.

"On the Monday evening before the final, we played a testimonial game at Upton Park for John Lyall against an ex-West Ham team. There was a decent crowd and I think John did fairly well out of it.

"Ron had already announced the team for Wembley – the same side that had won at Blackburn four months earlier, so there was no place for Martin Peters. We won the testimonial match 5-0 and in the second-half, Ron sent on a young unknown winger from our youth team in place of Peter Brabrook. It was the first time that he had played in the first team. His name was Harry Redknapp."

In 1964, it should be remembered that the BBC and, to an even lesser extent, ITV held a duopoly on the very restricted amount of live sport that was televised. It was a rare treat to see a live football match. The first flush of the colour television revolution was still five years away, whilst satellite TV with its saturation football coverage and rolling sports news was just an idle fantasy. As a result, the FA Cup final had a far bigger impact on the nation in those days, including the players themselves. It is fair to say that winning a FA Cup winners' medal in 1964 meant a lot more than it does to the players of today.

These days, when the reward for securing a place in the Premier League is at least £40million, it is not surprising that many clubs now only show a passing interest in the FA Cup. So far as the big four – Manchester United, Chelsea, Arsenal and Liverpool – are concerned, the FA Cup has been way down on their list of priorities for some years. It is an attitude that has spread throughout much of the Premier League and, sadly, even into the Championship as well. It has now got to the stage where some managers deliberately field weakened teams in FA Cup ties, so their players can be suitably rested for the league – as well as European Champions League – fixtures.

The prize money for the 2009 FA Cup winners was doubled to £2m, which is just a drop in the ocean when compared with the riches of the Premier League. The whole point is that the FA Cup has never been about finance. It's all about history and magnificent tradition. It is sad that those old fashioned virtues seem to count for very little these days and, tragically, the FA Cup has become an irritating distraction for some teams. It is a desperately sorry state of affairs.

When Jack Burkett was playing, the situation was quite the reverse. It seems incredible to think now that the FA Cup final was the only live game shown on TV in those days. In fact, there was very little football shown at all. The FA Cup final was the showpiece of the season and everybody wanted to watch it. The whole country came to a standstill on cup final day. There would be the build-up on TV starting in the late morning and everyone would watch the interviews with the players from their hotels before they left for the stadium.

There was the spectacle of the thronging crowds along Olympic Way and the great stone stadium with its majestic twin towers and the impeccable carpet of green turf.

There would be the community singing just before the kick-off. Somehow, even the cup final hymn *Abide With Me* seemed to be sung with more feeling and emotion than it is today. There was a great sense of anticipation because it meant kick-off – at the regulation time of 3.00pm on a Saturday, of course – was just minutes away.

In all probability and if they were given a choice, most players from that era would have chosen a FA Cup winners' medal above a League championship medal. It was the most glamorous, coveted trophy of all and there was a lot more glory attached to it than winning the league. The league title may say more about you as a team as you slogged your way through 42 league matches but except for that moment of final triumph, it could never match the excitement or emotion generated by the season's climax in the FA Cup final at Wembley.

As the big day approached, West Ham became even hotter favourites but Jack acknowledges that Preston were dangerous opponents: "They were a well organised side and had only just missed out on gaining promotion from the second division. Their main threat was centre-forward Alex Dawson, a big, bustling type of player and who was good in the air. He had previously played for Manchester United and we knew that Ken Brown, who would be marking him, was going to have a tough afternoon.

"Their mid-field consisted of two very skilful and industrious players, Alan Spavin and their captain Nobby Lawton, who was another ex-Manchester United player. The Preston manager, Jimmy Milne, caused a real sensation 48 hours before the game when he dropped their left-half Ian Davidson for disciplinary reasons. The 17-year-old Howard Kendall was brought in to replace him and, at the time, Kendall became the youngest player ever to play in a FA Cup final.

"In those days, the two cup final teams were allowed to visit Wembley on the day before the game. We went along on the Friday morning and Preston went in the afternoon. It allowed the players to get a 'feel' for the stadium and we could also walk on the famed Wembley turf. The pitch always looked so immaculate and as we were walking around, Jim Standen and myself noticed there was a member of the Wembley ground-staff down on his knees in the centre-circle. He appeared to be painting the turf.

"We walked over and asked him what he was doing. He explained that before any big game at Wembley, it was his job to apply green dye to the divots or parts of the pitch that were slightly worn. It suddenly became apparent why the Wembley turf always looked so lush and green!"

On the night before the game, West Ham stayed at the Hendon Hall Hotel in North London – the hotel that England usually frequented before games at Wembley. Jack admits to a sleepless night: "I was sharing a room with Martin, who slept like a log but, then again, he wasn't playing. I got up early and we all had breakfast together. Afterwards, a few of us – Geoff, Martin, Boycie, Sisso and me – went for a walk around the streets outside the hotel. Not a single person recognised us.

"The rest of that morning is a bit of a blur, including the journey to the stadium, but I do remember waiting in the Wembley tunnel for the signal to walk out on to the pitch. It was the biggest game of my career and I felt incredibly nervous."

Burkett was not the only one who was suffering a serious bout of nerves before the kick-off. Sitting high in the stands just behind the Royal Box were the West Ham players' wives and girlfriends.

Ann says: "I don't think I ever felt as nervous as I did before the FA Cup final. I was sitting next to Ron Boyce's fiancee, Dawn, and I was shaking with nerves. Before the teams came out, I prayed to God – literally – that West Ham would win and Jack would play well."

Unfortunately, God must have been otherwise engaged that afternoon or, perhaps, he was only partly listening to Ann's pre-match prayers. Within a few minutes of the kick-off, the future Mrs Burkett was earnestly praying yet again, this time that her fiancée would last the full 90 minutes on the pitch.

West Ham got away to a dreadful start. Preston took the initiative straight from the kick-off and Burkett, in particular, had more than his fair share of problems. In fact, he came perilously close to making football history, for all the wrong reasons, by almost becoming the first player ever to be sent off in a FA Cup final.

He looks back on those opening frenetic minutes at Wembley: "I was marking their right-winger, Davie Wilson, who was a small, tricky player. I was very nervous and as Davic went past me for the first time, I mistimed a sliding-tackle and brought him down right on the touchline. It looked bad but a few minutes later, he turned quickly and I obstructed him. A few minutes later, I brought him down again and I knew I was in trouble with the referee, Arthur Holland, a straight-talking Yorkshireman.

"He told me in no uncertain terms that I was close to being sent off. There were no red or yellow cards in those days and I was lucky to get away with it. I would definitely have been sent off in the modern game."

Nevertheless, Burkett settled down remarkably well after that early scare and, as the game progressed, proceeded to nullify the threat from Wilson which was a tribute to his cool temperament.

However, Preston's early pressure brought them a goal after just nine minutes when Standen failed to hold a shot from Alex Dawson and left-winger Doug Holden stabbed home the rebound from close range. The unavoidable truth is that Standen should not have conceded the Holden goal because he appeared to mistime his dive. It was a bad goal to give away but within a minute West Ham were level.

Moore broke out of defence and found Sissons, who played a one-two with Byrne before rifling home a shot from the edge of the penalty-area. At that moment, Sissons had become the youngest player in history to score in a FA Cup final.

"It was good to be level so quickly but Preston were still causing us all sorts of problems," admits Jack. "Our counter-attacks were not coming off and Spavin and Lawton were controlling the midfield.

"The real problem revolved around Bobby playing the sweeper role alongside Ken Brown. It was a tactic that had always worked well for us and it had got us to Wembley. It was good because Ken would always mark the opposition's main striker, while Bobby acted as the spare defender alongside him covering the threat in the air and also the knock-downs.

"But Preston played with two bustling strikers – Alex Dawson and Alex Ashworth – and they were making good use of Wembley's big pitch. As a result, Bobby was being left in no-man's land because he was being bypassed.

Above: Inspecting the Wembley pitch on the day before the game – Jack is flanked by Geoff Hurst and Jim Standen. Below: The West Ham WAGS leave for Wembley – back: Judith Harries (Geoff Hurst's fiancee) and Joan Brown. Front (left to right) Dawn Ames (Ron Boyce's fiancee), Ann Rivers (Jack Burkett's fiancee), Elise Standen, Doreen Brabrook and Tina Moore.

"Just before half-time, we conceded another bad goal when Dawson powered his way past Ken and headed home a corner-kick. Jim Standen slipped as he went for the ball, which didn't help matters.

"We went in at half-time 2-1 down and feeling very dejected. We weren't playing well and Ron told us that we were allowing Lawton and Spavin too much time and space. He told Eddie Bov to man-mark Spavin in the second-half and Boycie to look after Lawton. Almost immediately, we began to get the upper hand and both Spavin and Lawton lost their earlier effectiveness."

The change in West Ham's tactics began to turn the tide in their favour but when the equaliser came, it was somewhat fortunate. Brabrook took a corner on the right and Brown headed the ball onto Hurst whose own header hit the bar and bounced down before hitting the grounded goalkeeper Alan Kelly in the face and squirming over the line. The recording of the game shows that, strictly speaking, it could have been classified as an own goal by Kelly, but the record books have always credited Hurst with the goal.

Jack continues: "I felt that I was well on top of Davie Wilson in the second-half and I began to really enjoy the game. He didn't give me any more problems but in fairness, we were all playing a lot better. In particular, Jim was dealing with everything very comfortably now and confidence was spreading throughout the team. We had a number of chances and the longer the game went on, we were always going to be the more likely winners. But as the minutes ticked away, it looked as though there would be extra-time because we hadn't been able to make that vital breakthrough."

With 10 minutes remaining, Bovington collapsed with an attack of cramp in the centre-circle and play was held up before the indestructible 'Bov' could resume after treatment. It meant that the referee allowed three minutes of injury-time and it was during this period that the FA Cup was won. Although God didn't quite realise it, he was about to receive his third prayer of the afternoon from Ann Rivers – but this time it was a prayer of thanks.

With 60 seconds of injury-time remaining and extra-time looming, Standen's goal-

WEST STANDING ENCLOSURE

ENTER AT **H** TURNSTILES
(See plan & conditions on back)

ENTRANCE **57**

EMPIRE STADIUM, WEMBLEY
The Football Association
Cup Competition

FINAL TIE

SATURDAY, MAY 2nd, 1964
KICK-OFF 3 p.m.

Price 7/6

Chairman,
Wembley Stadium Limited

THIS PORTION TO BE RETAINED
This ticket is issued on the condition that
it is not re-sold for more than its face value.

WEST HAM

1964

The Official Publication
of the West Ham Players

Price **2/6**

*Above: A distinct lack of banners and
replica shirts in the crowd as managers
Jimmy Milne and Ron Greenwood lead
out their teams. West Ham players (left to
right): Moore, Byrne, Bovington (almost
hidden by Budgie), Bond, Hurst, Boyce,
Brabrook, Burkett, Standen, Sissons,
Brown.*

Top: Match ticket for Wembley.

*Right: The pre-Wembley brochure that
raised money for the players' pool.*

Above: Bobby Moore introduces the Earl of Harewood to Jim Standen, with Jack waiting next in line.
Below: John Sissons made FA Cup history when he scored Hammers' equaliser with this low shot inside the far post that gave Preston keeper Alan Kelly no chance.

Above: Ashworth (8) crashes into Jim Standen and Bobby Moore as the ball lands on the roof of the West Ham net. Jack Burkett watches anxiously from the far side of the goal while Ken Brown stays close to Dawson.
Below: Burkett, Standen, Eddie Bovington and John Bond can't prevent Preston's second goal.

Two views of Geoff Hurst heading Hammers' second goal, with Johnny Byrne (9) and John Sissons looking on.

Wembley winner: Ron Boyce heads Brabrook's pinpoint cross goalwards before (below) going on his memorable run behind the Preston goal, where the West Ham fans were waiting to acclaim the Cup final hero.

Johnny Byrne turns somersaults to celebrate Ronnie Boyce's Wembley winner.

Skipper Bobby Moore descends the 39 Wembley steps after lifting the most coveted silverware in British football.

Moments to treasure for the players as they get their hands on the FA Cup for the first time.
Above: Bobby Moore stands proud alongside Ken Brown, John Bond and Peter Brabrook, with John Sissons and Jim Standen in the background. Above left: Jack Burkett and Standen take a handle each as Geoff Hurst salutes the fans. Left: Burkett and Bond (2) stand alone in a moment of magic while Johnny Byrne embraces goalscorers Sissons and Hurst.

Secret behind West Ham's triumph

THE MASTER STROKE..

Greenwood gambled — and turned the match

One of the finest Finals for many a year

BANG ON HAMMERS

Last-minute goal K.O's Preston

IT'S WEST HAM A 3-2 VICTORY

Fantastic! When Hammers came riding home again..

kick looped high into the air and was neatly collected by Hurst just inside Preston's half. Despite the close attention of his immediate opponent, Tony Singleton, Hurst rode his marker's challenge and made a diagonal run towards the right-flank. As Singleton made another clumsy attempt to dispossess Hurst, he played the ball to the unmarked Brabrook, who crossed perfectly to the far post.

Boyce had judged his run to perfection from midfield and headed the ball into the opposite corner of the net past the stranded Kelly. As the ball crossed the line, Boyce leapt into the air but his momentum carried him past the near upright and he was forced to run around the back of the goal with his arms held triumphantly aloft before returning to the pitch and receiving the congratulations of his team-mates.

West Ham were 3-2 winners and had won a major trophy for the first time in their history.

Jack recalls: "As the final whistle sounded, the immediate reaction was one of overwhelming relief because we had won. I can't really remember going up the steps to the Royal Box to receive the cup and our winners' medals from the Earl of Harewood. It was all a bit of a blur.

"It was only on the lap of honour that I realised what it meant to West Ham's fans.

I'll drink to that!: John Sissons can't wait to follow Ken Brown in drinking from football's most famous trophy.

They were massed high on the terracing behind the goal where Boycie had scored the winner and as we ran towards them with the FA Cup in our hands, there seemed to be an explosion of noise. It was a moving moment and one that I will always remember. It was a real highlight for me.

"That night, we attended the club's official banquet at the Hilton Hotel in London's Park Lane and, afterwards, some of us went to Danny La Rue's night club in Hanover Square, which was a popular haunt for footballers in those days.

"We stayed the night at the Hilton and the next morning, we found out what winning the FA Cup *really* meant to the people of East London. It was estimated that a quarter-of-a-million people turned out to watch as we paraded the trophy from the roof of an open-topped coach. It edged its way through Whitechapel, Stepney and along the Mile End Road until it reached Upton Park.

"The crowds were 10-deep in some parts with supporters hanging from lamp-posts

Left: West Ham fans go wild with delight at the final whistle, while (below) back in the East End later that night the pubs were full of jubilant supporters enjoying a good, ol' knees-up.

and others leaning out of balconies. The journey took nearly four hours, on what is normally a 30-minute drive. It was an unforgettable experience. That was what winning the FA Cup was all about – knowing the fans were proud of what we had achieved."

West Ham were one of the youngest teams to win the Cup. The average age of the side was 24 and they were an all-English side. Eight members of the team had come through the junior ranks at Upton Park. Only Jim Standen, Peter Brabrook and Budgie Byrne had been signed from other clubs – an amazing statistic. It would be impossible for a team to win the FA Cup in similar circumstances in modern day football.

Jack continues: "Jim always looked like the 'complete sportsman' and I suppose he was exactly that, because a couple of days after our win against Preston he went

Thousands of fans lined the streets of East London and used every vantage point possible to get a glimpse of their homecoming Hammers heroes.

off to play cricket for Worcestershire throughout the rest of that summer. In those days, there were a few players who were able to play both games but with the growing pressures of top-class football, it was becoming increasingly difficult. Jim was one of the last players to do so and in the summer of 1964, he won the County Championship with Worcestershire and topped the bowling averages.

"It was a unique achievement coming off the back of our FA Cup victory and will never be equalled.

"Many years later, a good friend of mine pointed out that the 1964 FA Cup final was my 100th league and cup appearance for West Ham. It was not a statistic that I was aware of at the time but I was just thrilled to gain a cup winners' medal so early in my career. Over the years, there had been some great international players such as John Charles of Leeds United and Johnny Haynes of Fulham who had never even played in a final.

"I felt very privileged but at the same time, I think most of us were a little disappointed with our Wembley performance. We were proud of our football abilities and we wanted to show it on the biggest occasion of all. The fact that we hadn't done so was a bit of a let down."

There was an interesting postscript to West Ham's win against

Incredible scenes greeted the returning Cup winners around Upton Park and East Ham on the morning after the final. Then it was on to the Boleyn Ground, where there were even more jubilant supporters ready to salute their favourites. Left: Bobby Moore, John Bond, Eddie Bovington and Ron Greenwood look down from the directors' box

Preston, albeit some 40 years after the event. During a subsequent visit to the Lancashire town, Jack discovered that he was still known as 'The Cruncher' in those parts. At a Preston player's reunion dinner in 2004, their right-back George Ross made an amusing after-dinner speech which he concluded with the request: "Can I please ask Jack Burkett to return Davie Wilson's kneecaps!"

It was a neat reminder that they still had not forgotten the harsh treatment handed out to their diminutive winger at Wembley on that memorable day.

In truth, such a reputation is grossly unfair because Jack was a class act and he was never booked or sent off in his entire career. Nevertheless, it is abundantly clear that the good people of Preston have long memories and it is doubtful, even now, that Jack Burkett would win any popularity contests in that part of the world.

Above: 'Mooro' parading the FA Cup.

Left: Back at the Boleyn Ground, Jack Burkett leads the players on their walk around the stadium, followed by Bobby Moore, Geoff Hurst, Ken Brown, John Sissons and Ron Boyce.

Right: How the press covered the big East End celebrations.

THE EAST END GOES WILD

EAST LONDON'S 92-year wait for the F.A. Cup ended in a fusillade of flying champagne corks and a reservoir of pints last night as Cockneyland celebrated West Ham's last minute Wembley victory.

East Enders, who, over the years have suffered in silence while other London clubs have captured soccer's most elusive prize, really let down their hair and went to town.

Pubs were packed to the doors, and with their "booze" the Cockneys ate their jellied eels.

Centre of the Great Night Out was West Ham's "own" pub—the Boleyn, a few yards from United's ground. It was "Champers" all the way as hoarse-throated supporters streamed back from Wembley.

Rattles, horns and trumpets blared as the 35-year-old manager, Mike O'Sullivan, said: "We've never had a night like it. We're always busy after the team has a win but tonight they've gone mad."

Outside the crowd spilled out across the road linked arms and began to do "Knees up Mother Brown." Traffic on two main roads was brought to a standstill and extra police were called in.

Now turn to the Back Page.

Match of the Day: Ann and Jack are married on June 20, 1964.

11

Into Europe

EXACTLY seven weeks after the FA Cup final at Wembley, Jack Burkett and Ann Rivers were married at St John Vianney's Church in Harringay on Saturday, June 20, 1964. Ann vividly recalls her big day: "Some of the West Ham players had gone away on holiday but quite a few of them – Geoff Hurst, Martin Peters, Ron Boyce, John Sissons and Joe Kirkup – attended the wedding with their partners.**

"We held the reception at the Greyhound pub which was at the corner of Lawrence Road in Tottenham, where Jack lived.

"We went to Ibiza for our honeymoon and when we got back, we moved into the house that we had bought for the princely sum of £5,100. We were able to pay for the deposit with the money West Ham had been putting aside for Jack from his wages from the first day that he had joined the club, plus the other money that he had so meticulously added to it over the years.

"It was a very modest semi-detached house in Hatherway Gardens in Chadwell Heath, just a few minutes drive from the training ground. It was a perfect summer.

"There were three other 'West Ham weddings' that year because Geoff, Martin and Ron all got married as well. I suppose my closest friend was Dawn Boyce and when the team were playing away, Dawn and I would often stay with one another.

"All the girls used to sit together at home matches and we would always be shouting encouragement. Unfortunately, we also used to talk a lot amongst ourselves and, sometimes, we would miss a goal because we were so busy 'yapping' – but we didn't let on to our husbands!

"We tried to ignore the crowd if they were having a go at the players but on one occasion, Judith Hurst took particular exception to one fan who was giving Geoff a hard time. It was before Geoff became an England player and Judith was a very strong character. She shouted back at him. When he answered her, she went and hit him with her umbrella!

"I suppose there was a bit of rivalry amongst all the players' wives in terms of the clothes that we wore. Secretly, we were always trying to outdo one another but there was no 'designer labels' like Gucci or Versace for us. Our clothes just came from the local high street. The only problem was that none of us could compete with Tina Moore. She had a wonderful dress sense and she was an extraordinarily pretty girl."

It's 1964 and the West Ham WAGS are in town!
Top: Cheering on their men-folk at Upton Park are (left to right) Dawn Boyce, Kathy Peters, Ann Burkett, Judith Hurst and Jill Kirkup.
Above: In the players' lounge at Upton Park – Ron and Dawn Boyce, Jack and Ann Burkett, Geoff and Judith Hurst and Martin and Kathy Peters.
Above right: Kathy Peters shows her football skill as Martin watches, together with (left to right) Judith Hurst, Ann and Jack Burkett, Dawn and Ron Boyce and Geoff Hurst looking on.
Right: A night out at London's Talk of the Town in November '64. Left (from front): Jack Burkett, Ann Burkett, Dawn Boyce, Ron Boyce, Eddie Chapman (secretary), Mrs Chapman. Right: Eddie Bovington, Pauline Bovington, Martin Peters, Kathy Peters, Geoff Hurst, Judith Hurst.

Newly-married Ann admits that she had to quickly get used to her husband's preparations for matches and there was a distinct change in his normal laid-back attitude whenever a game was approaching.

She says: *"I imagine it's what most footballers' wives have to live with. On the day before a game, home or away, Jack would always get a bit edgy. He would have his meal at home on the Friday evening and be in bed by nine o'clock. I think he was a very dedicated player and always tried to look after himself.*

"On the morning of a game, he would be up quite early but he couldn't sit still. Around midday, he would leave the house and drive to Upton Park to meet up with the other players.

"It was also noticeable that it would take him a day or so to get back to normal after a game but if the team had lost or he had not played well, then he would be very down for a couple of days afterwards. Nevertheless, our life was very happy – but also very mundane. There was no stardom at all like the players of today receive. We were just a normal young couple living contentedly in our semi-detached house. They were wonderful times."

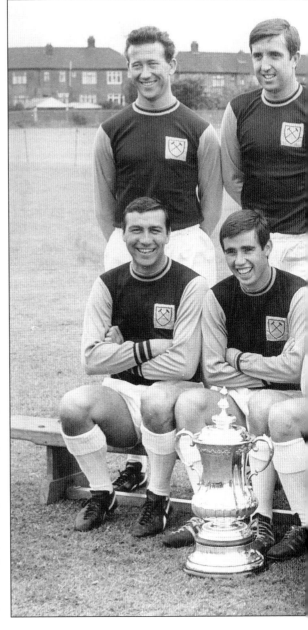

With a coveted cup winners' medal in his pocket, Burkett looked forward to West Ham's first ever participation in European competition. After their success at Wembley, Hammers had qualified for the prestigious European Cup Winners' Cup. However, before the season had got under way, Burkett learned that he was the subject of a transfer bid from Bill Nicholson, the legendary Spurs' manager.

At the start of the decade, Spurs had become one of the greatest club sides of all time when they became the first team in the 20th century to win the League and FA Cup double – a feat that had previously been considered impossible. Under Nicholson's astute management, Spurs had gone on to win the FA Cup yet again and also the European Cup Winners' Cup – the first British side to win a major European trophy.

Summer of '64 and Hammers parade the FA Cup alongside the Charity Shield, which they shared with Liverpool after the drawn game at Anfield. Back row, left to right: Ken Brown, John Bond, Jim Standen, Jack Burkett, Eddie Bovington, Bobby Moore. Front: Peter Brabrook, Ron Boyce, Johnny Byrne, Geoff Hurst, John Sissons.

West Ham were about to become the second team.

In the summer of 1964, Nicholson was gradually breaking up his side as they started to grow old and he began the process of rebuilding. He had already bought a young Irish goalkeeper called Pat Jennings from Watford to take over from Scottish international Bill Brown and his next objective was to replace the long-serving but ageing Ron Henry at left-back.

Jack says: "It had been in the newspapers that Bill was interested in me and, one day after training, Ron Greenwood called me into his office and said that Spurs had

Blackburn Rovers' Ronnie Clayton blocks Jack's cross during the 1-1 draw at Upton Park in November '64.

made an offer of £45,000. It was a decent fee but Ron said: 'I've turned it down, you are not going anywhere.'

"I was flattered that Bill wanted to sign me and, I suppose, equally flattered that Ron had been so emphatic in turning down the offer. As it turned out, Bill signed Cyril Knowles from Middlesbrough instead and Cyril went on to have a good career at White Hart Lane.

"If Ron had said I could have gone to Spurs, then it would have been a tough decision for me. Obviously, I was a Tottenham boy and it would have been nice to play for them but, then again, West Ham were the club with whom I had grown up and we had tasted success. Perhaps it is just as well that I never had to make that decision."

West Ham's first game of the 1964-65 season was against Liverpool at Anfield for the Charity Shield, the annual curtain-raiser between the League champions and FA Cup holders. Hammers fielded the side that had beaten Preston at Wembley and drew 2-2 thanks to goals from Budgie Byrne and Geoff Hurst. There were no penalty shoot-outs in those days, so the Charity Shield was shared, with each team keeping the trophy for six months apiece.

At the end of the game, skippers Bobby Moore and Ron Yeats tossed a coin on the Anfield pitch to determine who would keep the trophy for the initial six month period. It was Moore who called correctly and the Charity Shield thus accompanied the West Ham party back to London that night. Each player was presented with a miniature replica of the trophy. The following week, and for the only time in Hammers' history, both the FA Cup and Charity Shield were pictured together

Jack heads clear from Arsenal's George Armstrong (11) as Don Howe watches during Hammers' 3-0 win at Highbury in November '64.

during the team's photograph sessions with the enthusiastic press boys.

Burkett was in good form in the early weeks of the new season but the team as a whole were performing inconsistently. By the end of October, they were in mid-table and had been eliminated at the first hurdle in the League Cup when Sunderland beat them 4-1 at Roker Park.

However, they overcame the Belgian part-timers La Gantoise from Ghent in the opening round of the European Cup Winners' Cup by 2-1 on aggregate. It should have been about as routine as a first round match on Wimbledon's centre-court for Martina Navratilova in later years, but Hammers were lethargic, particularly in the second leg at Upton Park, which was drawn 1-1. At the final whistle, their fans were quick to let them know what they thought of such a disappointing performance.

Earlier in the day, reserve goalkeeper Alan Dickie had spent the afternoon relaxing at home before setting off to watch the game. He was caught in heavy traffic driving through the Blackwall Tunnel and only arrived at Upton Park 25 minutes before the kick-off to find the dressing-room area in a state of sheer panic.

Jim Standen had declared himself unfit to play and, in the days before mobile phones, club officials had found it impossible to contact their young keeper and were facing a real dilemma finding a suitable replacement. Fortunately, Dickie's late arrival solved the problem.

Hammers' next opponents were the powerful Czechoslovakian side Spartak Sokolovo from Prague. It promised to be a difficult tie and so it proved. Fortunately, West Ham turned in two excellent performances. In the first leg at Upton Park in late November, Hammers pounded the Czechs' goal but without success until right-back John Bond rifled home a shot from 30-yards to break the deadlock after 60 minutes. It was the veteran Bond's first goal for three years. A second goal from Alan Sealey eight minutes from time gave West Ham a 2-0 lead to take to the second leg but everyone at Upton Park was acutely aware that only their very best form in the return match would be good enough to see them through.

In modern times, the beautiful city of Prague has become one of Europe's most popular tourist attractions. It is picturesque and delightful, if one ignores the stag parties that have become an irritating blot on the city's landscape. However, in 1964, a somewhat different culture existed.

In those days, Prague was the capital of Czechoslovakia, which lay behind the Iron Curtain and the boundary that had symbolically, ideologically and physically divided Europe into two separate areas at the end of hostilities in the Second World War. As a result, a number of countries, including Czechoslovakia, remained under the political influence of the Soviet Union in the Eastern bloc. The Soviet Union imposed its repressive measures on all such countries and at the time, the city of Prague was a foreboding and depressing place.

Jack confirms: "It was early December when we played out there. The whole city was patrolled by armed guards. It was the way of life under a

communist regime and the people looked very downtrodden and poor.

"It was freezing cold and the pitch was icy with snow piled up behind the goals. The game was played on a Wednesday afternoon because they didn't have any floodlights. It was like a non-league ground because there was only one small stand and the rest of the ground was uncovered terracing. There was a decent attendance of over 40,000 crammed into the stadium and like most European crowds, they were

Eastern promise: With Bobby Moore injured, Ken Brown – carrying a very fetching bouquet of flowers! – led the team out in Prague for Hammers' first ever European tie behind the old Iron Curtain. Eddie Bovington, Ron Boyce Jack Burkett and Martin Peters are the Hammers immediately behind the stand-in skipper, while Johnny Byrne and Alan Sealey (7) seem preoccupied with Budgie's head.

very noisy and partisan.

"Bobby was missing through injury, so Boycie played in his place alongside Ken Brown. Ron had one of his best ever games for West Ham that day."

It was as tough a battle as Hammers feared. Fortunately, Sissons gave them an early lead but, thereafter, Spartak surged forward in an endeavour to reduce the 3-0 aggregate deficit. Standen saved a penalty but could do little to prevent two late goals which set up a nail-biting finale.

With the aggregate score at 3-2, Hammers' defenders faced a barrage of crosses as the Czechs poured forward in search of the equaliser. In the end, West Ham held on, but it was a desperately close call.

It didn't matter, though, because they were through to the quarter-finals of the European Cup Winners' Cup Suddenly, the Upton Park faithful were dreaming about the possibility of another glorious cup success.

Above: The ground-breaking Hammers before kick-off in Prague. Back row, left to right: John Bond, Jack Burkett, Jim Standen, Ken Brown, Eddie Bovington, Martin Peters. Front: Alan Sealey, Ron Boyce, Johnny Byrne, Geoff Hurst, John Sissons.

Left: Bond and Peters defend.

Right: Sissons scoring the vital away goal in Czechoslovakia.

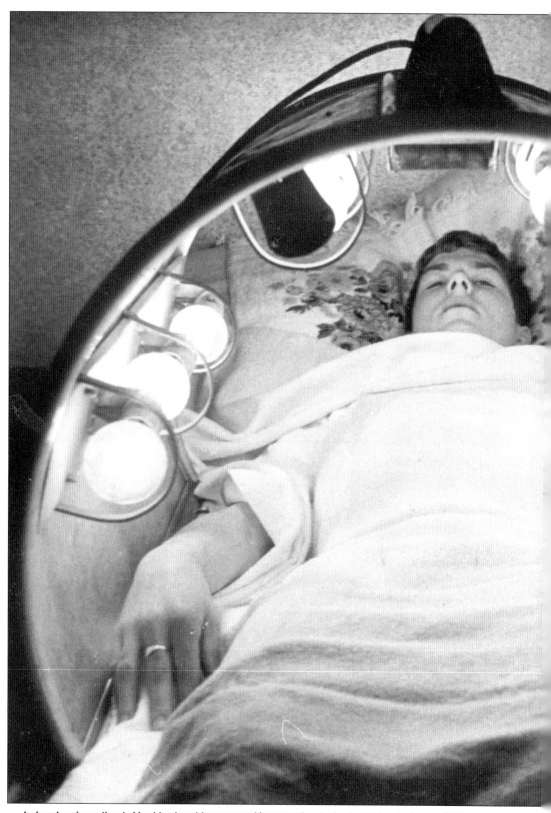

Jack undergoing antiquated heat treatment to overcome his career-threatening back injury in January 1965.

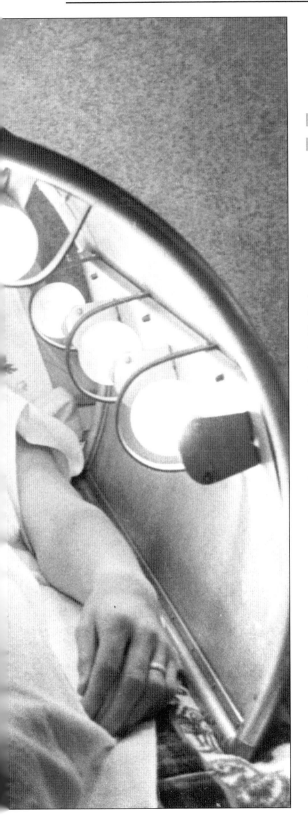

12

Every Footballer's Nightmare

AS Christmas approached, life was good for Jack Burkett because his form remained outstanding and the pre-season interest from Bill Nicholson had merely confirmed his increasing stature within the game. Also, he was being widely tipped for an England under-23 cap. Unfortunately, football has a nasty habit of producing some unexpected and unpleasant surprises.

On Boxing Day 1964, Hammers travelled to meet Birmingham City at St. Andrew's. It was a brutally cold day and the pitch was frosty. The Midlands side adapted to the conditions far better than West Ham and ran out deserving 2-1 winners.

"During the game, I seemed to jar my back on the hard pitch and it was quite sore on the train journey home," explains Jack. "The following day, the pain got worse and I reported to Upton Park for treatment from our physio Bill Jenkins but it didn't improve. A couple of days later, I was in serious pain and I was sent to hospital. After some tests and x-rays, I was told I had cracked a vertebra in my lower back.

"Suddenly, the seriousness of the injury

hit home when the Harley Street specialist said that I might need an operation. The problem was that, in his estimation, there was only a 50 per cent chance of success – and if it went wrong, which was a possibility, then I had to be aware that there was the potential danger of paralysis setting in.

"I was stunned. Just a few days earlier, I was 100 per cent fit and playing in the first division at the top of my profession. Suddenly, I was being told that at the age of 22, my career could be over and, worse still, I could end up being paralysed.

"The only other option was to be encased in plaster from the chest down to the hips for a minimum of two months, in the hope it would eventually heal itself. Given the paralysis warning, it seemed I didn't have much option other than to go for the plaster-cast option."

Ann takes up the story: "We were sick with worry. Jack was in plaster, although at least he was at home and not in hospital. He had to lie in bed as still as possible for eight weeks.

"We talked endlessly about what we would do if his career was finished because Jack didn't know anything else apart from football. It was the nightmare situation that every footballer dreads. The strange thing is that we never actually discussed other options and the reason was that Jack was so adamant that he would overcome the injury and get back into West Ham's first team.

"He simply refused to accept the possibility of the worse case scenario happening. He was incredibly determined – but it was still another occasion in my life when I did a lot of praying."

In the first week of March, Jack returned to hospital to have the plaster cast removed. Fortunately, the x-rays showed the cracked areas of the vertebra had fused together but the crucial question was whether or not it would be able to withstand the rigours of professional football. Although the specialist had given him strict instructions to rest as much as possible, Burkett made a 'secret' visit to West Ham's training ground after the playing staff had departed following that particular day's training session. He pulled on a track-suit and went jogging around the perimeter of one of the pitches.

Unfortunately, it transpired that Ron Greenwood was still at the training ground and the Hammers' manager was aghast to see him taking those first tentative steps in trying to achieve fitness again. Greenwood was aware of the specialist's instructions and was not impressed at the apparent obstinacy of Jack, who concedes his actions could have had serious consequences.

"I was actually in a lot of pain as I was running but I told Ron I felt OK. I was lying but I was determined that the injury was not going to beat me and that I would get my place back in West Ham's first team. On reflection, I accept it was foolhardy because I could have made things a lot worse. But I just wanted to play again."

In Burkett's absence, West Ham had enjoyed mixed fortunes. In the league, the team continued to hover around mid-table. As FA Cup holders, they had been drawn against Birmingham City in the third round at Upton Park which was their initial defence of the trophy. Unfortunately, 'Brum' raced to an early two-goal lead and as their jubilant fans roared out their anthem, *Keep right on to the end of the road*, it

The grounded Brian Dear can't see his shot entering the net in the victory over Lausanne in Switzerland.

seemed that the holders were going out at the first hurdle. However, inspired by Byrne and Hurst, Hammers staged a thrilling comeback and ran out 4-2 winners.

Sadly, inspiration was somewhat lacking when Tommy Docherty's Chelsea won 1-0 in the fourth round at Upton Park thanks to an early Bobby Tambling goal. West Ham had relinquished their hold on the FA Cup. It was a bitter pill for their fans to swallow as the Chelsea players celebrated a famous victory at the final whistle.

Fortunately, there was better progress in the European Cup Winners' Cup as Hammers overcame Lausanne of Switzerland 6-4 on aggregate in the quarter-final. They were drawn against Real Zaragoza from Spain in the semi-final with the first leg scheduled to be played at the Boleyn Ground. It was not the draw that West Ham wanted because the Spaniards were regarded as the strongest of the four teams left in the competition. In the other semi-final, TSV Munich 1860 from Germany had been drawn to meet the Italian side Torino.

Burkett was not the only Hammers' player who had been forced to miss a substantial part of that season through injury. In late October, Bobby Moore had pulled out of the home league game against Blackburn Rovers supposedly due to a 'groin strain'. Within a matter of days, Moore was in the London Hospital in Whitechapel undergoing an operation and he was missing from the team for three months.

Jack says: "So far as we were concerned, it was a hernia and when Bobby started training again, he didn't give us any indication to the contrary. What we didn't know was that Bobby had been diagnosed with testicular cancer and the operation was to remove a testicle.

"It wasn't until many years later that all of this became public knowledge and I always admired him for what he went on to achieve with England, particularly in 1966. At the time, I believe that only Ron Greenwood and physio Bill Jenkins were aware of Bobby's situation but nobody else at the club was told."

It is necessary to put the seriousness of Moore's diagnosis into perspective. Thanks to the advances of modern day medicine, more men than ever are surviving testicular cancer and the current survival rate is 97 per cent.

However, in the mid-60s when Moore was diagnosed with the disease, the survival rate was less than 50 per cent. Astonishingly, he was back in West Ham's first team by mid-February and looking as if he had never been out of the side. It was an incredible comeback.

Exactly one month later, Burkett's own comeback was under way. Despite Greenwood's undoubted concerns, he persevered and gradually stepped up his training programme under the watchful eye of Bill Jenkins.

Jack recalls: "While I was out of the side, Ron had played Martin in my position at left-back, although a very loyal reserve player called Eddie Presland had also come in and done well for a few games, including scoring the winner in a 2-1 win against Liverpool at Upton Park. It was Eddie's league debut. For the first time since I had got into the side three years earlier, my place was now seriously in doubt.

"There was also the monetary aspect. In modern football, players have these huge contracts and irrespective of whether or not they are in the team, they still receive their colossal weekly wages. If they are injured, there is no real incentive to overcome the pain and get back into the team as quickly as possible because their earnings are assured.

"At the time of my injury, I was earning £50 a week at West Ham, which was decent money in those days – probably twice the average weekly wage of the rest of the workforce in the country. The problem was that our contracts stated that if we were out of the first team for more than one month, then our wages were reduced to the equivalent of playing in the reserves – until we were back in the first team again on a regular basis. Roughly speaking, it meant that my wages had been reduced by 50 per cent, so I needed to get back into the first team.

"I felt better because I was back amongst the lads again, although I wasn't actually in full training. I was still in a lot of pain but I felt it was getting slightly easier. I kept having pain-killers, hot baths and massages. After a couple of weeks, I asked Ron if I could have a run-out in the reserves. All he said was: 'Are you sure?' but I said that I wanted to get a game under my belt. He reluctantly agreed and although I didn't play well, my back held up.

"The following week, I played another reserve game. This time, I felt that I had a good game although by this point, I was living with a considerable degree of pain all the time.

"Ron hardly spoke to me during this period. I almost got the impression that he was trying to avoid me. Obviously, the club were aware that I wasn't even supposed to be training, let alone playing, so I guess they were holding their breath in case I did some permanent damage.

None of the other West Ham players were initially aware of the full extent of Bobby Moore's 'groin' injury.

Hammers minus the injured Jack Burkett. Back row, left to right: Ken Brown, Martin Peters, John Bond, Jim Standen, Eddie Bovington, Bobby Moore. Front: Peter Brabrook, Ron Boyce, Johnny Byrne, Geoff Hurst, John Sissons.

"I played a third game in the reserves and this time, I played really well. But the following day, my back was very stiff and sore. I had more massages and took further pain-killers. By then, I had decided that I would just ignore the continuous pain and hope it would go away. In actual fact, that is exactly what happened, although it did have an impact on the rest of my career – there were many occasions when my movement was very restricted."

Jack remembers the day when his comeback was complete: "At the end of March, we were due to play Aston Villa in a rearranged league game at Villa Park. It was an evening match and Ron had a problem because there were a few injuries. I volunteered to play in my usual position at left-back. I actually approached Ron with a view to playing. He still hadn't spoken to me. I said that I was 100 per cent fit, even though that wasn't the case.

"When the team sheet went up, I was in the side. It was just over three months since I had cracked the vertebra on Boxing Day. I just prepared myself to withstand the pain and concentrate on playing well.

"We were 2-0 down at half-time at Villa Park but we fought back to win 3-2 with goals from Geoff, Budgie and Brian Dear. Even though I say it myself, I played a blinder that night and as we walked into the dressing-room at the end of the game, Ron just smiled at me. At that moment, I knew I had won back my place in the side and neither of us ever mentioned my back injury again. I kept my place for the rest of the season.

"But it came at a cost, because it still causes me problems to this day."

Apart from Burkett's brave and impressive display at Villa Park, it should also be said that Bobby Moore was back to his brilliant best. In separate ways and to their eternal credit, both players had overcome two harrowing ordeals with considerable fortitude and determination. They were now ready to play their part in the build-up to the greatest triumph in West Ham's history.

In those days, the European Cup Winners' Cup was second only in importance to the European Cup. In the modern era, it would be the equivalent of the Europa Cup and, with all due respect to the present incumbents at Upton Park, there appears to be little chance of them being successful at that sort of level, unlike their illustrious predecessors of the mid-60s.

Just prior to the beginning of the 1964-65 season, UEFA announced the venues for the finals of the various European competitions. Much to the delight of all at Upton Park, the final of the European Cup Winners' Cup was to be played at Wembley. West Ham were now in the semi-final and the highly dangerous Real Zaragoza stood between them and a return to the famous old stadium.

The city of Zaragoza is the fifth largest in Spain and lies mid-way between Madrid and Barcelona. It produced one of Spain's most famous painters, Francisco De Goya, and its castle was once the home of the Catholic monarchs King Ferdinand and Queen Isabella. In the mid-60s, Real Zaragoza also had a superb football team and they were reputed to have the best forward line in Europe. Each player in their attacking formation had been capped by his country and they were called *Los Cincos Magnificos* – alias 'The Magnificent Five.'

The first leg of the semi-final was played at Upton Park on April 7 – just seven days after Burkett's comeback match at Villa Park. It was a sell-out and the ground was packed to capacity as Moore led his team onto the pitch to the strains of the *Post Horn Gallop* which was the inspiring tune to which West Ham took the field in those days. Roared on by their fans, Hammers started like world beaters. They were two goals up within 25 minutes thanks to strikes from Dear and Byrne. The twin towers of Wembley were in their sights.

Unfortunately, Zaragoza began to claw their way back into the game and reduced the arrears early in the second half. In the end, West Ham were hanging on and were thankful to run out 2-1 winners on the night. The Spaniards had undoubtedly gained a moral victory and there were very few Hammers' supporters who thought the slender one goal advantage would be sufficient in the second-leg. It was a daunting prospect.

West Ham's fortunes were not helped the week before the return game in Spain when their talisman, Budgie Byrne, injured a knee playing for England in a 2-2 draw against Scotland at Wembley. He would not play again that season and all of Greenwood's immense tactical skills were required as he prepared his team, minus Byrne, for the second-leg.

Burkett explains Greenwood's formation that night by saying: "Ron decided we should play without an orthodox centre-forward with Geoff and Brian Dear in withdrawn roles. As usual, we had Sisso on the left-flank and Alan Sealey on the right. Ron's plan was to confuse their centre-half Santamaria, who was virtually redundant with no-one to mark. It worked perfectly.

"It wasn't until late in the game that Santamaria, a good player who had previously been with Real Madrid, realised what was happening and he started to make use of the acres of space in front of him. But by then, it was too late.

"Their ground was like a cauldron that night but we defended well and Bobby, in particular, had a great game. Even so, they scored mid-way through the first half to level the tie on aggregate and we were penned back for long periods.

"Before the game, Ron had said to Sisso and Alan that they would get very few chances and they had to make the most of any that came their way. That is exactly what happened. Brian set up a chance for Sisso with half-an-hour to go and he raced through to score.

"We were ahead 3-2 on aggregate and despite a late flourish from them, we held on to reach the final. The dressing-room was an ecstatic place. I had an additional reason for being so delighted at knocking Zaragoza out of the tournament. Their right-winger – the player who I had been marking in both matches – was Canario, who had nearly broken my leg with his over-the-top tackle during a game in our trip to America a couple of years earlier. Revenge was very sweet that night."

13

Touched by the gods

THE date was May 19, 1965 and it will go down as the greatest night in West Ham's history. It was the occasion when they faced TSV Munich 1860 from Germany in the final of the European Cup Winners' Cup.

Wembley was packed with 100,000 spectators – by far the largest proportion supporting West Ham. Around 20,000 German fans travelled to London and they would form an extremely vociferous part of the huge Wembley crowd with their Bavarian hats and flags.

The BBC had graciously relented from their usual intransigent stance and allowed the whole game to be shown live on TV. It was later estimated that 30 million television viewers throughout the UK and the rest of Europe would ultimately watch the match. It was a mouth-watering prospect with the Germans' athleticism, power and unimpeachable self-belief against West Ham's superior skill, quality and artistry. It promised to be a fascinating spectacle.

In the pre-match build-up, many of the press previews were of the opinion that the two teams were evenly matched but Hammers were installed as slight favourites, if only because the game was being played at Wembley and the majority of fans would be supporting them. These were the days before penalty shoot-outs decided drawn matches and UEFA had decreed that, if the teams were level at the end of extra-time, then a replay would be held at Feyenoord's stadium in Rotterdam exactly 48 hours later. Hundreds of intuitive Hammers' fans were already getting prepared for such an event by announcing to their employers that fictitious 'grannies' had suddenly died and they would need time off work to attend the funerals!

TSV Munich were the oldest club in Germany – the '1860' in their title denoting the year in which they were formed. However, for much of their existence, they had been the poor relations of the Bavarian city compared with the more successful Bayern Munich and Wacker Munchen clubs. During those years, German football was organised on a regional basis with the top two clubs in each area meeting in end-of-season play-offs for the overall championship. The idea of a German 'super league' was often discussed and it was ultimately agreed that a national league – the *Bundesliga* – would be formed at the end of the 1962-63 season based on final positions in the two regions.

The timing was perfect for TSV Munich, because their fortunes had dramatically improved the previous year when Max Merkel, a 43-year-old ex-Austrian international with SC Rapid, had taken over as their manager. Within two years, Merkel had built TSV Munich's greatest team and at the end of the 1962-63 season, they had finished as League champions in their region, thus giving them qualification into the new *Bundesliga*.

In 1963-64, their first season in the new German elite league, they finished in a highly creditable seventh place – but they also won the German Cup beating Eintracht Frankfurt 2-0 in the final. It had been a magnificent season for TSV and as German Cup holders, they qualified for the following season's prestigious European Cup Winners' Cup competition. On their way to the final and their historic meeting with West Ham, they beat US Luxembourg (10-0 on aggregate), Porto of Portugal (2-1), Legia Warsaw of Poland (4-0) and Torino of Italy (2-0 in a play-off after both teams had drawn 3-3 on aggregate). They would be formidable opponents.

Jack remains impressed when he thinks about the players of TSV Munich, saying: "Because they had to play-off against Torino in the semi-final, it gave us the chance to go and watch them. The game was played in Switzerland and about eight of us, together with Ron Greenwood and trainer Albert Walker, flew out on a spying mission. Ron had already seen them beat Chelsea 2-0 in a pre-season friendly and he left us in no doubt that they were a very good side.

"Ron wanted each of us to take particular note of the player who we would be marking. My immediate opponent was right-winger Alfred Heiss who had already played for the German national side. He was a fast, tricky winger very similar to Davie Wilson of Preston. I was determined that he would not be allowed to cause me the same problems that Wilson had done in the FA Cup final exactly 12 months earlier."

On the evening of the final of the ECWC, it was warm and humid. The atmosphere inside Wembley was quite extraordinary. Unlike the FA Cup final when so many people in the crowd are invariably neutral supporters, the stadium was packed with true football fans, albeit the majority fervently supporting West Ham.

Before the game, a telegram was delivered to the Hammers' dressing-room. It was a message from their great North London rivals, Spurs, who had dominated English football to such a huge extent in the early-60s and the club that Burkett could possibly have joined earlier in the season. The somewhat wistful telegram merely said: 'Those were the days. Hope they are yours too.' It was a nice sentiment from a club who had a touch of class about them in that era, both on and off the field.

There were four changes to the West Ham team that had beaten Preston in the previous year's FA Cup final. The stylish Joe Kirkup had regained the right-back spot from the veteran John Bond, while Martin Peters was at right-half after the unfortunate Eddie Bovington had broken a kneecap against Sunderland two months earlier. Alan Sealey had taken over the right-wing spot from Brabrook.

Sealey was a more direct player than Brabrook and a good runner off the ball. Just a week before the final, Sealey had got married and most of his team-mates attended the ceremony. The 'new' Mrs Janice Sealey was a local beauty queen.

Brian Dear (left), watched by Peter Brabrook, came in for the injured Byrne and scored vital European goals.

The re-emergence of Peters with his intelligent play and clever running had given Hammers a new dimension that season and he constantly made good use of the decoy runs made by Sealey.

Also, the robust Brian Dear had become a more than useful replacement for the injured Budgie Byrne. In fact, Dear had scored 14 goals in 14 league and cup games after breaking into the side in mid-March, including an astonishing, record-breaking five-goals-in-20-minutes in the 6-1 thrashing of West Bromwich Albion at Upton Park on Good Friday.

In the final against Munich, Greenwood adapted his tactics once again. Hurst wore the number nine shirt and played a deeper role reminiscent of his days as a marauding wing-half, while Dear was the front man supported by Sealey and Sissons on the flanks.

There was a crescendo of noise as skippers Bobby Moore and Rudi Brunnenmeier led their respective teams onto the Wembley pitch. The tunnel end of the stadium was engulfed by the rays of the setting sun which seemed to add to the magnificence of the occasion. It was an electrifying moment as the teams emerged into the cavernous bowl of the stadium. Moore and Brunnenmeier – the latter graciousness personified – exchanged pennants in the pre-match formalities as referee Istvan Zsolt from Hungary looked on. At the toss-up, Moore called incorrectly – virtually the only thing that he got wrong all evening. His team prepared to kick-off and West Ham were 90 minutes away from European glory.

From the outset, it was clear that the game was going to be a classic with adventurous, attacking and inventive football. Initially, it was almost chess-like as both teams probed for weaknesses in the opposition's ranks but there was a captivating flow about the game that enthralled the Wembley crowd and the millions of watching television viewers.

Early on, it was noticeable that West Ham had pulled left-winger Sissons away from the touchline, taking the German right-back Wagner with him. It was a tactic designed to create space down the left-flank through which Burkett made numerous runs and overlaps. There were no pre-match Wembley nerves for him on this occasion, just a quiet determination to impress on the greatest stage of all.

A teasing cross from Moore almost allowed Dear to put Hammers ahead in the 12th minute but Munich scrambled the ball away. Then Boyce and Dear made a chance for Sissons who shot wide when well placed. Dear had a goal disallowed, although in fairness, there were no protests about the linesman flagging for offside.

The Germans survived the onslaught and inspired by skipper Brunnenmeier, they created their own chances but, on this night, Jim Standen's handling was faultless. Twelve months earlier, he had looked distinctly nervous in the first-half of the FA Cup final against Preston but against Munich, his performance was one of sheer excellence.

Dear and Sealey both went close before half-time but as the teams went into the dressing-room for the break, there was a nagging doubt amongst Hammers' fans because their team had not turned their overall superiority into goals.

The Wembley crowd had been held spellbound by a gripping first-half and, so too, had the millions who constituted the huge BBC television audience. Unfortunately, the viewers had to endure an error strewn commentary by Kenneth Wolstenholme who, amongst other things, repeatedly pronounced Joe Kirkup's name as "Keirkup" throughout the entire match. In later years, Wolstenholme came to be regarded as the doyen of football commentators but it was entirely due to getting lucky with his famous "They think it's all over . . . it is now" comment at the end of the 1966 World Cup final. In truth, his commentaries often left much to be desired and the constant mispronunciation of the experienced Kirkup's name during the final of the

Captains Rudi Brunnenmeier and Bobby Moore before the greatest game in Hammers' history.

European Cup Winners' Cup showed an abject lack of knowledge and preparation.

The second-half began with Sissons hitting a post but Munich continued to threaten and Standen made an excellent save as he came off his line to deny Brunnenmeier. Then a close range shot from Grosser bounced off Standen's knees and a rare mistake from the otherwise majestic Moore almost let in Kuppers. Again, Standen dived at the German's feet to avert a goal.

Apart from his up-field forays, Burkett kept a tight rein on the dangerous Heiss. In truth, the Munich right-winger was conspicuous by his absence throughout the whole 90 minutes as Burkett gave another classic full-back display with a series of perfectly timed tackles and forward runs.

As the minutes ticked away, West Ham imperceptibly moved into another gear and

Alan Sealey fires Hammers ahead against TSV Munich 1860.

began to take complete control. The constant roars of encouragement from their fans massed on the Wembley terraces seemed to gather momentum with each passing moment and swept over the stadium like a tsunami. After 69 minutes, Hammers got the breakthrough that they wanted.

The perceptive Boyce won possession in midfield and with the briefest of glances to his right, played the ball to the unmarked Sealey. The Hammers' right-winger, so often the target of the Upton Park boo-boys, needed just one touch to bring the ball under control before rifling an unstoppable shot into the roof of the net past the Munich goalkeeper, Petar Radenkovic. Wembley erupted as Sealey turned a somersault in celebration before being submerged under a pile of jubilant colleagues.

Moore and Burkett were the only out-field players who did not join in the celebrations. A team is at its most vulnerable when it has just scored a goal and they merely reverted to their defensive positions in order to prepare for the crucial minutes that lay ahead. Their concentration was total. It was professionalism of the highest order and it paid off within two minutes of the re-start.

They worked the ball between them deep inside their own-half, which resulted in Hurst firing a raking 30-yard pass over the Munich defence to allow Dear to burst through. However, Radenkovic came racing from his goal and pulled down Dear with a rugby tackle that would have made Jonny Wilkinson proud. In the modern era, it would have produced an instant red card but in those far-off days, it merited no more than a free-kick. Dear showed remarkable restraint by accepting Radenkovic's hand-shake as both players climbed to their feet – but justice was about to be done.

Sealey strikes again, nipping in before Martin Peters to make it 2-0.

The resultant free-kick routine was a product of previous hard work carried out on the West Ham training ground. It was a relatively simple move but it completely confused the Munich defenders. Hurst appeared to be preparing to unleash a fierce shot but, instead, he ran over the ball. Almost inevitably, it was Moore who floated the free-kick into the German goalmouth aimed at Peters coming in at the far post on a late run. As usual, he timed his movement expertly but, for once, Peters was unable to make proper contact. The ball bounced off his legs to the unmarked Sealey who was on hand to jubilantly score again, this time from six-yards, to put Hammers 2-0 ahead.

West Ham went into overdrive. Sissons hit the crossbar and Dear had a shot blocked by the outstretched legs of Radenkovic. They were in complete control and displayed a brand of football that was stunning in its grace and quality. The whole team was industrious and expansive, impressively solid in defence, marvellously creative in attack and simply sensational in midfield.

The strains of Hammers' haunting anthem *I'm Forever Blowing Bubbles* echoed around the famous stadium. It is doubtful if it has ever been sung with such emotion. As if to accentuate the moment, thousands of bubbles – illuminated by the floodlights – floated high into the night sky courtesy of dozens of 'wire-blowers' in the huge crowd who watched, spellbound, at the sheer brilliance of West Ham's football. In that pulsating second-half, the Germans were systematically taken apart, piece by Teutonic piece, by a Hammers' side showing imagination and discipline that was simply majestic in its execution.

In the dying minutes, Dear again fired a shot against the legs of Radenkovic when it seemed easier to score and the ubiquitous Martin Peters went close with an overhead-kick. In fact, Peters' spectacular effort was the last action of this enthralling match. Suddenly it was over. The referee, Istvan Zolt, blew the final whistle and Wembley erupted into a cacophony of sound as Hammers' delirious fans celebrated an unforgettable 2-0 victory.

For the second time in 12 months, skipper Bobby Moore led his team up the 39 steps to Wembley's Royal Box to receive another trophy – this time from Gustav Wiederkehr, the president of UEFA – and their winners' medals. The deafening chant of *Ee-aye-addio, We've Won the Cup* accompanied the players as they made their triumphant way to the summit. It was a chant the Hammers' fans had shamelessly 'stolen' from their counterparts on Liverpool's Kop. It was well justified because West Ham had created their own piece of football history. They were – and, indeed, still are – the only team to win a major European trophy consisting entirely of English-born players.

It was a unique achievement and will never be equalled.

However, despite the euphoria on the pitch that night, other matters proved to be something of an anti-climax for the heroes in claret and blue. Jack explains: "It was the greatest night of our careers and, yet, it ended on a strange note. Wembley had laid on a buffet in the restaurant afterwards but it was only for the players, officials and directors of both teams. No provision had been made for our wives and girlfriends who, to say the least, were not best pleased.

"Also, we realised that our cars were still at Upton Park, where we had left

WEST HAM ARE CUP KINGS OF EUROPE

THE greatest Cup team in Europe. That's West Ham United.

They proved it at Wembley last night, when they "hammered" Munich 2—0

The London club were spurred on by the Liverpool Soccer chant "Ee-aye-addio."

But the football that won the cup was very much West Ham's

into victory was right winger Alan Sealey, who scored both goals in a two-minute blitz.

Prime Minister Harold Wilson, who saw the match on television, last night sent a telegram congratulating West Ham on a "splendid match and...

Kings of Europe: Bobby Moore holds the ECWC aloft and is joined by (clockwise, left to right) two-goal hero Alan Sealey, Martin Peters, Geoff Hurst, John Sissons, Ken Brown, Jack Burkett, Ron Boyce, Brian Dear.

them before going to the hotel on the night before the match. It meant that instead of heading off to celebrate at a nightclub in London's West End, we all went back to Upton Park in a coach and arrived around midnight at a totally deserted ground which was in complete darkness.

"It didn't cause us a problem, though. We each had a couple of beers in the players' lounge and then went our separate ways. Ann and I got back to our house by 2.30am and I was asleep within minutes."

The following morning, the normally reticent Greenwood was still ecstatic at his team's display and, somewhat unusually, he singled out two players for particular mention. He said: "I thought Bobby Moore was magnificent and, also, Jack Burkett did a first class job at left-back, fitting in with marvellous efficiency behind his captain. In their separate ways, both of them played huge parts in a momentous victory. In fact, when Burkett returned to the side after his serious back injury in time for the semi-final against Real Zaragoza, it was then that I thought we started looking like a team again."

In his own typically quiet and unassuming way, Greenwood was paying tribute to the bravery of two players who had overcome highly personal battles against serious injury and frightening illness earlier in the campaign.

The game itself had been a wonderful spectacle for West Ham's loyal fans. What drama and emotion it had generated. What unbridled happiness and electrifying excitement. It was the stuff of which dreams are made as the Upton Park faithful lived out their football fantasies during 90 spellbinding minutes.

After Hammers' victory, the whole of Europe applauded their performance and messages of congratulation poured into Upton Park. One came from their West London rivals, Chelsea, which said: "Well done, you East End lot. A real West End show." Another came from Liverpool's manager, Bill Shankly, whose injury-hit

The players enjoyed another rapturous homecoming and their WAGS also got their hands on the European trophy.
Left to right: Jan Dear, Judith Hurst, Ann Burkett, Mrs Albert Walker, Jill Kirkup, Kathy Peters, Dawn Boyce.

team had been beaten by Inter Milan in the semi-final of the European Cup the previous week. Shankly's typically aggressive message said: "Well done. I feel that British teams are more than ready for these European people."

Even the Prime Minister, Harold Wilson – a big football fan – who had watched the game on television from Downing Street, sent a telegram of congratulations saying: "Splendid match and a wonderful victory."

A certain Dr. Murgel, who had been part of the Brazilian back-room squad which had won the World Cup three years earlier, was at Wembley to see Hammers' victory. Post-match, he prophetically vouchsafed: "If the football of the England team is like this display by West Ham, then England will be a real danger in the World Cup next year. West Ham's football was brilliant – so clever and so quick."

The praise for Hammers' performance in the following day's newspapers was almost overwhelming. The sports pages across Europe were magnanimous as they heralded West Ham's triumph. The leading French sporting newspaper *L'Equipe* ran a headline stating: 'West Ham have discovered a new football formula.' Similarly, the Fleet Street press boys went into raptures. The *Daily Express* carried a banner headline on the front page of its paper saying: 'Forever Blowing Bubbles – Night of Glory.' One of the match reports announced: 'There could have been no greater match to place before the greatest night audience in English football history.'

The highly respected reporter, Bryon Butler, graphically wrote: "Moore and company used Wembley's green carpet as an artist uses his canvas. Their movements were precise, their designs bold and imaginative. They were a credit to themselves and English football." The esteemed J.L. Manning described it as: "The best football match I have seen at Wembley since the stadium opened 42 years ago."

A report in another paper announced: "West Ham lifted the roof off super Wembley when they won the European Cup Winners' Cup in probably the greatest night of soccer splendour England had ever seen."

Another soccer scribe said: "West Ham's display was so majestic that, at times, it seemed they were touched by the gods. They are going to be greater than Bill Nicholson's double-winning Spurs and greater than the pre-Munich Manchester United." It was praise indeed and given the exultation rightly being accorded to West Ham, it was difficult to disagree with such a proud sentiment. After all, never before had the club experienced such euphoria and success. It was not unreasonable to assume that winning the FA Cup and European Cup Winners' Cup in successive seasons would be the beginning of a long period of unbroken success.

However, perhaps the most meaningful post-match tribute came from the former Wolves and England captain Billy Wright, who was the first man to gain 100 caps for England. He said: "West Ham have the potential to dominate the English game for years to come. They are a young team and there are no limits to the heights that they can attain." It was a magnificent compliment from one of England's most respected and esteemed players. Unfortunately, it is an eternal paradox of sport that the most expert practitioners tend to be the least reliable pundits. This is especially true of football and, sadly, Wright's words ultimately proved to be way off the mark.

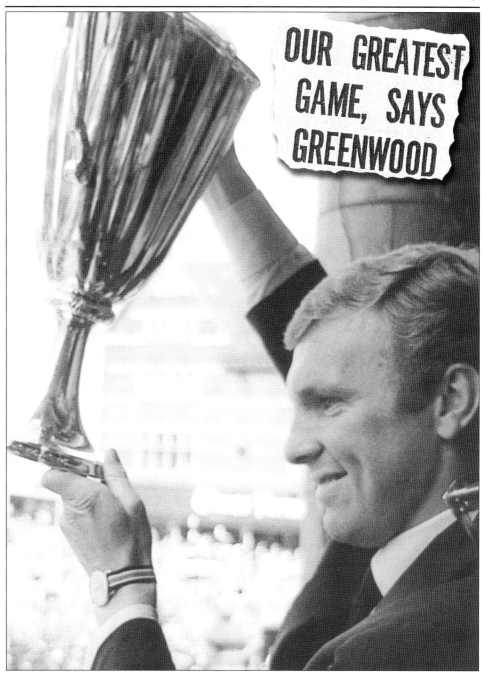

OUR GREATEST GAME, SAYS GREENWOOD

The skipper shows off the European silverware from the balcony at East Ham Town Hall.

Incredibly, West Ham were about to drift into years of decline and mediocrity. It would be exactly 10 years before they won another trophy, by which time virtually all of the successful team from the mid-60s had departed from the club. The sole exception was Ron Boyce, who became a member of the club's coaching staff.

It would prove to be a spectacular fall from grace and the resultant pain for their disbelieving fans would be insuperable. Just like one of the lines from their famous theme song, West Ham's dreams were about "to fade and die."

Jack Burkett tackles Magdeburg winger Klingbiel during Hammers' defence of the ECWC in March 1966.

14

Where did it all go wrong?

ONE of football's most enduring stories relates to the well documented demise of Manchester United's genius George Best. After the Irishman had prematurely retired from football and begun his tragic descent into alcoholism, he continued to lead the good life. At the time of this alleged story, Best's girlfriend was the reigning Miss World, the delectable Mary Stavin who, inevitably, was a stunning blonde from Sweden.

After a particularly successful night's gambling in London, the couple lay on their bed in one of the most luxurious hotels in the West End, drinking the most expensive champagne with their winnings spread on the bed around them. The story goes that Best rang down for more champagne which was thus delivered by a middle-aged employee from room service. After pouring the champagne, the man duly noted the aforementioned scene with considerable envy and before departing, he turned to Best and famously said: "George, where did it all go wrong?" Many years after the event, it still remains a good story and those immortal words have been applied and repeated on numerous occasions.

On reflection, it was a question that should, perhaps, have been slightly modified to read: "Ron, where did it all go wrong?" and directed at West Ham's manager, Ron Greenwood.

Even today, it still angers Hammers' fans from that era because, after their two unforgettable victories at Wembley in the mid-60s and for the only time in their history, the club stood on the edge of greatness. Yet, inexplicably, they allowed it to pass them by.

Perhaps a biblical tale epitomises what happened to West Ham. It says in the Bible that Joseph told the Pharaoh that it was necessary to make provision in the good years for the bad years that may follow. The Pharaoh chose not to heed such advice and disaster duly ensued. So far as Hammers' frustrated fans were concerned, that was exactly the same path that Ron Greenwood followed because, during those all-too-brief glory years, the club did not bring in any quality players to ensure that the success was maintained over a longer period.

Jack Burkett has no doubt that this was the case: "*That* was the time to buy. When a club is successful, great players will always want to come and join you but West Ham didn't follow that golden rule.

"We had done well to win the FA Cup and European Cup Winners' Cup in successive seasons but what we needed after that was a couple of big name signings who could have taken us to the next level. The squad was lacking in depth as well and when we got a few injuries, we were immediately in trouble.

"Also, the quality of some of the younger players coming through the ranks was not as good as in previous years. In essence, we tried to battle on with the same squad of players when, in fact, considerable strengthening was necessary."

It is a correct assertion regarding the lack of signings. It is a fact that after signing goalkeeper Jim Standen from Luton Town in November 1962, West Ham did not buy another player for almost three years. Astonishingly, their next purchase did not take place until October 1965, when the ageing midfielder Jimmy Bloomfield was bought from Brentford for a small fee – and that was only a stop-gap signing because of a lengthy injury to Ron Boyce.

In truth, the signs were ominous for West Ham in the weeks immediately after their European triumph against TSV Munich. They had been invited to return to America the following month to take part in the International Soccer Tournament in New York which they had won two years earlier. At the time of their initial visit, their participation had rightly been regarded as a steep learning curve which had subsequently paid rich dividends, but now they were returning as 'double' Wembley winners. It would not be unreasonable to suggest that, perhaps, they were not quite as hungry for success as they had been on their earlier trip across the Atlantic.

Also, West Ham's return trip to America in the summer of 1965 caused some resentment so far as Jack Burkett was concerned. He says: "I had been a late inclusion in the England under-23 squad for a short end-of-season European tour which was my first international call-up. The World Cup finals in England were only 12 months away and it was a good opportunity to stake my claim for a place.

"The problem was that the American organisers had previously gained an assurance from West Ham that all of the squad would make the trip and there would be no absentees. Usually, the club were very good at releasing players for international duty but this was one occasion when they weren't prepared to do so. It was a difficult situation because West Ham were my employers and, in the end, I wasn't given a lot of option.

"I pulled out of the England trip on the basis that I wasn't fully fit following the problems with my back. Needless to say, the news filtered back to FA headquarters that I had gone to America with West Ham and, to all intents and purposes, it appeared that I had snubbed my country.

"I knew I wasn't exactly top of England manager Alf Ramsey's popularity poll and I was never picked again. It was quite obvious Alf didn't take kindly to rejection and I knew that my England 'career' was over before it had even started.

"In the circumstances, I suppose it was almost inevitable that our return trip to America turned out to be something of a disaster. We won only one match throughout the whole tournament and finished bottom of the group. I think a bit of reaction had set in after all the glory and excitement of winning at Wembley. It was a tired bunch of players out there and we were pleased to get home."

As the 1965-66 league season got under way, worrying cracks were beginning to appear from the outset in West Ham's team. Injuries had indeed taken their toll since Budgie Byrne was still trying to recover from the knee injury received playing for England against Scotland the previous April. In addition, Brian Dear and two-goal Wembley hero Alan Sealey were both out with broken legs sustained in pre-season training. Incredulously, Sealey's injury occurred when he fell over a wooden bench in an impromptu cricket match during a lunch-break at the training ground. Although he didn't realise it at the time, that farcical injury was the beginning of the end of Sealey's career.

Most crucially, Ron Boyce would suffer a serious back injury early in the season. It was yet another back injury to a West Ham player who had lifted heavy weights during his time as a young player at the club. The underrated Boyce was a vital member of the side and his lengthy absence would prove to be a devastating blow.

Hammers' opening three games of the campaign resulted in a disastrous 3-0 defeat at West Bromwich Albion; a 1-1 draw against Sunderland at Upton Park when 18-year-old right-winger Harry Redknapp made his league debut; and a hard-earned 2-1 home victory over Don Revie's rapidly emerging Leeds United. It was in the latter game that Burkett was involved in a small piece of West Ham history.

The 1965-66 season had seen a major change in English football when the Football Association allowed substitutes to be used in league football for the first time. Clubs were allowed to name one player as substitute for each match and on August 28, 1965, Jack became the first West Ham player ever to be substituted in a league game, albeit as a result of an injury. He was replaced by young Peter Bennett early in the second-half.

Incredibly, the following week's match day programme contained a full-page explanation regarding the substitution. Clearly, the club were concerned about accusations of the new rule being 'abused' and went to great lengths to explain the situation, saying: "The new ruling on substitutes in league matches came under discussion when Ron Greenwood met the press after the match against Leeds United. In that game Peter Bennett became the first Hammer to be used as a substitute in a competitive game, although three minutes were to elapse before Peter filled the vacancy caused by Jack Burkett's departure.

"It was this time gap that brought the first question from the press and Ron made the point that until it was certain that Burkett could not return to his position, then there was no intention to replace him. To ensure this our physiotherapist, Bill Jenkins, examined the injured player while the substitute had a precautionary warm-up under the stands."

The detailed explanation went on: "There had already been indications that a substitution might become necessary, as at half-time, Burkett had complained that his muscle was causing trouble. The examination after he left the field during the second-half confirmed that for him to continue would only aggravate the injury; then, and only then, was the decision taken to use the substitute.

"The reasons for this line of thought were then developed by Ron who pointed out that the subject of substitutes had been thoroughly gone into before the commencement of the season. It had been decided that as far as Hammers are concerned, a player sustaining an injury would not be replaced unless it was certain that for him to continue would be to his physical disadvantage. Ron then went on to say that, in his opinion, this was the true interpretation of the League ruling and if the Football League called for a report on any substitution, then it could be adequately justified."

The programme notes continued: "When further questioned on the possibility of abuse of the rule, Ron stated that he considered the substitution of one player by another because the original choice was having a below-par day was bad for club spirit. It would cause a lowering of mutual respect among those concerned and any organisation which was built upon team spirit would only suffer in the long run if it made such a decision."

In modern times, it seems ridiculous that West Ham should have gone to such lengths to justify Jack's substitution, particularly when, in later years, certain England managers virtually substituted their entire starting line-ups during the course of friendly internationals. The irritating policy of giving fringe players a brief run-out in the second-half became the subject of fractious debate. In essence, it completely devalued England caps. It meant that a journeyman player like Phil Neville ended up with considerably more England caps than immortals like Jimmy Greaves, Johnny Haynes and Stanley Matthews. There are some injustices in football that truly take the breath away.

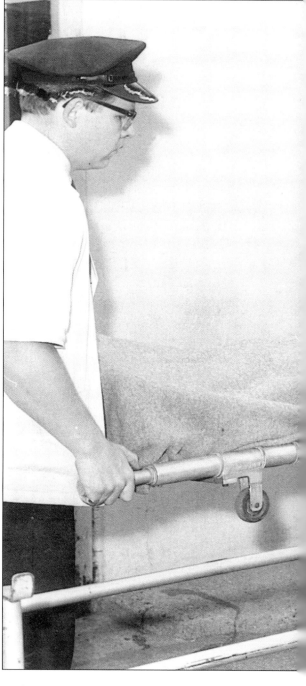

It is also a system that certainly went against all the principles that Greenwood so scrupulously applied in his use of substitutes during his time in charge at Upton Park.

It quickly became apparent in the early weeks of the 1965-66 season that West Ham were on the slide. By mid-October, they were third from bottom and on four

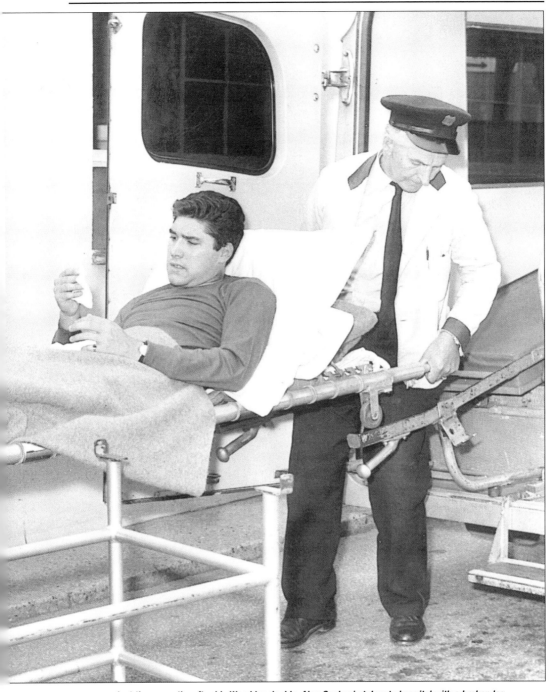

Just three months after his Wembley double, Alan Sealey is taken to hospital with a broken leg.

occasions they conceded five goals – in matches against Sheffield United (a) 3-5, Liverpool (h) 1-5, Leicester City (h) 2-5 and Nottingham Forest (a) 0-5. Things had reached pantomime proportions and the night of glory against TSV Munich only five months earlier seemed like a world away.

Jack acknowledges the team as a whole were showing a collective loss of form and he was not immune to the demise that was affecting his team-mates.

171

John Charles – Jack's replacement at left-back – is far right of picture in this shot of the players on their training run. Others in view are (left to right) Peter Brabrook, Jack Burkett, Eddie Presland, Ken Brown, Brian Dear, Jimmy Bloomfield, Dave Bickles, Eddie Bovington, Johnny Byrne, Ron Boyce, John Sissons.

He says candidly: "Looking back, I relaxed slightly and for a brief period, I seemed to lose my competitive edge. I wasn't getting close to my immediate opponent and I lacked a bit of sharpness. In fact, we all seemed to take our foot off the accelerator and Ron had to make changes.

"I was dropped and John Charles took over from me for a while, although I managed to get back into the side later in the season. No player likes to be dropped and I was no exception. I was seriously upset at the time but when I look back now, I have to concede that Ron was absolutely right to leave me out."

Burkett and Charles virtually shared the left-back spot throughout the campaign, playing in 29 and 36 league and cup matches respectively.

Local boy Charles had captained West Ham's youth team when they won the prestigious FA Youth Cup two years earlier and he became the first black player to play in Hammers' league side. Admittedly, many more black players would follow at Upton Park in the ensuing years but Charles was an historic trailblazer. Barring injury, Burkett had been an automatic choice for more than three years but the emergence of the tough tackling Charles had suddenly put pressure on him to retain his place.

However, there was a reminder of somewhat happier days when the club's players and officials were invited to attend the BBC's prestigious Sports Personality of the Year programme in recognition of winning the European Cup Winners' Cup seven months earlier. The event, which was screened live to a huge television audience, took place at the BBC Television Centre in London on December 16. As usual, the 'great and good' of British sport were in attendance, including the victorious Hammers' team together with Ron Greenwood.

There was a specific reason why they had been asked to attend. It was a proud moment for all at Upton Park and their thousands of watching fans when it was announced that West Ham had won the Team of the Year award as a result of their spectacular display at Wembley. Bobby Moore received the trophy and expressed his thanks on behalf of everyone at the club. Fittingly, it was Rudi Brunnenmeier, the captain of TSV Munich, who presented the award.

It was the fifth trophy that Moore had collected in two-and-a-half years: American International Soccer League, FA Cup, Charity Shield, European Cup Winners' Cup and BBC Team of the Year award. Although he didn't realise it at the time, the greatest prize of all – the World Cup – awaited him less than eight months later.

West Ham's league form remained disappointing throughout the entire season. They would eventually finish in 12th position but conversely, they made good progress in the League Cup and European Cup Winners' Cup. It added fuel to the ongoing argument that their style of football was only suitable for success over a shorter span of games, like a decent cup run, and it could not be sustained throughout the marathon-like league programme with its interminable onslaught of fixtures. In later years, Greenwood acknowledged the problem but, by then, it was too late.

By his own admission, it appeared that when West Ham were playing well, they were able to use space in the most sublime fashion, just as Greenwood had expertly coached them to do so. However, when they were under-performing, then their obsession with creating space worked against them. In other words, when they lost possession, they also lost the space that they had worked so diligently to create and their opponents took advantage of it. It meant other teams suddenly found a freedom in playing against West Ham that they did not enjoy against other opponents. Ironically, the success that some of them consistently achieved against Greenwood's team in that era was not of their own making. It often came about because of an inherent weakness in Hammers' armoury and it was never rectified.

Nevertheless, in the latter months of the 1965-66 season, West Ham reached the final of the Football League Cup before losing 5-3 to West Bromwich Albion on aggregate. It was the last time the League Cup final was held over two legs because, the following season, it was switched to Wembley.

Burkett played in the first leg of the final at Upton Park which Hammers won 2-1 thanks to goals from Moore and Byrne, the latter coming in the last minute. However, injury prevented him playing in the second-leg a fortnight later when Albion tore West Ham apart and won 4-1.

He admits: "I was too honest with Ron that night because I had taken a knock in the previous game. It wasn't too serious and I could probably have got away with it but because it was such a crucial match, I felt that it wouldn't have been fair to take a chance with the injury. I told Ron I was unfit and he switched Martin Peters into my place.

"What I didn't realise until afterwards was that it was only the players who took part in the second-leg that got a medal, so I missed out. It was a ridiculous ruling and one that still rankles to this day."

As holders of the European Cup Winners' Cup, West Ham made good progress in their defence of the trophy. In the first round, they beat Olympiakos of Greece 4-0 at Upton Park in the first leg and drew 2-2 in the return in Athens to win 6-2 on aggregate. The referee in the second leg was Tofik Bahkramov from Russia. The following summer, the moustachioed official would become famous – or infamous depending on one's nationality – when he was the linesman at the 1966 World Cup final at Wembley who allowed England's controversial third goal.

In the quarter-finals of the ECWC, Hammers eliminated Magdeburg from East Germany by 2-1 on aggregate in two dour games. West Ham's semi-final opponents were the powerful West German side Borussia Dortmund and, sadly, Hammers were about to say farewell to the trophy that they had won in such spectacular fashion at Wembley almost 11 months earlier. In the other mouth-watering two-legged semi-final, Bill Shankly's Liverpool were paired with Jock Stein's Celtic.

However, a bombshell was about to explode in early April just prior to Hammers' semi-final, first leg tie against Dortmund at Upton Park. Bobby Moore had become disillusioned with West Ham's poor form in the league and, crucially, his contract with the club had only three months left before it expired on June 30. There was a considerable amount of conjecture in the newspapers that Moore could be on his way out of Upton Park. Moreover, Spurs were not exactly denying the rumours that they would be Moore's preferred choice, if a transfer materialised.

The situation was further complicated because, although the possibility of a new contract had been briefly discussed between Moore and Greenwood, there was considerable disparity in their respective positions. The player was seeking more money than the club were prepared to offer.

Furthermore, there was the little matter of the 1966 World Cup finals on the horizon with England as the host nation. The tournament was due to commence on July 11. Moore and Greenwood agreed to place further talks in abeyance, if necessary until after the World Cup. It was also agreed that their discussions should be treated on a strictly private and confidential basis.

On the eve of the first-leg against Dortmund, Moore was outraged to learn that Greenwood had 'gone public' on the matter and the story had broken in the newspapers. A furious Moore stormed into Greenwood's office stating that he would not now be signing a new contract, whatever West Ham offered. It was a clear indication that Moore considered that he had no future at the club.

Greenwood had thus created a difficult situation for himself because he knew that he could ill-afford to leave Moore out of the team to face Dortmund in such a crucial game. At the same time, he could hardly allow a disgruntled player to lead the side. As a result, Moore was stripped of the West Ham captaincy. On the night of the match, it was a strange sight for the Upton Park faithful as Budgie Byrne led out the team with Moore following him.

It was also a strange scenario for the Hammers' players as well. Jack recalls: "Ron had told us that Budgie would be the new club captain and none of us could argue with his choice. Budgie was always a great talker, both on and off the pitch, and he was also very popular with the lads.

"I always felt that he was much closer to Ron, whereas there was a degree of

Captains Bobby Moore and Constantine Polychroniou of Olympiakos with that 'Russian linesman'.

coolness between Ron and Bobby. At the time, we all understood that Bobby had a contract issue with the club and it was most likely that he would be on his way, probably to Spurs, at the end of the season.

"It was disappointing because he was such a great player but these things happen in football. Bobby never discussed the matter with any of the other players. He was a very private person which is unusual in football because, generally speaking, players are often prepared to discuss all sorts of things, even private issues, with their team-mates."

Sadly, Borussia Dortmund proved too strong in the semi-final and beat West Ham 5-2 on aggregate. The only consolation for Hammers' fans was that the Germans went on to beat Liverpool 2-1 in the final at Hampden Park, so they had the satisfaction of knowing that their team had been eliminated by the eventual winners.

Hammers' played out the last seven league matches of the season and eventually finished in mid-table with Byrne as their new skipper. It was a tame end to a bitterly disappointing season. Nevertheless, this was 1966 and Moore, together with Hurst and Peters, were about to help England in their quest to win the World Cup. It is an amazing fact that when Moore captained England to victory during that historic summer, he was not even captain of West Ham.

However, a major problem arose for England on the eve of the tournament. It came about as a result of the earlier meeting between Moore and Greenwood because they had overlooked the fact that Moore's contract with West Ham had expired on June 30. At that point, Moore was not registered as a player with any team in the Football League – but it was a FIFA ruling that all participating players in the World Cup had to be affiliated to a league club. In effect, any player who was not registered on this basis was ineligible to play in the tournament.

With the opening of the World Cup on July 11, it meant that Moore could not be selected. When this startling fact became apparent at England's training camp, manager Alf Ramsey was almost apoplectic. Greenwood was instantly summoned to the team's hotel with strict instructions to bring a one-month contact with him. This document, once signed by the player, duly extended Moore's contract with West Ham until July 31, just long enough for duration of the tournament. The rest is history.

Moore went on to attain immortality as England's World Cup-winning captain when West Germany were beaten 4-2 in that never-to-be-forgotten World Cup final on July 30. It was just one day before his 'extended' contract with West Ham was due to expire.

The new 1966-67 season kicked-off exactly three weeks after the World Cup final, so Moore, Hurst and Peters were only given a few days' rest before returning to Hammers' training ground. Jack says: "England had won the World Cup and Bobby had been voted Player of the Tournament, which backed West Ham into a corner. After the success Bobby had achieved that summer, there was no way that they could let him go to another club, particularly Spurs. There would have been uproar amongst the fans.

"In the end, they made him an offer that he couldn't refuse and, a few days later,

The day West Ham 'won' the World Cup.

he signed a new long-term contract. He had been reinstated as West Ham's captain by the time that we went to Germany on a short pre-season tour."

It later transpired that Moore had signed a three-year contract with a further three year option on his services, which almost doubled his weekly wage to £150 per week. It made him the highest paid player in the club's history and, ultimately, he would remain at Upton Park for another eight years.

While in Egypt for the friendly against Zamalek in November 1966, the players took the chance to take in famous sights such as the Sphinx and Pyramids. Left to right: Johnny Byrne, Martin Peters, Bobby Moore, Geoff Hurst, Jim Standen, Eddie Bovington, John Charles, Jack Burkett, Ron Boyce, John Sissons.
It was on this trip that most of the players went down with 'Egyptian Tummy' – hence the 5-1 defeat!

15

Hammers in decline

IN the early weeks of the 1966-67 season, the glow of England's victory and the fact that West Ham had provided the three most prominent members of the World Cup-winning side tended to gloss over the deficiencies in Hammers' team.

Admittedly, they lost their opening three games – the first at home to Chelsea by 2-1 when the three England heroes received a rapturous reception before the kick-off from the Upton Park fans. This loss was followed by two away defeats, by 2-1 at Arsenal and 5-4 at Leicester City.

Hammers then began to find some decent form and climbed up the table with good wins, most notably at Sunderland by 4-2 and a highly impressive 4-1 victory at Manchester City who were beginning to emerge as a major force in the game under the managerial partnership of Joe Mercer and Malcolm Allison, the mentor to so many players at West Ham in earlier years.

However, Jack has some unhappy memories of a league game at Sheffield United towards the end of October. He recalls: "Sheffield United had a tall, lanky centre-forward called Charlie Bell playing for them and after just 10 minutes, we went up for a header together. He led with his elbow which caught me on the side of the head. It would probably have been a straight red card in the modern game. I was knocked unconscious and, apparently, it was a few minutes before I came round."

After extensive treatment on the pitch from physio Rob Jenkins, Burkett continued with the game, but remembers nothing about it. It was 15 minutes later when the 'delayed action effect,' which is typical of concussion, saw him sink to the ground with nobody near him. He was led – not carried – from the field and confirmed Jenkins' fears by asking in the dressing-room: "Where are we, Rob?"

Jack says: "Rob had taken over from his dad, dear old Bill Jenkins, who had died just before the start of the season. I was very groggy and I was later told that the Sheffield United doctor examined me and said I should be taken to hospital by ambulance.

"In that era, teams were not accompanied to matches by a large back-room staff as they are today. Apart from Ron and the 11 players who had been selected for the Sheffield United match, the only other personnel who travelled that day were Rob, plus substitute John Sissons and Albert Walker, who looked after the kit.

Martin Peters advancing from midfield to fire a shot at Chelsea keeper Peter Bonetti.

"So far as I can recall, I went on my own in the ambulance to the hospital. Obviously, Rob couldn't accompany me because he had to stay in the dug-out in case there were any more injuries. I ended up in an emergency ward. I was still covered in mud and wearing my playing kit. I was given some pyjamas and my kit was wrapped up in a plastic bag which was left by the side of the bed.

"I was really concerned about my West Ham shirt going missing because it was regarded as a sin to lose your kit. The players' names weren't shown on the backs of the shirts in those days and we were strictly forbidden to exchange them with our opponents at the end of games.

"There were only four first team shirts produced for each position during the course of a season. They consisted of two home shirts, one long-sleeved and one short-sleeved, plus two away shirts, which was the pale blue strip with two claret bands across the chest. Again, there was one long and one short sleeved, so it was important not to lose any of them. The only time the club let us keep our shirts was after the two Wembley finals, because they had been specially made for each occasion.

"I was examined by a hospital doctor who said that I had to stay overnight for observation. Everything was a bit hazy but I recall seeing someone bring my clothes into the ward and lay them on the chair next to the bed. I assume my clothes had been collected from the dressing room and brought in the ambulance with me.

"I asked one of the nurses if someone could telephone Ann. I slept a lot during the evening and the next morning, another doctor examined me and said that I could go home – even though I felt absolutely dreadful. My head was throbbing and I felt

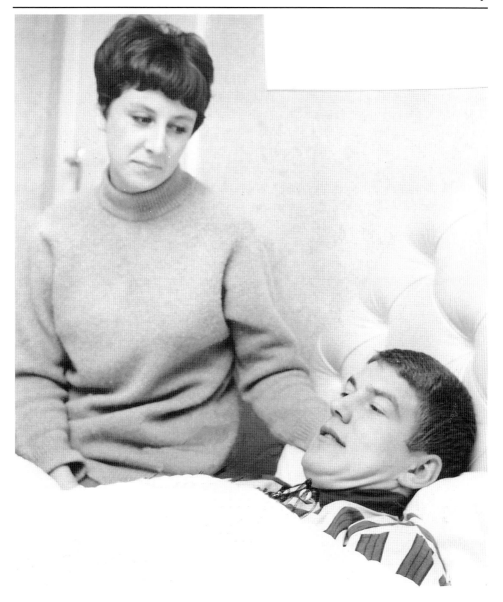

Ann attends to Jack as he recovers from concussion sustained at Sheffield United.

nauseous. It was then that I discovered that I didn't have any money.

"The procedure in the dressing-room before a game was that the players would put their money and valuables into a bag which Albert Walker kept with him throughout the game. It was done for security reasons – there had been a number of instances over the years where there had been break-ins at dressing-rooms while matches were taking place.

"Although my clothes had been brought to the hospital, nobody had thought to collect my wallet, watch and wedding ring from Albert's bag. I was stranded in a hospital in Sheffield, on a Sunday morning and about 250 miles from home, with no money and still muddied from the previous afternoon.

"I got dressed and asked a nurse from the admissions office if I could borrow some money. She gave me £10, which was enough to get me home. I was told that it was a five-minute walk to the railway station, so I made my own way there after asking a couple of passers-by for directions. My West Ham kit was still in the plastic bag and I carried it under my arm all the way to the station. I was fearful of losing it.

"When I got to the station, I telephoned Ann and said that I was on my way home. I asked her to arrange for my brother-in-law to pick me up when I arrived back at St Pancras station in London later that afternoon.

"I stayed at home on the Monday and Ann phoned the club to let them know I couldn't train. A local reporter came round to take a picture of me lying in bed. The next day, I went to the ground to return my kit. I was relieved when I handed it back. I collected my wallet and valuables, which were still in the care of Albert Walker.

"On the Wednesday, I saw the club doctor and he said that I could start training again. In fairness, I was feeling a lot better. Before I left hospital on the Sunday, I had taken the name and address of the nurse in the admissions office and I sent the £10 back to her with a note of thanks."

The telling of this story is not intended as a criticism of any member of the West Ham personnel who were in attendance at Sheffield United that day. It is how things were at the time. Nevertheless, Burkett's potentially serious injury shows how things have improved in modern football. These days, a player with a head injury would be immediately immobilised on a stretcher in a neck brace and rushed to hospital with the team's medical staff in close attendance and monitoring every move.

It is unthinkable that a Premier League player would be left to his own devices in hospital and have to borrow money from a nurse, so that he could make his own way home from a railway station in the north of England, with his playing kit in a plastic bag under his arm!

During the 1966-67 season, West Ham had become highly attractive opposition in terms of lucrative friendly matches, bearing in mind that there were now three World Cup winners in their ranks. One such game created a piece of unique football history and it came against, arguably, the most glamorous team in the world, the Spanish giants Real Madrid.

It had been arranged to promote the newly-formed North American Soccer League. The game was played at the Houston Astrodome in Texas, USA and it made history because West Ham and Real Madrid became the first teams to play a game on a full-sized pitch completely under cover.

The Astrodome had been opened in 1965 and was heralded by the jingoistic American press as being the 'Eighth Wonder of the World.' The huge dome-shaped structure was visible for miles around. It was situated seven miles outside the city centre and could only be reached by several specially built freeways. The entire complex, including exhibition and parking areas, covered 260 acres. It had car parking space for over 30,000 vehicles with free transport from the parking area to the stadium itself. The awe-inspiring Astrodome had a maximum capacity of 60,000 – all seated, which was a phenomenon in itself at that time – and it had already played host to such events as American football, baseball, polo, a rodeo and a Billy

Graham evangelical crusade.

Also, the irrepressible Muhammad Ali had defeated Cleveland Williams and Ernie Terrell in two brutal world heavyweight championship fights just prior to West Ham's visit.

Jack has vivid recollections of that memorable trip: "We stayed at the Shamrock Hilton Hotel in Texas and we trained at the Astrodome on the night before the game. The surface was astroturf, which was a new invention in those days, and Ron stressed the need to stay on our feet because if we went to ground when making a tackle, then we were likely to end up with severe burns.

"There was a decent crowd –

nearly 35,000 – to see the game and Real Madrid were captained by the legendary Francisco Gento. He was nearing the end of his career and had lost a bit of pace, but he was still a great player.

"It was exceptionally hot in the Astrodome during the game, although there was air-conditioning. There was music blaring out and a running commentary over the loud-speaker system, so it was a surreal atmosphere. In the end, we lost 3-2 but it was one of those occasions when the result didn't really matter. It was a fantastic experience to play at the Houston Astrodome."

Another prestige friendly match came in early December against the Egyptian champions Zamalek from Cairo. However, Jack admits that this was a trip that was not exactly enjoyed by the West Ham part: "We had four days out there and because it was the depths of winter back home, it was good to get some sun on our backs. We managed a short sight-seeing tour to the Sphinx and ancient Pyramids at Giza, on the outskirts of Cairo, and returned to the hotel to prepare for the game which was being played the following afternoon.

"Unfortunately, that night, most of us went down with a bad attack of diarrhoea. It was a classic case of 'Egyptian tummy.'

"The next day, there was an attendance of more than 50,000 to see the game and they were one of the most partisan and volatile crowds that I ever faced in my career. We lost 5-1 – but it was a joke. Some of us kept leaving the field to go to the toilet but we had to go back on the pitch and carry on playing because the substitutes kept going to the toilet as well!

"We were in a sorry state when we flew back to London the next day. The following Saturday, we played West Bromwich Albion at Upton Park and Ron had some difficulty in finding 11 players who were able to stay on the pitch for 90 minutes. Incredibly, we won 3-0."

Despite the difficulties encountered in Cairo, West Ham had struck a rich vein of form in the weeks leading up to Christmas. They scored an incredible 42 goals in 11 league and cup games, with Hurst and Peters plundering 23 goals between them. The highlights were a 6-1 demolition of relegation-threatened Fulham in the league and an astonishing 7-0 victory against Don Revie's formidable Leeds United in the fourth round of the League Cup, both matches being played at Upton Park.

In the latter game, Hammers gave a magnificent attacking display. The Leeds team, comprising of such illustrious names as Billy Bremner, Norman Hunter, Jack Charlton and John Giles, were simply torn apart by a rampant West Ham. Over the Christmas period, Hammers twice faced Blackpool, winning 4-1 at Bloomfield Road and 4-0 in the return at Upton Park. It seemed that they could not stop scoring goals and they were in seventh place in the league table at the turn of the year.

In many ways, the dip in the team's form that had occurred the previous season seemed to have been overcome but, in fact, this was almost entirely due to the incredible performances of the three World Cup heroes. It appeared that Moore, Hurst and Peters continued to be inspired by all that they had achieved with England six months earlier but there was simply too much reliance being placed upon them.

Indeed, the more astute West Ham fans were particularly concerned as to what would happen if the goals from the Hurst-Peters partnership dried up because, surely, it was not possible for them to maintain such a degree of lethal finishing throughout the remainder of the campaign. The fans' worst fears were well founded, for in the early weeks of the New Year Hammers experienced one of the most traumatic periods in the club's history.

In the third round of the FA Cup, West Ham had been drawn at home to third division Swindon Town. A crowd of 37,400 watched the tie – the biggest attendance at Upton Park for seven years. Jack acknowledges the occasion seemed to inspire the visitors. He says: "The pitch was very heavy but they had a left-winger called Don Rogers who appeared to float over the mud. He caused us all sorts of problems but we managed to salvage a 3-3 draw thanks to a hat-trick from Geoff. We had got away with it but we knew that we had a tough game on our hands in the replay the following Wednesday evening."

It seemed the whole of Wiltshire turned up at Swindon's ground that night. It was bulging at the seams as expectation amongst the locals reached fever pitch. Here was an opportunity for Swindon to create one of the greatest shocks in FA Cup history. They were facing a team who, less than two years earlier, had achieved European glory at Wembley and now had three members of England's World Cup-winning side in their ranks. First division scalps did not come much bigger than that. As the kick-off approached, it was just possible to hear the expectant licking of thousands of Swindon lips all the way back to East London.

A nightmare was about to unfold.

Right from the kick-off, Swindon hustled and chased every ball. Their players seemed to hunt in packs because every time a West Ham player was in possession, he was immediately surrounded by two or three opponents who tackled with staggering ferocity. Moore and Burkett held off a succession of Swindon attacks down Hammers' left side, whilst on the other flank, Bovington was striving to control the elusive Don Rogers.

After constant early pressure, Swindon deservedly took the lead through Andy Penman in the 18th minute. Hammers tried in vain to settle but they could not create the space that was so crucial to their game. The midfield area was a battle ground and Swindon were in complete command. West Ham's players breathed a sigh of relief as they retreated to the sanctuary of the dressing-room at half-time with Swindon leading by only a single goal.

Sadly, the second-half did not bring any respite to their beleaguered defence. Every time that Swindon crossed the half-way line, there was danger mainly due to the brilliance of Don Rogers. He was beginning to run West Ham ragged and one mazy dribble that took him past four Hammers' players was only foiled by a last-ditch tackle by Bovington.

Swindon continued to pour forward and Burkett cleared off his own goal-line with Standen beaten. Hammers had been forced to play reserve centre-half David Bickles in place of the injured Ken Brown and Bickles endured a torrid time at the heart of the defence. Even Moore's icy coolness could not quell the enthusiasm and work-rate of the Swindon players.

Briefly, West Ham seemed to get back in the game. Peters and Boyce began to find some space and, completely against the run of play, West Ham scored an equaliser in the 78th minute. A rare attack earned a corner-kick which was taken by Byrne and rifled home by Sissons. It brought a fleeting ray of hope that Hammers might escape a humiliating defeat but it was not to be.

Within six minutes, Rogers dived between Bovington and Standen to restore Swindon's lead and, with two minutes remaining, Skeen scored a third goal to complete an unforgettable 3-1 victory. The roar that greeted the final whistle could be heard for miles around as West Ham's dejected players trudged off the field with abject misery written all over their faces.

When the Hammers' party arrived back at Upton Park just after midnight to collect their cars, the degree of anger felt by a small number of their fans at such a disastrous defeat was blatantly obvious. The windows of the sports shop owned by Bobby Moore, situated opposite the ground, had been completely smashed. Success in football is supposed to be cyclical but West Ham had waited a long time for their place in the sun. The realisation amongst their fans that the sun had already set on their future hopes and aspirations was clearly too much to bear.

Unfortunately, another disaster awaited them in the semi-final of the League Cup. Hammers had been drawn against West Bromwich Albion who had beaten them in the final of the competition the previous year. The 1966-67 semi-final tie was held over two-legs with Hammers travelling to the Midlands for the first leg. It was yet another nightmare. Albion were 1-0 up after 50 seconds and 4-0 up by half-time, with striker Jeff Astle notching a hat-trick.

West Ham's full-backs Dennis Burnett and Jack Burkett strove to quell the threat of Albion's fast raiding wingers, while Ken Brown was given a tough time by the irrepressible Astle. In effect, the tie was already over at half-time. Although there were no further goals in the second-half, Albion knew they were taking a comfortable four-goal lead back to Upton Park.

Hammers' fans created an electric atmosphere before the kick-off in the second-leg but miracles rarely happen in football. Although Byrne and Hurst scored either side of half-time, Albion equalised on both occasions and the game ended 2-2, with the Baggies going through 6-2 on aggregate. Unfortunately for them, their joy was short-lived – they were surprisingly beaten 3-2 in the League Cup final at Wembley the following month by a Rodney Marsh-inspired Queens Park Rangers from the third division.

After their aggregate defeat at the hands of Albion, Hammers' shell-shocked players travelled to Southampton for a first division fixture at The Dell. West Ham were becalmed in mid-table whilst Southampton, a poor side, were involved in a desperate relegation battle. Once more, Hammers' enfeeblement was extreme as they received another severe 6-2 beating with Saints' strike partnership of Martin Chivers and Ron Davies creating havoc in their defence. Hammers' second-half consolation goals came from Hurst and Burkett.

In the space of three weeks, West Ham's entire season lay in ruins. They had been humiliated by Swindon Town, annihilated by West Bromwich Albion and mutilated by Southampton. It was crisis time. Ron Greenwood faced the press and admitted: "It is the blackest month that we have ever known at this club."

For Hammers' tortured fans, it was the understatement of the century. The lack of activity in the transfer market in previous seasons had come back to haunt Greenwood with a vengeance. In truth, he had no option but to break up the side and attempt to rebuild. However, he now had to do it at a time when the team was in terminal decline. It would have been so much easier if he had strengthened the side with some top quality signings when his team were in the ascendancy and winning trophies.

A gloom descended over Upton Park and it was a depressing time at the club. It was clear that the team was over the hill and in the next few weeks, Greenwood gave a number of youngsters a chance in the side, including defenders George Andrew, Paul Heffer and Billy Kitchener together with Scottish winger Doug Eadie. Only Heffer looked as if he might make the breakthrough on a permanent basis but his career would be cruelly cut short by injury after just 15 league appearances.

As the disastrous 1966-67 season drew to a close, there were still two more games that epitomised the demise of West Ham and the disenchantment that existed within the dressing room. In early April, Greenwood gave a reserve team run-out to nine members of the senior squad because there was no first team match on the day in question. Hammers' reserves were duly beaten 3-0 by Southampton's second-string and their performance brought scathing criticism from reserve team manager Ernie Gregory. When his report reached the desk of Greenwood, the Hammers' manager fined nine of the players £5 each for their lack of effort. The nine 'offenders' were Jack Burkett, Ken Brown, John Sissons, Peter Brabrook, John Charles, Billy

Kitchener, Colin Mackleworth, Peter Bennett and Doug Eadie. Only Jimmy Lindsay and Barry Simmons escaped punishment, which was the first of its kind handed out to under-performing players.

Even today, Jack fails to understand the reasoning behind the decision to fine the players: "It was petty even though £5 was a fair amount of money in those days. Admittedly, it was a bad performance but there had been plenty of other bad performances over the years and nobody had ever been fined before.

"I failed to understand how we had lost 8-2 at home to Blackburn Rovers on Boxing Day 1963 and the manager had not said a word and, yet, we lost 3-0 to Southampton reserves and that warranted a fine. It didn't make sense and did more harm than good. I lost a bit of respect for Ron over that decision."

The final ignominy came on the penultimate day of the season when West Ham faced Manchester United at Upton Park in a first division game. Hammers were now in 17th place in the table but, fortunately, they were safe from relegation with Aston Villa and Blackpool already doomed. Conversely, Manchester United needed one point to clinch the League championship and, on this day, all of their stars – Bobby Charlton, Denis Law, George Best, Nobby Stiles, Pat Crerand *et al* – were in the side and suitably fired up for their final push for glory.

Apart from season-ticket holders, there were no advance ticket sales in those days and it was a question of first come, first served. Thousands of fans began queuing outside the ground more than five hours before the kick-off. There were some isolated skirmishes between rival fans but once they were inside the ground, it virtually became a powder-keg with a rapidly burning fuse. In soaring temperatures, the gates were closed an hour before the kick-off with more than 38,000 spectators crammed inside. It was not a day for the faint hearted as opposition fans clashed violently on the sun-drenched Upton Park terraces.

While things were fiery off the field, it is true to say that they were equally explosive on the pitch as well. Manchester United came out of the blocks like an Olympic 100 metre sprinter. After just two minutes, Burkett tackled Law on the edge of Hammers' penalty area. The ball ran loose to Charlton who came roaring in like an express train and his thunderous shot threatened to break the back of the net as young goalkeeper Colin Mackleworth stood rooted to the line. Mackleworth was only playing because of an injury to Standen and, at times, he must have felt as if he was under mortar attack.

Best and Law, in particular, were in rampant form and at half-time United led 4-0. It could have been 10. Mercifully, they relaxed in the second-half and ran out easy 6-1 winners. They were the champions and their fans celebrated in the grand manner at the final whistle.

It was another humiliating defeat for West Ham at the end of a catastrophic season. It was difficult to comprehend that the team could have descended to such depths in just two short years after that night of European glory at Wembley.

It was the end of an era.

John Charles, who took over Jack's left-back position, and keeper Bobby Ferguson under pressure at Stoke City.

16

A sad farewell

JACK acknowledges that it was the beginning of a period of considerable change and transition at Upton Park. He says: "John Bond had reached the veteran stage and had been transferred to Torquay United. Joe Kirkup had gone to Chelsea because he had fallen out with Ron after being dropped from the side. After our defeats against Swindon, West Bromwich Albion and Southampton, there was also a lot of talk that Jim Standen, Ken Brown and Budgie Byrne would be leaving the club.

"In fairness, they were probably past their best – but they were our goalkeeper, centre-half and centre-forward, which was the spine of the team, and that was a major cause for concern."

Byrne was the first of the trio to leave when he returned to his former club, Crystal Palace, just a month after the heavy defeat at Southampton. The ebullient Budgie had never fully recovered from the knee injury sustained whilst playing for England against Scotland two years earlier. His return to Crystal Palace was a good move for him because he was thus entitled to a signing-on fee.

At the end of the 1966-67 season, the loyal Ken Brown rejoined his former Hammers' colleague John Bond at Torquay. However, goalkeeper Jim Standen stayed with West Ham for another nine months before flying out to America to play for Detroit Cougars. Ironically, it was Greenwood's attempts to find a replacement for Standen that created a furore amongst Hammers' fans that exists to this day.

Despite the criticism of Greenwood for not previously strengthening the team, it should be acknowledged that he had made a tentative enquiry for England's goalkeeper Gordon Banks before the 1966 World Cup. At the time, Banks was playing for Leicester City but their manager, Matt Gillies, told Greenwood he was not available. West Ham were then linked with Chelsea's Peter Bonetti and Millwall's up and coming goalkeeper Alex Stepney but neither transfer materialised. Standen retained his place in the side but the nature of the goals conceded in the disastrous defeats at Swindon, West Bromwich Albion and Southampton convinced Greenwood that the signing of a new keeper was a major priority.

In March 1967, he made a move for Kilmarnock's 21-year-old keeper Bobby Ferguson who had played for Scotland on seven occasions. The clubs agreed a fee of £65,000 – a then world record for a goalkeeper. Kilmarnock's manager was Malcolm McDonald who had been a former team-mate and good friend of

Above: Billy Bonds, one of the club's greatest-ever signings, shielding the ball from John Whitfield of Nottingham Forest. Below: The 'new boys' defending at Burnley. Bobby Moore looks on as (left to right) John Cushley, keeper Bobby Ferguson, Frank Lampard (in Jack's customary No.3 shirt) and Billy Bonds come under siege at Turf Moor.

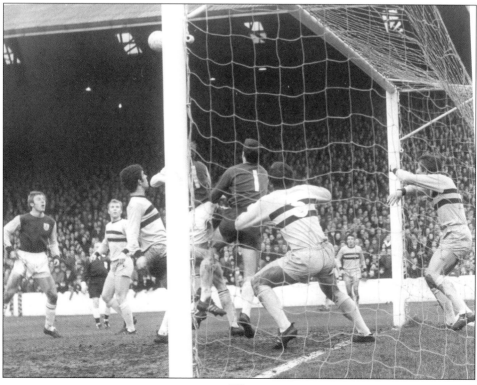

Greenwood during their playing days at Brentford in the early-50s. The only stumbling block to the deal being finalised was that Kilmarnock were still involved in European competition – the Inter-Cities Fairs Cup – and they were reluctant to release their goalkeeper while they still had an interest in the competition. However, Greenwood was prepared to wait for his man and he entered into a 'gentlemen's agreement' with McDonald that the deal would be completed once Kilmarnock had been eliminated.

Meanwhile, back in Leicester, Matt Gillies was faced with a difficult situation because although he had Gordon Banks – now a World Cup winner – in his side, he also had an outstanding 17-year-old keeper in the reserves who was showing astonishing form for one so young. His name was Peter Shilton. The pragmatic Gillies accepted that it would be impossible to keep Shilton in the reserves for much longer. He had to make the incredibly difficult choice between the 30-year-old Banks or the much younger Shilton who, obviously, had considerably more years in the game ahead of him.

Gillies pondered long and hard on his decision and eventually chose Shilton on the basis that he was the better long-term option. Because of Greenwood's enquiry the previous summer, Gillies duly 'tipped-off' the Hammers' manager by telephone to tell him that the legendary Banks was now available for £52,000, which was considerably less than the fee that had been agreed on the pending transfer of Ferguson.

Meanwhile, the story had broken in the newspapers that Leicester were prepared to sell Banks and, bearing in mind West Ham's defensive problems at the time, it was assumed that Hammers would be interested in signing him.

Kilmarnock manager Malcolm McDonald was hugely perturbed to read such reports and quickly telephoned Greenwood to establish if the deal for Ferguson was still on. As a man of great integrity, Greenwood reminded McDonald that they had already shaken hands on the deal and, as promised, West Ham still wanted to sign Ferguson.

Whilst one must acknowledge Greenwood's principles, it must also be said that his decision to decline the opportunity to sign Gordon Banks, the greatest goalkeeper in the world, was an error of monumental proportions. One can only imagine what West Ham could have achieved with Moore, Hurst, Peters and Banks in their team. Greenwood's mitigation was that he had "given his word" to a close friend but more than 40 years after the event, it still infuriates many Hammers fans.

In truth, the failure to sign the legendary Gordon Banks completely and utterly defied logic.

It transpired that Kilmarnock enjoyed a good run in the Inter-Cities Fairs Cup and were not eliminated until the semi-final stage, so Ferguson did not join West Ham until the close season.

In a further endeavour to begin the rebuilding process, Greenwood made two more signings in the summer of 1967. A 20-year-old right-back called Billy Bonds was signed from Charlton Athletic for £47,500 and Scottish centre-half John Cushley joined Hammers for £25,000 from European champions Celtic, where he had been

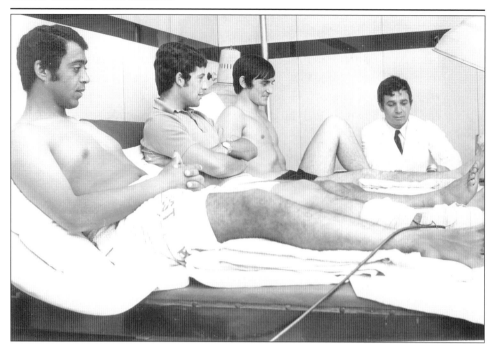

Above: From left – John Charles, Bobby Howe and Frank Lampard in the treatment room being tended to by physio Rob Jenkins. Below: Lampard spends time with two young fans while recovering from his broken leg. This picture was taken alongside the old wooden cricket pavilion, which then served as the players' dressing rooms at the club's Chadwell Heath training ground, following the move from Grange Farm.

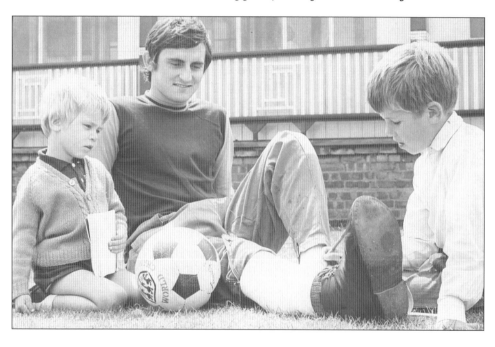

an understudy to Billy McNeil.

It was Greenwood's intention that Cushley would be a suitable replacement for Ken Brown. At the time of signing him, the West Ham manager perversely described Cushley as having: "A long body and short legs." As things turned out, the unfortunate Cushley was 'short' on other attributes as well, notably the ability to win aerial battles with some of the tall centre-forwards of that era. Although he was positive and strong, he was too short for a centre-half. He could never dominate in the air in the way that Brown had done for more than a decade at the heart of West Ham's defence.

Nevertheless, Jack has distinct memories of Cushley's debut in the claret and blue. He says: "We went to Germany on a pre-season tour and our first opponents were Borussia Dortmund. Obviously, 'Cush' wanted to make a big impression and he went charging about all over the field, kicking anything that wore a yellow shirt. Ron was a bit aghast and at half-time, he told him to calm down. I think Cush was totally bemused because that was what his game was all about – getting stuck into opponents."

So far as Greenwood's pursuit of Ferguson was concerned, it was cruelly ironic that after the furore of signing him – not Banks – had died down, it quickly transpired that Ferguson was never going to be the answer in goal. Although he went on to make over 250 league and cup appearances for the club, he failed to inspire much confidence throughout his years at Upton Park.

On the other hand, Bonds was a magnificent signing – one of the greatest in the club's history. Jack says: "Billy was an introverted lad when he first joined us and I think that he was a bit overawed, but he was a fantastic buy for West Ham.

"He was a tremendous athlete and was always up front in cross-country runs. His fitness level was amazing.

"Billy joined us as a right-back but I felt right from the start that he would make a good central defender. After a while, Ron switched him into a midfield role and, later in his career, my instincts proved correct because Billy did play in central defence – under John Lyall – with great success."

Despite the impetus of three new signings, West Ham got away to their usual disappointing start when the 1967-68 season commenced. They won only one of their opening six games and managed to concede 18 goals in the process. The only thing that Ferguson and Cushley appeared to have in common was the fact that they both came from north of the border. Apart from that, there was a woeful lack of understanding between them.

Suffice to say, Cushley's tenure as a first team regular was relatively short-lived and he was replaced by Alan Stephenson, who was signed from Crystal Palace for £80,000 exactly eight months later.

Nevertheless, Cushley was highly popular amongst his team-mates. Jack says: "He was a good lad and I got on very well with him. I was very sorry to hear that he passed away in 2008 after a long battle against motor neurone disease."

During the 1967-68 campaign, John Charles became the first choice left-back and Burkett spent the early weeks of the season in the reserves. He was brought back

The summer of 1968 and Jack has gone to Charlton. Back row, left to right: Paul Heffer, Billy Bonds, Martin Peters, John Cushley, Bobby Ferguson, Eddie Bovington, Geoff Hurst, Bill Kitchener, Bobby Moore. Front: Harry Redknapp, Peter Brabrook, Ron Boyce, Brian Dear, Peter Bennett, John Charles, John Sissons.

into the side at the end of October, when Hammers won 3-1 against Chelsea at Stamford Bridge, but his days at Upton Park were numbered.

In mid-December, West Ham travelled to Sheffield Wednesday and were comprehensively beaten 4-1. It was another poor display from a team who were languishing in 19th place in the first division. Jack looks back on that game which turned out to be his final league appearance for the club: "Afterwards, Ron was critical of my performance and said that I wasn't getting forward enough. I disagreed with him but I sensed that my time at the club was coming to an end.

"The following week, I wasn't surprised when I was left out for the game against Spurs at Upton Park. Ron picked Frank Lampard in my place and he also brought Trevor Brooking into the side. The team went on a decent run and I remained in the reserves for the rest of the season.

"Despite my disillusionment, I worked hard at my game and I felt that I was getting my form back. A couple of weeks before the end of the season, Frank broke his leg in a league game at Sheffield United and although no player likes to get back into the side in those circumstances, I felt that I had done enough to be selected again. Unfortunately, Ron had other ideas and when the team-sheet went up, he had picked a midfield player, Bobby Howe, in the left-back position.

"That was the final straw and it confirmed to me that I had no future at the club.

"I met with Ron and he said that he was going to build a new team around the likes of Bonds, Brooking and Lampard. It was clear that I wasn't part of those plans and at the end of the 1967-68 season, I received a letter from the club saying that my contract was not going to be renewed. Ironically, it was exactly 10 years to the day since I had received my first letter confirming that I was being taken on as a ground-staff boy.

"I was sad that my time at West Ham had come to an end but nothing is permanent in football. I completely understood Ron saying that he wanted to rebuild the side. I was officially placed on the transfer list and my name was circulated to all the other league clubs.

"I liked Ron as a person but I felt my relationship with him changed over the years. I never fell out or had a big argument with him, even when I was dropped from the team, but it seemed that a gulf grew between us. I know that some of the other players felt the same way.

"I believe that it stemmed from our 'clear the air' meeting after the 8-2 home defeat against Blackburn Rovers in 1963 when some of us were critical of him. It wasn't a problem in the next couple of years because we were successful and winning trophies but it manifested itself when things started to go wrong.

"Ron was a decent, honest man with high morals and he was one of the greatest coaches of all-time. It didn't surprise me that he was relatively successful as England's manager in later years.

"But it is a fact that, at times, his man-management skills often left a lot to be desired. The fine that he handed out to the players after our 3-0 defeat to Southampton reserves was a classic example. It didn't achieve anything and Ron lost respect because of it. Basically, I think he had also lost his way a bit.

"Despite that, I owe Ron Greenwood a huge debt of gratitude because he had faith in my ability and gave me the opportunity to make the breakthrough into the first team. He also made me a better player and I shall always be grateful for that.

"I was very saddened by his death in 2006 but Ron left a great legacy. He helped us to become the most successful team in West Ham's history."

Burkett set for Wolves

Above: The press were convinced that Jack was heading for Wolves . . . but he's seen here (below) in August 1968 making his debut for Charlton against Millwall's Derek Possee.

17

Unhappy years in South London

JACK recalls the events during the summer of 1968 as he prepared to leave West Ham – the club that he had joined as a 16-year-old exactly 10 years earlier. He says: "After being placed on the transfer list, I heard that Wolverhampton Wanderers were interested in signing me.

"Potentially, it was an exciting move. They were a first division club and had some outstanding players in Derek Dougan, Mike Bailey, Peter Knowles and Frank Wignall. Their manager was Ronnie Allen and I travelled up to the Midlands to meet him. I was very impressed with everything that he said about the club. The deal was a good one because it was more money than I was earning at West Ham and, since I hadn't asked for a transfer, I was entitled to a signing-on fee. I told Ronnie that I was keen to sign but wanted to go home and talk it over with Ann.

"I promised that I would contact him again the following day but when I got home, Ann told me that Charlton Athletic had been on the telephone and wanted to speak to me. I spoke to their manager, Eddie Firmani, the following morning and we arranged to meet later that day.

"I was in a quandary. A move to Wolves definitely appealed but although Charlton were in the second division, they were a London club and if I joined them, it meant that we wouldn't have to move house. Our two sons, Darrell and Dean, had been born in 1965 and 1967 respectively and because they were still so young, we didn't want the upheaval of moving at that particular time.

"I met Eddie and he did a good job in 'selling' the merits of his club to me. They were offering slightly less money than Wolves but I was still entitled to a signing-on fee. I went home and discussed both offers with Ann. In the end, we decided that I should sign for Charlton purely because we wouldn't have to move house.

"I telephoned Eddie Firmani and he was delighted. I also called Ronnie Allen at Wolves and explained the situation. He was a good man and completely understood my decision. He wished me well and although we didn't realise it at the time, we would work together some years later, albeit in a far-off foreign land."

Eddie Firmani was something of a legend at Charlton. He had been born in South Africa and was one of a number of Springboks who had come to England to play league football in the early-50s. He was a prolific goal scorer, including once netting five goals in a game against Aston Villa in 1955. Later that year, he moved

Charlton Athletic 1968-69: Jack is second from left in the middle row, with manager Eddie Firmani in the centre of the front row.

to Italian team Sampdoria for £35,000 which, at the time, was a record transfer involving a British club. He spent eight hugely successful years in Italy and gained three caps for the Italian national team, qualifying because his grandfather had been born there. Firmani later played for Inter Milan and Genoa, before returning to Charlton in 1963. After two years, he had a brief spell with Southend United before going back to Charlton for a third time.

During his three spells with Charlton, he made a total of 177 league appearances, scoring 89 goals. In later years and in recognition of his talents, he was named as Charlton's greatest-ever overseas player. Even today, he remains the only player to have scored 100 league goals in both English and Italian football.

Unfortunately, Burkett was soon at logger-heads with his new manager. He explains: "I signed a two-year deal with Charlton. It was agreed that I would get a £1,500 signing-on fee but I fell out with Firmani just a few days after joining the club.

"The team went on a pre-season tour of Holland and on the first night, all the players sat down together for a meal at the hotel. I ordered a lager, which is what I had always done during my time at West Ham. I had never been a big drinker but I always enjoyed a lager with my dinner. Firmani came over and said: 'What the hell do you think you're doing? Who gave you permission to order a lager?'

"This was in front of the other players and there was no way that I was going to be belittled like that in front of my new team-mates.

"I told him that I was a grown man and I could see no problem in having a drink with my evening meal. The rest of the lads kept quiet but I suddenly realised that all of them had orange juice, even the likes of Matt Tees and Graham Moore, who liked a beer or two.

"The following day, Firmani told me that he thought I was a trouble-maker and I knew immediately that my career at Charlton was going to be a very unhappy and relatively brief affair.

"Firmani had been schooled in the regimented Italian way of doing things and he was trying to implement that sort of discipline at Charlton.

"A further example came later that evening when I told my room-mate, goalkeeper Charlie Wright, that I was going out for a stroll to get some fresh air. Charlie said: 'Don't do that, Jack. You will really upset the boss. We can only go out for walks when we are all together and, also, we have to walk along in pairs.'

"I thought Charlie was joking, because that is how young schoolchildren are often seen walking along the street with their teacher, but I realised he was deadly serious. I thought back to the manner in which Ron Greenwood had done things at West Ham. He treated players in the way that he wanted to be treated himself. It was a matter of mutual respect and I had quickly discovered that 'respect' was something that was sadly lacking in my relationship with the new manager.

"In fairness, Firmani's rules seemed to be accepted by the rest of the players and, as things turned out, the team had a decent season. In those days, it was only the top two teams who were promoted and there were no end-of-season play-offs. In the final placings, we lost out on promotion by finishing third behind Brian Clough's rapidly emerging Derby County and our South London rivals Crystal Palace. We would have got promotion but we managed to miss five penalties during the season, which must be some sort of record.

"I wasn't at all pleased with my own form throughout the season, although my mood was not helped because the signing-on fee that I had been promised did not materialise. I later discovered that four other players who had been signed just before me were in the same position. We were still waiting for payment by the time that Christmas arrived and we were just not getting any satisfaction from Firmani. We kept being told that we would be getting our money but it seemed that the club was stalling.

"In the end, we demanded a meeting with the chairman and I threatened legal action. Eventually, we got our signing-on fees but it was nearly a year after we had signed for the club, which was completely unacceptable. It was unsettling and I wasn't enjoying my football at Charlton which was reflected in my form on the pitch.

"In my second season there, I was completely out of favour. On more than one occasion, Firmani repeated his earlier comments about me being a 'trouble-maker.' I think that I was regarded as the ring-leader of the players who had forced the club to pay the long overdue signing-on fees. I was always querying things on the training pitch.

"Ron had always encouraged West Ham players to have their say on such matters but that was not Firmani's way and he clearly felt that I was undermining him. I spent all of that season in the reserves but in a strange way, I quite enjoyed it. The reason was that there were a number of untried youngsters in the reserves and I was using my experience to help them. I was playing in central defence and, in some cases, I was literally talking them through matches. I suddenly felt that I was beginning to make good use of the coaching qualifications I had gained during my time at West Ham. I tried to impart the coaching philosophies that I had learnt under Ron Greenwood.

"Half-way through the season, Firmani said he was aware that I was having a big influence on the development of some of the reserve players and, in particular, on the youngsters. He asked if I would be prepared to take some of those players for extra coaching sessions during the afternoons, once the normal training day was over. I said that I would be delighted to do so and for the rest of the season that is how I spent my afternoons.

"It is strange and somewhat ironic that despite my problems with Firmani, it was he who first set me on the road to a coaching career. He had seen something in my ability to relate to other players and I am very grateful to him for that."

Despite his perception in appreciating Burkett's coaching potential, Firmani's time as Charlton's manager was rapidly coming to an end. The team were unable to replicate their excellent form during the previous campaign. Indeed, the 1969-70 season was almost disastrous – they were embroiled in a season-long relegation battle. In March 1970, Firmani was sacked, although he probably felt that he had the last laugh on Charlton because he later moved to North America, where he successfully managed Tampa Bay Rowdies and New York Cosmos.

Charlton turned to first team coach Theo Foley, who was made caretaker manager following Firmani's departure. Foley was a knowledgeable football man who had played with distinction for both Northampton Town and the Republic of Ireland. He later briefly managed Northampton before joining the coaching staff at Charlton.

When he took over as Charlton's caretaker manager, there were only four games left – but Foley pulled off a minor miracle by steering the team to safety. Their record in those four matches was: one win, two draws and a defeat. It was the 2-1 home victory against Bristol City on the last day of the season that ensured Charlton escaped relegation to the third division. At the end of the game, their fans celebrated as if they had won the League championship but, unfortunately for Jack, the team's successful bid for safety had been made without him. He remained in the reserves throughout the entire season.

"I got on well with Theo and I was pleased when he was made manager on a permanent basis in recognition of keeping Charlton in the second division," admits Jack, "but, basically, I was unhappy at the club. My contract was about to expire and I wanted to get away.

"I had a chat with Theo and stressed that I wanted to leave. He had a lot of contacts within the game and he said that Millwall were looking for a youth team coach. Theo said that he had watched me working with the youngsters at Charlton and he felt that was the area in which my long-term future lay. There was no opportunity to step into a similar role at Charlton because they were in considerable financial difficulties at the time and Theo had been instructed to reduce the wage bill.

"He suggested that I contact Millwall manager, Benny Fenton, and apply for the job. Ironically, Benny was the younger brother of Ted Fenton, my first manager at

West Ham all those years earlier. I regarded that as a good omen.

"I met Benny in the summer of 1970 and I got the job as youth team coach at second division Millwall, although I didn't have a contract. The money was OK and it was convenient because, once again, I didn't have to move house and uproot the family. Also, I knew a few of the Millwall first-teamers – Harry Cripps and Dennis Burnett, who were former team-mates at West Ham.

"Although I was only 28, I had more or less accepted that my days as a player at the top level were virtually over because I was getting a huge amount of satisfaction from coaching the youngsters.

"But towards the end of the season, one of the first-team full backs, Brian Brown, broke his leg and Benny asked me if I

Burkett aims for break at Millwall

FORMER WEST HAM defe
training hard at Millwall after b
with his eye set firmly on follow
and Dennis Burnett into the M

The 27-year-old Burkett arr
Cup and European Cup winner
the determination to prove his
future as well as a great p

would take over from him. The reason was that it would save the club having to buy another defender because money was so tight. I had managed to retain a decent level of fitness but I wasn't match-fit, so I played a couple of games in the reserves with a view to a first-team call up.

"In the meantime, Millwall's long-serving winger, Billy Neill, had temporarily taken over the running of the youth team from me. Unfortunately, my return to league football never materialised. Benny explained the club needed to register me as a player and I would have to sign a contract with my wages being renegotiated. That seemed OK until I realised that they were offering me less as a player than I was earning as youth team coach – even without a contract!

"The chairman was conscious of the fact that Billy Neill had been a good servant to the club and he wanted Billy to retain the job as Millwall's youth team coach. I didn't have any problems with Billy, who I liked a lot and he continued to serve the club for many years thereafter. I just felt that Millwall's principles on the matter left a lot to be desired.

"The season was almost over and I just walked away from the club. So far as I was concerned, I had just spent three wasted years in South London with Charlton and Millwall. For the first time in my life, I was very disillusioned with football. But I had a young family and a mortgage, so I needed to find work again – and quickly."

The early summer of 1971 was a depressing time for Jack who, with the benefit of hindsight, now bitterly regretted his departure from West Ham exactly three years earlier. Unfortunately, regret can be a pernicious emotion and at the age of 29, his career as a player in top class football seemed to be over.

Even more worryingly, his ambition to become an aspiring coach had stalled after the unhappy events at both Charlton and Millwall. However, it transpired that the ever-reliable Charlton manager, Theo Foley, would be his saviour. Once again, it proved that news travels fast in football and within days of Burkett's unhappy departure from Millwall, Foley made contact with him.

Jack recalls that conversation which, ultimately, had a huge influence on his life. He says: "Theo spoke to me and said he was sorry things hadn't worked out at Millwall. He reassured me by saying that I still had a future in the game. It was then that he took me totally by surprise by asking if I fancied working in the Republic of Ireland. At first, I turned it down flat, saying I wasn't interested, but Theo insisted that it was a great opportunity. He had been born and raised in Dublin and he was a wily old-pro, so I was aware that he knew a lot about the game in Ireland.

"Theo explained that there was a club just outside Dublin called St Patrick's Athletic who were looking for an ambitious player-manager. He seemed to know a lot about them and he later admitted that his parents lived near their ground. Theo insisted that it would be a good move and he gave me the name and telephone number of the chairman. I talked it over with Ann and it seemed that I had nothing to lose. I picked up the phone and made the call to Ireland."

18

Guns and balaclavas

ST Patrick's Athletic FC – nicknamed St Pat's – was founded in 1929. They progressed through the junior and intermediate ranks of Irish football and by the end of the 40s, they were established as the top non-league side in Ireland.

After winning the FAI Intermediate Cup in 1948 and 1949, they applied to join the premier ranks of Irish football – the League of Ireland – and were duly admitted in 1951. Astonishingly, St. Pat's made an immediate impact by winning the League championship in their first season. It was an amazing achievement and this was followed by two more title successes in 1955 and 1956. In 1959, they won the FAI Cup – Ireland's equivalent of the FA Cup – for the first time in their history and repeated that success in 1961. The latter victory enabled them to qualify for the following season's European Cup Winners' Cup, although they were eliminated in the preliminary round by Scottish club Dunfermline Athletic.

In a relatively short period, St Pat's had come a long way from being an inauspicious non-league team to one of the most successful sides in the League of Ireland. But, perhaps not surprisingly, they were unable to sustain that success. They struggled throughout the next 10 years, although they maintained their position in the top sphere of Irish football.

By 1971, they were a struggling side with all of their players being part-timers. In their best years, the crowds for home matches at Richmond Park had averaged around 4,000 – a decent attendance in Irish football – but, now, they had dwindled to around 600 a game. The club badly needed an injection of cash and enthusiasm plus the coaching expertise of an ambitious young player-manager. It was under these circumstances that Jack Burkett applied for the vacant job in the summer of 1971.

He was impressed by the structure of St Pat's even though he had not previously heard of them. "The most famous teams in Ireland have always been the likes of Shamrock Rovers, Dundalk, Bohemians and Shelbourne," explains Jack. "I flew over to Dublin and met the St Pat's chairman, Paddy Monroe, and his directors at a hotel in the city centre. I was told that they had received a number of applicants for the job but they said that they were impressed by my pedigree in terms of having played for West Ham under Ron Greenwood.

Ann and sons Darrell and Dean help Jack pack his boots in preparation for his move to Ireland as player-manager of St. Patrick's Athletic in July 1971.

"They had also done their homework and were aware of what I had achieved as a player and, also, my coaching qualifications. They set out their future plans for St Pat's and, despite the fact that they had clearly been struggling in the league and the club was being run on a shoe-string budget, I thought that they had a very progressive outlook and it was good that they were so ambitious.

"It was also apparent that the chairman and directors were prepared to invest some money because they were desperate for St Pat's to become successful again. We talked for a long while and at the end of the meeting, they said I was the most suitable applicant and I was offered the job. We discussed my contract which was to run for three years with a further one year option. It was a substantial increase on the money that I had been earning at Millwall plus there were additional bonuses if we were successful.

"I gave my agreement there and then – it was as simple as that. At the age of 29, I was player-manager of St Patrick's Athletic in the League of Ireland.

"The following morning, the chairman picked me up from the hotel and drove me to the ground. At first, I didn't realise what was happening because he pulled up in a street with rows of terraced houses down either side. 'We're here,' he said, but I couldn't see any sign of the ground.

"He led me up to the front door of one of the houses, which I later learnt was owned by the club. In fact, the groundsman lived there and he let us in the front door. We walked right through the house and out of the back door into the garden which backed on to St Pat's tiny ground. I think I looked a bit shocked because it wasn't quite what I was expecting.

"There was a small stand but little else. The rest of the ground was just an uncovered standing area for spectators with a low wall around the perimeter of the pitch. The chairman told me that they held their board meetings in the front room of the groundsman's house and walking through the house could be used as a short-cut for me to get to the main stand and dressing-rooms.

"I had been a player with West Ham for 10 years and I had been used to playing at some of the biggest stadiums in the country, so St Pat's ground was a bit of a culture shock. But it didn't matter. I had only been in Ireland for 24 hours and I had fallen in love with the place. The people at the club were incredibly charming and friendly. Instinctively, I knew I had made the right decision."

Despite Burkett's confidence in the decision to uproot his family and move to Ireland, it should be stressed that he was taking an enormous risk and it had nothing to do with his ability to re-establish St Pat's as a force in Irish football. It had far wider implications than that.

Two years earlier – in the summer of 1969 – the simmering religious troubles had erupted in Northern Ireland. At the time, 6,000 British troops were sent to separate the Protestant and Catholic militants. There was appalling violence, riots and arson attacks throughout the Province which was in ferment as the long-dormant IRA unleashed a rein of terror. Tension continued to escalate and, in due course, the violence would spread to mainland Britain with IRA bombers targeting major towns and cities. Tragically, hundreds of people were killed, maimed and injured during that dark and dreadful period.

Admittedly, Burkett and his family were moving to the relatively trouble-free south of Ireland but in the summer of 1971, violence across the border in the north of the country was beginning to reach frightening proportions. In the very week of their arrival, tensions were cranked up several notches as two rioters were shot dead by the British Army in the Bogside area of Derry. In retaliation, an IRA sniper from Derry's Creggan Estate killed a British soldier who thus became the first of many army personnel to die during the troubles. Shortly afterwards, 21 people died during three days of riots as they clashed with the army in protests at the introduction of internment without trial.

The degree of hatred and anti-British feeling throughout the whole country was on the increase. In a sense, Northern Ireland was staring into an abyss but, more worryingly, the anti-British feeling was growing in the south of the country as well. It was not exactly the ideal time for an English family to be taking up residence across the Irish Sea.

Nevertheless, after the disappointment of three wasted years with Charlton and Millwall, Burkett was prepared to ignore the dangers and bigotry that existed in the Emerald Isle. It is fair to say that, despite the terrible troubles that were overwhelming the country, setting foot in Ireland gave him a breath of new football life.

Unfortunately, Ann was not so impressed.

She says: "My heart sank when he told me that we were going to live in Ireland.

I was so happy in our house at Chadwell Heath and the boys were settled there but it was Jack's career and we had no option.

"The religious troubles had flared up a couple of years earlier, so that was another reason why I was so concerned about going to live there. We sold up and moved to Clondalkin in County Dublin – about 20 minutes from St. Patrick's ground. I suppose that I was expecting something like Upton Park and I was quite shocked when I first saw the state of their little ground with its tiny ramshackle stand.

"Initially, we lived in a club house, which we rented, and I must admit that Clondalkin was a nice little town. It was very rural and the pace of life was much slower than I had been used to but this was 1971 and, not surprisingly, some parts of Ireland – including that area – seemed a bit behind the times when compared to London.

"Even so, I surprised myself because I settled very quickly into our new way of life and so did our two sons who ended up being able to speak Gaelic. My Mum came to live with us because Dad had died earlier that year and, in effect, she was returning to her roots. Mum had been born and raised just a few miles from Clondalkin and I think that moving back to the area helped her get over the loss of my Dad.

"I also think that having Mum with us helped me because, inevitably, Jack was away a lot of the time with the team. Eventually, we bought the house we had been renting – a beautiful property with a large garden. It cost us £8,000 and more than 30 years later, I heard that the same house was sold again for £500,000. Perhaps we should have stayed there a bit longer!

"Fortunately, most of the problems and troubles were confined to Northern Ireland but there was always the constant worry in the back of our minds that something terrible could happen to us. The most ironic thing is that in the summer of 1974, we went back to London to see all the family – and we were nearly blown up by the IRA.

"By this time, our daughter Elizabeth had been born and we decided to take the children to the Tower of London for a day out. We were about 50 metres from the entrance when there was a huge explosion from inside the Tower. At first, I thought it was a cannon firing off a 21-gun salute – but it was an IRA bomb. There was choking smoke everywhere and suddenly people were running in all directions. Sheer panic had broken out.

"I later heard that one person had been killed and 41 badly injured, including a number of children. It was horrifying. We just got away from the area as quickly as possible. It was a lucky escape. After that, London was on high security alert and because we had gone over in our car with an Irish number plate, we kept getting stopped by the police. It was amazing that there was so much violence in Ireland at the time and, yet, we could so easily have been badly injured or killed on a short visit to London."

As the Burkett family settled in Ireland in 1971, Jack was determined to make an immediate impression on the players of St Patrick's Athletic.

He explains: "They were all part-timers and worked as postmen, firemen or in the docks. A couple of them were office workers and they all trained on Tuesday and Thursday evenings. The standard of football was the equivalent of the present day Conference League.

"At the first training session, I told the players that if they could get some time off work and come in for extra training during the day, then I would arrange for the club to make up any loss of earnings and, also, get some extra money for them. They were all for it and I sensed that I had got them on my side right from the start.

"I told them that we would sometimes be staying in a hotel on the night before important matches because I wanted our preparation to be absolutely spot-on. St Pat's chairman was a bit aghast when I told him but I said that I wanted the club to be more professional in its approach. I also said that if I could get the team fitter and spend more time with them on the training ground, then we had far more chance of becoming successful. I stressed that if we achieved that objective, then the crowds would increase and so would the club's revenue. It was a bit of a gamble on my part but I wanted to give myself every opportunity to succeed.

"It paid off handsomely. In my first season, we won the LFA President's Cup – Ireland's equivalent of the League Cup. Our attendances increased to around 2,000 – a big improvement on the average of 600 when I had taken over. I was playing at centre-half or in midfield and although I had a dual role as player-manager, I felt my own form was good. St Pat's had given me back my appetite for the game.

"In the league, we finished in fifth place, which was an improvement on

The new boss ready for work at St Pat's in August 1971.

207

the previous season. Also, we reached the FAI Cup semi-final, where we were beaten by Cork Hibs, and two of the youngsters in our team were selected for the Irish under-18 youth side. All things considered, it was a very successful first season in charge for me.

"It was all the more satisfying because three of our senior players missed a lot of matches during the season and it wasn't anything to do with football matters. When I first joined St Pat's, I was talking with the chairman about the ability of some of the playing staff. I was a bit concerned when he said that there would be occasions when three members of the squad would sometimes be away 'on business' and that they would be unavailable for training or selection for matches. He stressed that I should not ask any questions about their whereabouts but when they returned, they should be allowed to carry on training and be included in the selection process, just like the other players.

"When I remonstrated and said that it was totally unacceptable, he told me in no uncertain terms that it was something I would have to live with and, again, impressed the need for me to show the utmost discretion. I was most unhappy about the situation and decided that I would deal with the matter in my own way when the opportunity arose.

"But during an early-season training session, I noticed that one of those players had left his kit-bag open. Clearly visible and lying on top of the gear in his bag was a balaclava and a revolver. I realised the reason why the chairman had stressed I should not question the three players when they had been away 'on business.'

"They were members of the IRA!"

Six months after Jack joined St Pat's, the tension in Ireland reached an unprecedented level after one of the bloodiest days throughout the troubles. The infamous date was January 30, 1972 and it will forever be known as Bloody Sunday, which became a centrepiece for IRA propaganda. It was on this day that British soldiers opened fire on crowds, killing 14 people and seriously wounding 12 others. Republicans maintained that the troops had shot innocent demonstrators, whilst the army said that they had come under fire from the IRA. In either event, it was one of the blackest episodes in Ireland's history. Once again, tensions in the Province attained frightening new heights.

The following week, St Patrick's Athletic had arranged to play an evening friendly match against Derry, which is situated just across the border in the north of the country near County Donegal. It was staunch Republican territory and the IRA had established menacing 'no-go' areas for the British Army throughout Derry with the use of armed barricades and road-blocks.

Jack recalls: "The three IRA members in our team weren't playing because they were away 'on business.' It was the middle of winter and night had already fallen as we drove along a deserted country road towards the town. I was sitting at the front of the coach with the chairman when I suddenly saw some lights ahead of us. The driver slowed right down and then we stopped completely.

"It was an IRA roadblock and there were several members of the paramilitary wearing balaclavas and holding guns. The chairman turned to me and said: 'Keep your mouth shut, Jack. Don't let them hear your English accent.'

"Two of the IRA members menacingly boarded the coach brandishing their firearms and wanted to know who we were and where we were going. Their tone was aggressive and intimidating. The chairman explained that we were St Pat's FC and we were on our way to fulfil a fixture against Derry. The IRA men told us to get off the coach and we had to line up alongside the vehicle. They carried out a full search of the coach and the chairman later told me that they were looking for weapons and also checking to see if we were hiding anyone on board.

"It was cold and pitch-black on the road-side that night. It was eerie, although I didn't feel frightened. It was a sign of the times but it was a surreal situation. As I watched the IRA searching our coach, it did occur to me that my years at West Ham seemed an awfully long time ago.

"Once they had completed their search, we were allowed back on the coach and they waved us on our way. There was an audible sigh of relief from everyone on board as the coach pulled away. The rest of the journey was completed in total silence.

"There were some occasions when I encountered a serious degree of bigotry during games themselves. We were playing a league game against Finn Harps and as I tackled one of their players near the touchline, I heard a voice in the crowd shout out: 'Go home, you f*****g English pig.' I kept getting the same abuse throughout the entire game but I just ignored it.

"At the end, I shook hands with the Finn Harps players and, as I was walking off, the fan who had apparently been hurling the abuse climbed over the wall and came running across the pitch as if he was going to attack me. One of the stewards saw what was happening and laid him out with a punch to the head.

"Afterwards, the 'assailant' was taken away by the police and I was asked if I wanted to bring charges against him – but I declined. There was no point because it wouldn't have made any difference to the antagonism that he felt towards me.

"There were other instances when some of the Irish lads in opposing teams would try to wind me up by saying: 'You English bastard, you're gonna get shot tonight,' but it was just typical of the verbals that occur between players during matches. At the end of the game, you shake hands and forget all about it.

"In my second season with St Pats, I felt one or two members of the team were beginning to reach the veteran stage and I brought in some new players from other Irish clubs as well as giving debuts to some of the youngsters from the junior side. We began to get a nice blend of youth and experience and I felt my reputation as a coach was growing."

That is something of an understatement because early in the 1972-73 campaign, Jack was given the chance to coach the Republic of Ireland international side on a part-time basis in conjunction with his player-manager role at St Pat's. It was an exciting opportunity because Ireland were about to begin their World Cup qualifying campaign with the finals due to be held in Germany in 1974. The legendary Irish international midfielder John Giles of Leeds United fame had just taken over as player-manager of the national team and he was looking to revamp the coaching set-up.

Jack received a telephone call from John Jarman, the head coach of the Irish Football Association, asking if he would like to join the new regime under Giles. It was a considerable compliment to Jack's coaching skills and it was also a huge honour for St Patrick's Athletic.

Ireland were in a small qualification group for the World Cup finals but, unfortunately, the two other teams were France and the powerful Soviet Union. It was deemed that only the winners of the group would qualify, so the odds were heavily stacked against the Irish team from the very outset. At the time, the Republic were able to call on famous names such as Steve Heighway (Liverpool), Joe Kinnear (Spurs), Paddy Mulligan (Chelsea), Jimmy Conway (Fulham), Don Givens and Gerry Daly (both Manchester United).

There were some useful victories in warm-up and friendly matches, notably against Poland, who were beaten 1-0 in Dublin and Chile, who were overcome 2-1 in Santiago. However, Ireland ultimately failed in their bid to qualify for the World Cup finals in Germany. While they performed creditably in beating France 2-1 at home and drawing 1-1 in Paris, they lost both games to the Soviet Union by 1-0 in Moscow and 2-1 in Dublin. As a result, it was the Soviets who went to the finals.

Burkett reflects on his relationship with the Irish player-manager John Giles by saying: "During his time as a player with Leeds, he always had a lot to say for himself on the pitch and he was very unpopular with opponents. John was well known for trying to wind up other teams and, although he was very skilful, he also had a reputation for having a real hard streak.

"Even so, I got on OK with him during our time together with the Irish team. He let the coaches get on with the training without interruption because he was still heavily involved on the playing side but he was very astute so far as tactics were concerned. I helped coach the Irish national side for two years which covered the World Cup qualifying matches.

"There was a good spirit amongst the players but I don't think they always took international football as seriously as the players who were called up by England or Scotland at the time. Over the years, the Republic had become accustomed to being the 'whipping boys' for some of the major football nations and it was the influence of John Giles that began to change that mindset. It was the start of the Republic of Ireland becoming a force in international football.

"Later on, John also got me involved in coaching the Irish under-18 youth team. It was a great experience and I enjoyed working with players of international quality.

"My third season with St Pat's was memorable because we reached the final of the FAI Cup against Finn Harps at Dalymount Park. On the night before the game, I arranged for the team to stay at a top-class sports and leisure resort on the outskirts of Dublin. It had once been a monastery but, unfortunately, there was no divine intervention for us on this occasion. We lost 3-1 in front of 30,000 spectators.

"It was a big day for the club and, although we lost, I felt we acquitted ourselves well and played some good football. I played at centre-half but I substituted myself with 10 minutes to go, so that we could bring on an extra attacker.

Jack (far right) steers the ball away from danger during the FAI Cup semi-final win against Drogheda in 1974.

"I took up the further one-year option on my contract and spent a fourth season with St Pat's during which time we finished third in the league and reached the semi-final of the FAI Cup. The club was now on a sound financial footing and we had been relatively successful during my time there. A number of good youngsters were coming through the ranks and the future looked bright but I was missing English football.

"There was some talk in the papers that two clubs, Cork Hibs and Drogheda, were keen for me to take over as their manager but I felt that I needed to get a coaching job back home. I told St Pat's that I would be leaving at the end of the season. I was sad to leave but I think that I had taken them as far as I could given the resources that were available.

"The former Chelsea and England striker, Barry Bridges, took over from me as player-manager of St Pat's and he did a good job. Barry even managed to get Gordon Banks to briefly play for the club, although Gordon left soon afterwards to join Fort Lauderdale Strikers in America.

"I believe the youth policy that I tried to develop at St Pat's paid off in the longer term because, in later years, Paul McGrath came through the ranks and went on to enjoy a great career with Manchester United and the Republic of Ireland.

"I always reflect on my time with St Pat's as an immensely enjoyable period in my football career. The people at the club were marvellous and I look back on my time there with great memories."

Above: Southend United 1975-76. Jack is second from right in the back row, with manager Arthur Rowley at the opposite end of the same row. Below: Jack (second row from back, just right of centre) in the summer of '75 on the FA coaching course at Lilleshall. Geoff Hurst is seated at the far right end of the front row.

19

The Scapegoat

JUST prior to his departure from St Patrick's Athletic in the summer of 1975, Jack Burkett went on a one-week 'refresher' FA coaching course at Lilleshall back in England. Apart from the benefits of gaining some extra coaching acumen, it presented a good opportunity for players and coaches to make contact with other people from within the game.

Also on the course was Geoff Hurst who was about to set off on his own coaching career as player-manager at non-league Telford United. Apart from catching up with his former West Ham colleague, Burkett also met Southend United's full-back

Re-united in 1975: Players from the Cup-winning teams of the mid-60s returned to Upton Park to play in the Wally St. Pier Testimonial match. Standing, left to right: Peter Brabrook, Jack Burkett, Ken Brown, Martin Peters, John Bond, Bobby Moore, Jim Standen. Front: Geoff Hurst, Johnny Byrne, Eddie Bovington, Ron Boyce.

Tony Taylor who was endeavouring to gain his own preliminary coaching badge. Scottish-born Taylor was a good professional who had begun his career with Morton before moving to Crystal Palace and, eventually, Southend.

They struck up a conversation about their respective careers and when Taylor realised that Jack was looking for a job in English football, he pointed out that a coaching vacancy existed at his own club.

At the end of the coaching course at Lilleshall, Burkett duly applied for the job of player-coach at third division Southend United. At the time, the club were managed by Arthur Rowley who had gained a unique place in Football League history during his own playing days. Rowley was a bustling striker who had served West Bromwich Albion, Fulham, Leicester City and Shrewsbury Town during his 19-year career but his claim to fame was that he held the record for the greatest number of goals in the Football League – an astonishing 434 in 619 games. At the end of his playing career, Rowley had managed Shrewsbury and Sheffield United before taking over the reins at Southend in 1970.

During their meeting, the redoubtable Rowley made it clear that he wanted Jack to join the coaching staff but he was brutally honest, admitting that Southend were in dire financial straits. The wage that they were prepared to offer Burkett was considerably less than he had been earning in Ireland. Nevertheless, the 'pull' of a return to English football was too great and, in July 1975, he accepted the offer of a one-year deal as first team player-coach at Southend United.

He explains: "My contract with St Pat's had expired and I was able to start work almost immediately. Initially, I stayed with my sister who lived near Southend, while Ann was left to sell the house in Ireland. After the sale was completed, Ann returned with the children and we bought a house on the outskirts of the town.

"I accept that it was a lot of upheaval for the family but I felt that it was worth it because I could pursue a coaching career in English football. Unfortunately, it turned out to be a bad move and my year at Southend was a very depressing experience.

"They had some decent players, especially full-back Dave Worthington and midfielder Graham Moore, who had played for Manchester United and Wales in the early-60s. I knew Graham because we had been at Charlton together and on the first day's training at Southend, he said: 'You're going to have a few problems here, Jack.'

"He also made a few disparaging remarks about Rowley's style of management. It wasn't quite what I wanted to hear but an example of the players' general dissatisfaction came early in the season. We beat Brighton 5-1 at Roots Hall and Peter Silvester scored all five goals. After the game, he proudly sat in the dressing-room with the match ball and all the players were in a buoyant mood.

"But Arthur came in and infuriated Silvester by saying: 'Peter, if I'd been playing today, I'd have scored 10.'

"Bearing in mind Arthur's goal-scoring record, it is most likely that he would have done so but this wasn't the time to belittle what Silvester had achieved in that game. It was a classic way of turning players against him and it was one of the reasons why Arthur was so unpopular.

"I started to have my own problems with him as well and we clashed a number of times during the season over tactics and training. Basically, he was a decent enough man but we just didn't get on – it was one of those things that occur in all walks of life. It was a dire season and the bad feeling that existed in the dressing room ultimately affected performances on the field."

Southend fought a season-long relegation battle. In March and in a desperate bid to beat the dreaded drop into the fourth division, Rowley was made general manager and Burkett was put in charge of team affairs. However, the damage was irreparable and at the end of a depressing season, Southend suffered the ignominy of relegation to Division Four.

On Monday, May 3, 1976, the local *Evening Echo* newspaper carried the banner headline: 'Blues to sack boss Burkett'. The full length report stated: "Jack Burkett, Dave Worthington, Ken Foggo, Tony Taylor and Stuart Brace – these are the heads that will roll when Southend announce their retained list tomorrow and leading scorer Peter Silvester will be up for sale. The biggest shock from crisis-torn Roots Hall is that Burkett, who took charge of the team less than two months ago, looks like being made a scapegoat for the club's relegation to the fourth division."

The axe fell the following morning and Burkett responded in the following day's edition of the local paper. Under the headline, 'It's a sick joke fumes Burkett,' he was unusually vociferous, saying: "I was told that I was not to blame for relegation but that doesn't ring true. In fact, I regard that as a sick joke. The thing is that I have

BLUES TO SACK BOSS BURKETT

More bad news from Southend.

been sacked and I feel I've been made a scapegoat.

"I could have accepted it if I had been in charge for three seasons but it was only two months. Naturally, I am bitterly disappointed at the way things have turned out."

Suddenly, Burkett's decision to leave Ireland a year earlier didn't seem to have been such a good idea after all. He was out of work but football is a strange profession. It can be hard and brutal but it is also a sport in which life-long friendships are forged, even during the heat of battle.

Over the years, a mutual respect had built up between Burkett and Birmingham City's midfielder Malcolm Beard. During their playing days, they had both been dedicated professionals who had served their respective clubs with distinction. Whilst they had played against each other on numerous occasions, it was because Burkett had spoken up for Beard over a harsh sending-off that a friendship had subsequently developed between them.

It was during the long, hot summer of 1976 that Beard made a telephone call to Jack that would lead to him taking a coaching job in the most unlikely of destinations – oil-rich Saudi Arabia.

20

The Ultimate deterrent

NEWS travels fast in football and Malcolm Beard was aware that Jack Burkett had left Southend in acrimonious circumstances and was looking for work. During the phone call, Beard explained that former Coventry City manager and PFA chairman Jimmy Hill had set up a company called World Sports Academy – and they were looking for qualified coaches to go out to the Middle East and coach the Saudi Arabian national team and youth sides.

Beard said all interested coaches were required to register at Warwick University the following week for interviews and selection process.

Jack says: "Malcolm was going to attend and since I was out of work, I had no option but to give it a try as well. Ronnie Allen, who nearly signed me for Wolves eight years earlier, was eventually chosen as national team manager and I was selected as one of his coaches, along with Malcolm, plus Dave Woodfield (ex-Wolves), Geoff Vowden (ex-Birmingham City), John Manning (ex-Bolton) and Ian King (ex-Leicester) – all good former professional players and first class coaches in their own right.

"It was a three-year contract and it was all geared to the Gulf Games which were due to be held in Iraq in 1979. It was a major tournament and in Europe, it would be the equivalent of the European Championships, so there was a great deal of prestige to be gained if Saudi Arabia were ultimately successful.

"The wages were good because I would be earning £12,000 a year, which was tax-free. It was more than twice what I had been earning in Ireland and it was double the average annual wage in the UK at the time. The downside was that I would be away from the family. Ann and I discussed the situation and we agreed that we couldn't uproot the children again because they were very settled back in England.

"There were other aspects to consider. Saudi lies between the Persian Gulf and the Red Sea and it is one of the few countries in the world where summer temperatures exceed 50 degrees centigrade. I didn't think that I could subject my family to that sort of climate.

"Another reason is that women in Saudi are regarded as second class citizens and it is the only country in the world where they are banned from driving on public roads. They can drive off-road or in private housing compounds but that is all.

It was not a lifestyle that would have suited Ann.

"I flew out on September 12, 1976 and the contract required me to work in Saudi for three months at a time before returning home for a two-week break. I would then go back to Saudi and the process would begin all over again. I found it very difficult being away from the family – I virtually missed three years of my children growing up but I just had to make the best of it.

"Malcolm Beard and myself were given the job of coaching Saudi Arabia's under-20 team. During the initial three-month period, we travelled around the country mainly to Riyadh and Jeddah watching games and looking at young players who were good enough to be selected for the side, with a view to them eventually progressing to full international level in time for the Gulf Games.

"Once we had assembled the under-20 squad, we took them on numerous tours and gradually the team began to take shape. Most of the players spoke reasonable English, so the language wasn't a problem, but we were always provided with an interpreter so that we could ensure that our coaching sessions and tactics during matches were fully understood.

"We flew everywhere in the Prince of Saudi Arabia's private jet, which was the ultimate in luxury. We undertook tours to France, Germany, Belgium, Spain, Austria, Tunisia, Thailand, Iran, Malaysia and Iraq.

"At the end of each trip, I had to report to the Prince at the Royal Palace in Riyadh where he lived with one of his wives who, somewhat surprisingly, originated from Leicester. He had three other wives and they all lived at other palaces elsewhere in the country.

"The opulence in the palace at Riyadh was quite staggering. I had to give the Prince a complete run-down on each trip including our results and the form of the individual players. He was very knowledgeable about the game and wanted to know every detail of the tour matches. But he made it abundantly clear that he expected success in the Gulf Games, so the pressure to succeed was constant.

"In my second year, we continued touring and on one occasion, we returned to Germany for a friendly against Hamburg's first team which included Kevin Keegan, who had been signed from Liverpool a few months earlier. We lost 5-2 but it was still an impressive performance from the Saudi youngsters. I spoke briefly with Kevin at the end of the game and it was clear that he was settling down well in Germany.

"That game showed how much the Saudi under-20 youngsters had improved in just over a year. It was also very satisfying watching some of them make their debuts for the full national team later that season

"It was a fascinating experience living in Saudi Arabia, particularly having to get used to the different customs and cultures that existed in their country. For example, Saudi culture mainly revolves around the religion of Islam whose two holiest sites, Mecca and Medina, are located in the country. Muslims are called to prayer five times a day and we had to arrange training sessions and matches around the players' prayer time.

"Saudi's dietary laws forbid the eating of pork and the drinking of alcohol and this

Jack (extreme right, back row) as manager of Saudi Arabia's under-20 team.

law is enforced very strictly throughout the country. It was quite amusing, though, because the Prince would sometimes call a meeting with all of the coaches and, afterwards, he would hand out a few beers. As we were about to leave, he would say: 'Remember, if you are stopped by the police on your way home, you haven't been here!'

"Another major aspect of Saudi culture is that law and order are enforced very strictly and the fear of punishment was brought home to me during the under-20 squad's first trip to Europe. Most of the young players left their rooms unlocked with their Rolex watches and other valuables lying on their beds. When I told them to make sure everything was locked away, they looked at me as if I was mad. They said that there was hardly any thieving in Saudi Arabia because of the severity of punishments in their country.

"They automatically assumed that things were the same the whole world over. I had to impress upon them that was definitely not the case.

"The Saudi legal system allows capital punishment, usually beheadings or stoning to death, for murder and adultery. There is also corporal punishment, including amputation of hands and feet, for certain crimes such as robbery, rape, drug smuggling and homosexual activity. The courts can impose less severe punishments, like floggings, for crimes against public morality such as drunkenness.

"On one occasion, I witnessed the brutality of the punishments administered to offenders. We were in Jeddah one Friday which was 'punishment day.' The local police liked foreigners to witness punishments being administered because it ensured that they wouldn't break any Saudi laws themselves. The police usually pushed foreigners to the front of the crowd to make sure that they got the best view and didn't miss anything.

"Hundreds of people from surrounding areas converged on Jeddah each Friday to watch the punishments which were carried out in a square in the city centre. There was shouting and chanting rather similar to a football crowd. The arena was square-shaped and was about half the size of a football pitch. The surface was covered with sand and the middle part of the arena was stained with the blood of previous victims.

"I saw one man, who had been found guilty of thieving, have his hand cut off. As the man screamed in agony, the medics plunged the stump of his arm into a bucket of ice before he was rushed to hospital.

"Another man, who was hooded and had his hands tied behind his back, was dragged in and forced to kneel down. I realised that they were going to behead him. The executioner's sword glinted in the sunshine and as it flashed downwards, I looked away. There was a great roar from the crowd and when I looked back again, the executioner was holding the severed head high into the air. It was all over in a matter of seconds.

"A couple of women in the crowd fainted. It was a horrifying spectacle but it is the Saudi's way of doing things and it ensures that crime is kept to the absolute minimum. Without doubt, their punishment regime is the ultimate deterrent."

Perhaps it is just as well that such severe retribution is not administered in Saudi Arabia when it comes to football matters. Burkett's under-20 team continued to improve and the national side managed by Ronnie Allen was also doing well but, by this time, the 1979 Gulf Games were fast approaching. The tournament was being held in Iraq and it was the culmination of three years' hard work by Allen and his team of coaches.

As a result of their considerable progress during that period, Saudi Arabia were considered strong favourites for the tournament. All went according to plan as the competition got under way – host nation Iraq were eliminated and the Saudi's serenely marched on to reach the final in Baghdad against their arch rivals Iran.

Unfortunately and as so often happens with odds-on favourites, Saudi failed at the last hurdle. In a hostile and intimidating atmosphere, Iran won 2-1 in front of 100,000 spectators. It was a devastating blow to have come so close and the whole of Saudi Arabia went into a period of mourning. They take their football seriously in that part of the world.

The following day, all the coaching staff together with Ronnie Allen were summoned to the Royal Palace where the Prince was waiting to hold court with them. "He was a very charming man," says Jack. "Despite his immense disappointment, he was most courteous as he thanked us for all we had done over the previous three years and for the way that we had helped improve his country as a football nation. But the bottom line was that we had failed in our quest to win the Gulf Games and he told us that our contracts were not being renewed.

"It had been an incredible experience but I was consoled by the fact that I could go home and be with my family again. I do believe that we created a fantastic football legacy because, in later years, Saudi Arabia qualified on four occasions for the World Cup. I still get a lot of satisfaction when I think back to what we achieved during our time there. It was an unforgettable period in my life."

21

Player power rules

ON the journey home from Saudi Arabia, Jack Burkett made a stop-off in Germany in order to keep a promise that he had made 18 months earlier, when the Saudi under-20 team had been involved in one of their numerous European tours. It had included a stay in the German city of Frankfurt where he had met Karlo Herbert, the owner of second division side, Offenbach Kickers.

Herbert was a great admirer of English football and he remembered West Ham's spectacular triumph against TSV Munich in the final of the European Cup Winners' Cup 14 years earlier. They struck up a friendship which resulted in Herbert offering Burkett a job on the coaching staff at Offenbach. Unfortunately, it was not possible for Jack to accept because, at the time, he was under contract to the Saudi's, but he promised that he would help with the coaching at Offenbach if the opportunity ever arose in the future.

Hence, the journey home from Saudi in the spring of 1979 allowed him to keep that promise, if only for a short period. "I spent a few weeks there," explains Jack. "It was another good experience and I could have stayed on a permanent basis subject to passing the German FA's coaching badge, which wouldn't have been a problem, but I had been away from home for too long. I wanted to get back and be with my family again. I also wanted a job in English football."

The coaching role at Offenbach Kickers was another good addition to Burkett's CV. However, one of the obstacles to obtaining coaching and managerial jobs in the English game is supply and demand. For every job that becomes available, there are invariably dozens of applications from former players who are anxious to remain in the game. It is a problem that has existed for decades and it was such a difficulty that faced Burkett upon his return from Saudi Arabia via the short stay in Germany in 1979. He applied for numerous vacant positions but such was the massive interest in the various jobs that, sometimes, the clubs concerned did not even bother to acknowledge the majority of applications.

One major disappointment was failing to get a job on the coaching staff at Chelsea which was being advertised at the time. Burkett felt that he was in with a chance because, apart from his extensive coaching experience, the newly-appointed Chelsea manager was his former West Ham team-mate and good friend, Geoff

Hurst. "At Geoff's request, I went over to Chelsea's training ground near Heathrow Airport and had an interview with him," says Jack. "He said he would get back to me but I never heard any more from him about the job."

It was a hugely frustrating time and Burkett began to consider the possibility of working abroad again. It was under these circumstances that he applied for the player-manager's role at Orsta, in the second division of Norwegian football, in January 1980.

"I flew out to Norway – land of the Vikings – and met with the Orsta officials," says Jack. "I was offered a two-year contract and, although it meant being away from the family again, I accepted the job because there was nothing forthcoming back home. Basically, I had no other option.

"Orsta is a small town situated north of Bergen, in a very isolated part of the country surrounded by mountains and fjords. The players were part-timers who trained a couple of evenings a week and although the facilities were good, the attendance for home matches was very sparse – probably averaging no more than 500 a game."

As far as Burkett was concerned, it was a situation far removed from the blistering temperatures and opulence that existed in football-crazy Saudi Arabia. In fact, Orsta was typical of the Nordic region as a whole and its inhabitants dealt with their isolation through a tight-knit community spirit. It was a very insular town and it seemed that the locals did not take kindly to outsiders infiltrating their 'territory'.

This was particularly true of their football team who were somewhat upset that the previous manager – a highly popular local man – had been sacked after a series of poor results. When Burkett walked into the dressing room for the first time as their new player-manager, the reception afforded to him was decidedly cool.

In truth, it never improved. It seems that 'player power' is much in evidence all over the world, even in the remotest of football outposts.

"I didn't get on with the players from the very outset," admits Jack. "There was a distinct feeling of animosity amongst them because of the sacking of the previous manager. I was never able to win them over like I had with the players of St Pat's.

"Also, I was a bit too hard on them. I was determined to improve the results of the team but at the same time, I sometimes overlooked the fact that they were part-timers and my expectations of their capabilities were too high. It was abundantly clear throughout my time there that I was not exactly the most popular manager in the world.

"The Norwegian season runs from April until September because the conditions are too severe to play football during the winter months. I spent two years with Orsta and we finished in the lower half of the table on both occasions.

"It was during my second season out there that my Dad died after a long battle against stomach cancer, which made things even harder for me. In the end, I was glad when my contract eventually expired, so that I could return home to England. It was decent money and it was another of life's experiences – but it wasn't a particularly enjoyable time for me."

Ann has equally mixed feelings about life in Orsta.

Jack Burkett hadde Ron Greenwood som Læremester:

Nå vil han lære Ørsta-spillerne arbeidsfotball

Stadig flere norske fotballklubber har de senere år satset på utenlandske trenere, og spesielt synes de engelske å være populære på det norske markedet. Lokalt var vel Hødd først ute med utanlandsk læremester, og senere har både Aalesund og Molde fulgt etter, med Ørsta som ...

Frosty reception: How the Norwegian press greeted Jack's appointment at Orsta in January 1980.

She recalls: "Early on, I went out and stayed with Jack. It was during the summer holidays, so I was able to take the children with me. He lived in a beautiful chalet situated high on the mountain and the views were fantastic – but it was in the middle of nowhere. It is a stunning country with magnificent scenery but it was also very boring because Orsta is such an isolated town.

"Obviously, I couldn't understand the Norwegian language on TV, so I ended up ploughing through dozens of magazines that I had taken with me. The children enjoyed it and went fishing in the fjords for salmon but as far as I was concerned, it was the most boring six weeks of my life."

Early in 1982, Burkett returned home to the UK to be with his family after his two-year sojourn in Norway but he needed to find work again. Initially, he did some part-time scouting for Birmingham City and Aston Villa – thanks to Malcolm Beard, yet again – which kept him in touch with the game. He also spent a few weeks selling sports clothing from an outlet in Southend near his home.

Ann admits: "It was great that Jack was home again but I had got used to running the house on my own for virtually five years while he was working in Saudi Arabia and Norway. Suddenly, he was back and we had to readjust to the situation of being together again on a full-time basis.

"Although Jack was only out of football for a few months when he returned home, he missed it dreadfully and I was very relieved when he told me that he had applied for a part-time coaching job with the youth team of Southend United.

"It is true that he had left the club on bad terms in 1976 after all the problems with Arthur Rowley and the team being relegated, but all of the personnel from that era had now left. By this time, Southend's manager was Dave Smith and I was thrilled when Jack got the job in the summer of 1982."

At last, Burkett was back in English football and, in a relatively short space of time, it would also give him the chance to link up once again with his great friend and former West Ham colleague – the iconic Bobby Moore.

Bobby Moore, the manager, in his time as boss of cash-strapped Southend United.

22

Bobby Moore – frustrated manager

UNFORTUNATELY, things had not improved for Southend United over the years because they had always remained in the lower reaches of the Football League. Just like Arthur Rowley before him, the unfortunate Dave Smith had also struggled to turn Southend's fortunes around and it came as no surprise when he was sacked in 1983.

Smith was quickly replaced by former Ipswich midfielder Peter Morris who, sadly, met a similar fate within a few short months. Throughout all of this managerial carnage, Burkett continued with his role as part-time coach to Southend's youth team – quietly and with a degree of success.

Meanwhile, the club were now looking for their third manager in two years and it seemed the next incumbent of the job should not be someone who intended making any long-term plans. A radio station announced that Southend were looking to make "A big name appointment," but since a similar message had been circulated prior to the tenures of Smith and Morris, it is true to say that their disillusioned fans did not give much credence to such a statement.

Imagine their amazement then when, within a few days, the club announced that Bobby Moore was the new manager. 'Big name' appointments did not get much bigger than that.

Whilst Moore's 21-year playing career had been one of football's greatest success stories, it is also true to say that parts of his life after he had retired as a player were a juxtaposition of immense disappointment and regret. He had spent 18 years with West Ham where he had attained God-like status and the final three years of his career were successfully spent with second division Fulham. His final appearance as a player came on May 14, 1977 when Fulham lost 1-0 at Blackburn Rovers. Moore was 36-years-old at the time and, fittingly, it was his 1,000th first class match.

It was generally accepted that a managerial career would quickly follow. That seemed to be the case during the summer of 1977 when Moore enjoyed a lunch in London with Watford's flamboyant new chairman, Elton John, who offered him the vacant manager's job at Vicarage Road. Although Watford were in the fourth division, a prospective partnership between two such world famous personalities from the showbiz and football industries seemed almost too good to be true.

They shook hands on the deal and agreed that the matter would be finalised once Moore had returned from the impending Spanish holiday with his family.

Unfortunately, Watford's board of directors were apparently insistent that an experienced manager should take over and Elton John was allegedly overruled in his decision to appoint Moore. Instead, they went for Graham Taylor who had already been very successful managing in the lower divisions, notably with Lincoln City. Upon his return from holiday, Moore was devastated to discover that the Watford job had gone to Taylor. It was a sad sequence of events that set the pattern for Moore in the ensuing years.

He briefly coached at Seattle Sounders and, also, the quaintly named Carolina Lightning in the USA. Thereafter, Moore held a similar position with Eastern Athletic in Hong Kong for just five months. He later became player-coach to Herning, a third division club in Denmark, for an even briefer period – 10 matches to be precise – where the sparse crowds were separated from the playing area by nothing more than a rope tied to posts around the perimeter of the pitch. He might as well have been playing at Hackney Marshes.

However, perhaps the greatest ignominy came when he took over as manager of non-league Oxford City – with a certain Harry Redknapp as his assistant – where the crowds usually consisted of the proverbial two men and a dog. It was hardly the scenario that England's World Cup-winning captain could have envisaged when he retired from playing. By comparison, the manager's job at lowly Southend United must have seemed like the Holy Grail. In fact, it was a dual role because Moore was also made chief executive as well as team manager.

Burkett has no doubt that the debacle over the Watford job had dealt Moore a sickening blow. "Bobby was bitterly disappointed at what happened. He was a man of great integrity and felt very let down because they had apparently reneged on their verbal agreement with him.

"Nobody could argue that Graham Taylor wasn't successful there but he did it playing a long-ball game. There is nothing to say that Bobby wouldn't have been equally successful at Watford but it would have been with a totally different style of football."

Moore took over as manager of Southend United in August 1984 on a wave of optimism but, typically, he chose his words extremely carefully. As his new playing-staff completed their pre-season training, he was quoted in the local paper thus: "The players have worked very hard since I arrived and gone about things in a very professional manner. If they can take that attitude into the league matches, then we should give ourselves every chance of picking up honours."

Jack was also suitably buoyant: "It was great to team up with Bobby again and his appointment definitely raised levels of expectation in the town. He immediately revamped his back-room team. He brought with him ex-Hammer Harry Cripps as first team-coach and made my position with the youth team a full-time job. But Bobby stressed that he wanted me to assist Harry in training the first team as well. It suited me down to the ground, although Bobby realised that I would need some back-up with the youth squad.

"We talked it over and decided to approach our former West Ham team-mate, Paul Heffer, who lived in the area. He was gaining a good reputation as a coach in local schools. Paul agreed to join us on a part-time basis and did a good job – youngsters like Spencer Prior and Justin Edinburgh came through the ranks before being sold to Norwich City and Spurs respectively, which brought in some much needed cash."

Unfortunately, Ann has some unhappy recollections of her husband's spell at Southend alongside Moore.

She says: "The club paid very low wages and to supplement our income, I got a job as a receptionist at a local physiotherapist's practice. It was the first time I had worked since we had got married nearly 20 years earlier.

"The problem was that Southend were in dire financial straits and even when Bobby took over as manager, I don't think that he earned a great deal either. I guess he was just pleased to be back in football with a league club again.

"Bobby moved down to the Southend area and lived quite close to us in Mountdale Gardens but by this time, he was in the process of splitting up with Tina. It must have been a very difficult period for him."

Despite Moore's problems in his personal life, Burkett saw a distinct change in him, albeit for the better. "When Bobby took over as manager at Southend, I sensed that he had become slightly more relaxed than when we had been team-mates at West Ham," says Jack. "He was always a very private person but he seemed to have opened up a bit and was more inclined to discuss things. He would seek my opinion on players and ask for my assessment of future opponents.

"At the time, Southend didn't have a recognised training ground and most of the sessions were conducted in the public park opposite our home ground at Roots Hall or at the army garrison at Shoeburyness. It was hardly satisfactory but Bobby was always very upbeat about everything.

"Clearly, he wanted to be successful but the odds were stacked against him with no money being available for players. We had to make do with what was already available and that wasn't very much. If we did succeed in bringing any new players into the team, they were invariably from the youth side, free-transfers or players whom we had snapped up from non-league football.

"Despite his enthusiasm, Bobby got very frustrated at times working with players who, generally speaking, were of limited ability. In many ways, he was like Ron Greenwood – he had an expectation that all players should have been able to aspire to greater heights but that wasn't always the case. Sometimes he would get annoyed on the training ground if the players were unable to carry out a specific instruction or tactic that he wanted to bring into their play. In fairness, it wasn't their fault because they just weren't good enough to reach the heights that Bobby expected of them.

"Bobby always used to join in the training sessions – he was never going to be a manager who stood on the touchline barking out instructions to his players. He always wanted to be involved and I got the impression that he was at his happiest when he was involved on the training ground.

"As one would expect, he was particularly good at getting the players to practice defending set-pieces such as corner-kicks or throw-ins. He would concentrate on their running and movement in marking opponents. In all the time I worked with Bobby at Southend, there was never an occasion when one of the players disagreed with him.

"In many ways, they were completely in awe of Bobby – not only because of his reputation, but also due to the fact that when he demonstrated something on the training ground, it was invariably done perfectly. Sometimes, we held a practice match and Bobby would be at the heart of the defence making interceptions and winning possession just like he had done throughout his career. It was as though he was turning the clock back.

"There was one occasion when an opposing player in a practice game actually applauded him for making one of his classic tackles!

"As we all know, Bobby had turned tackling into an art form during his playing days. But if any of the Southend players conceded a free-kick for a clumsy challenge or were booked for a late tackle in league games, then he would get really upset. He hated seeing defenders 'diving in' at opponents. The art of tackling was something that mattered greatly to him and, afterwards, he would stress the need for them to control their tackling or 'jockey' an opponent into a position so that a tackle could be made successfully."

Despite the mighty presence of Moore at the helm, the team was still struggling on the pitch. Even more worryingly, it was apparent that things were going from bad to worse in terms of off-the-field matters. The club were threatened with bankruptcy which prompted Moore to amusingly say to his great friend and biographer, Jeff Powell, the highly respected Fleet Street journalist: "We've got so many bailiffs knocking at the door that every night I go round collecting all the televisions, lock them in my office and keep the keys in my pocket!"

Jack gives a further indication of the dreadful financial constraints at Southend: "We could never stay away on the night before a game – there was no money for luxuries such as that. We always travelled by coach on the morning of a game and on the way home afterwards, we would stop off and buy fish and chips for the players which they ate on the coach. Bobby always 'mucked in' and there were many occasions when he was first off the coach to buy fish and chips for everyone.

"I always admired him for that but it also occurred to me that while Bobby was queuing up in fish shops somewhere in the north of England on bitterly cold winter nights, his great friend and rival, Franz Beckenbauer, was back home in Germany managing the national team on their way to qualification for the 1986 World Cup finals in Mexico. The difference in the way their respective careers had evolved could not have been greater.

"I believe Bobby didn't get any big jobs in football because certain clubs felt that they would not be able to handle someone with such a big name and huge reputation. It was a sad indictment of the English game at the time.

"He would have been a fantastic ambassador. Nobody has a divine right to a job in football, whatever their reputation, but the Football Association should have created such a role for him in the same way that the German FA later created an ambassadorial role for Beckenbauer. Those roles are important in football but very few players are capable of making a success of such high profile positions. They must have achieved at the very highest level – but the way they conduct themselves is equally important.

"Just like Beckenbauer, Bobby had the total respect of everyone. It was always noticeable that whenever Southend were playing away from home – it didn't matter where – Bobby always got a fantastic reception from the home supporters, which showed just how much people from all over the country thought of him.

"He also had charisma. It is something that money cannot buy and very few people are lucky enough to have been born with it. Bobby had charisma by the bucket load. He definitely got a raw deal from the hierarchy of English football after he retired from playing.

"We lived very close to each other on the outskirts of Southend and some mornings, I would pick him up in the car. We would talk about the day's training that lay ahead of us and Bobby would explain the type of session that he wanted the coaching staff to organise with the players. When we arrived at the ground around 9.00am, he would go to his office and clear up some paperwork, while I would get everything ready for the training session together with the rest of the staff. Bobby was always very meticulous in dealing with the paperwork and after training had finished, he would often go back to his office to clear up any outstanding issues.

"In his private life, Bobby was having some problems at the time because he had left Tina and moved in with Stephanie Parlane-Moore (they had the same surname) who he had met in 1979. He had also been involved in a number of unsuccessful business ventures including an Essex country club called Woolston Hall in which he invested – and lost – a small fortune.

"Even so, Bobby never let those personal problems affect his role as Southend's manager. He always had an ability to put things into compartments in his mind and deal with them one at a time. Nothing could break his concentration and nothing ever seemed to faze him, either on or off the field.

"I am sure that Bobby felt the manager's job at Southend would be a stepping stone for him and it would ultimately allow him to move on elsewhere and manage at a higher level. Bobby knew that he was regarded as a figurehead and he would never let himself down in front of other people. Even as a manager, he always conducted himself properly and correctly.

"He never shouted or screamed at players in the dressing room. He might swear occasionally but that was more for effect than anything else. If he was upset by a particular performance, then he would let the players know about it in no uncertain terms but he was able to do it in a manner that commanded respect. Bobby was firm but very fair in his assessment of players and their performances.

"As one would expect, he was very tactically aware but he was often let down because many of the players were limited in their technical ability.

"The wages at Southend were very poor and at the end of the 1984-85 season, I asked Bobby if there was any chance of getting a rise. I felt that I had a good case because I was putting in a lot of hours at the club. Bobby said that he would see what

Page 28   EVENING ECHO Monday, July 22, 1985   QS

Echosport... is first again with the latest news on Blues

BURKETT QUITS

SOUTHEND United suffered a major blow today when youth team coach Burkett quit.

By HOWARD SOUTHWOOD

good local talent."

Manager Bobby Moore said that Burkett's first-team presented

"I am obviously putting in a lot of time with the

it."

Moore said he was sorry to see Burkett go. "I understand it from Jack's point of view — he has been offered a golden chance," he ad-

"He did a tremendous amount of work here laying the foundations for a good youth policy. It is important that we carry on where he left off and appointed a right person.

fered a good increase on his money from last season, but he did not feel he could accept it."

Moore's hopes of having a pre-season

he could do for me but a couple of days later, he told me that the directors had said there was no money available.

"Around this time, I went to Bisham Abbey for a summer coaching seminar and I got chatting to Ray Harford, who was Fulham's manager. I told him that things weren't great at Southend and he asked if I wanted to join him at Fulham. They were in the second division but had been struggling near the foot of the table. He was looking for a new youth coach.

"We talked about a salary and it was considerably more than I was earning at Southend. I didn't hesitate to accept the offer. I had been working at Southend without a contract, so I could start almost immediately. I was very excited about it but there was only one problem. Ray had omitted to tell me that Fulham were completely bankrupt and, if it were possible, they were in an even worse financial state than Southend. I told Bobby of my decision the following day."

It was July 22, 1985 and that evening, the local Southend newspaper carried a banner headline saying: 'Burkett Quits.' Jack was quoted: "Obviously, this is a step up for me – going to a club in a higher division – but I leave with some regrets. I put in a lot of hard work at Southend building up the youth policy and I felt it was getting well organised and bringing some promising youngsters to the club. Unhappily, I couldn't agree terms and I decided to try my luck elsewhere."

Jack recalls Moore's reaction: "He was quite taken aback when I told him I was leaving. He asked me to reconsider but my mind was made up. I packed up my things, shook hands with him and walked out of Roots Hall for the last time."

Indeed, Moore's disappointment at Burkett's decision was apparent the following day when he was quoted in the local press saying: "I am very sorry to see Jack leave the club but I understand it from his point of view. He has been offered a golden chance at Fulham. We were not in a position to satisfy his personal demands and this opportunity came up which was too good for him to turn down.

"He did a tremendous amount of work here laying the foundations for a good youth policy. It is important that we carry on where he left off. Jack goes with our good wishes."

Bobby Moore accepted the situation with good grace but, in truth, he was also becoming seriously disillusioned with life at Southend United. He lasted just one more season before resigning. It was his last job in football and epitomised the tragic waste of the great man's talents.

23

Hard times at The Cottage

AT the time of Jack's departure from Southend United in the summer of 1985, Bobby Moore may have stated that the move to Fulham was a "golden chance" for him but, in fact, it turned out to be more like a poisoned chalice. Ann Burkett's perceptive comments accurately describe the problems that faced her husband in his new job.

She says: "It was great that Fulham had approached Jack because they were a bigger club than Southend and the wages were better but getting round the M25 motorway became a bit of a nightmare. He was spending a minimum of four hours a day getting to and from work. We didn't want to move across to West London because, again, it would have meant uprooting the children, so he commuted every day. Also, it was a pity that Ray Harford hadn't forewarned him about Fulham's perilous financial situation because, arguably, it became the most stressful period in Jack's career."

Harford had been a determined central defender during his playing days with Charlton Athletic, Exeter City, Lincoln City, Mansfield Town, Port Vale and Colchester United. He amassed around 350 league appearances for his various clubs. After retiring as a player, he began his coaching career with Colchester and quickly gained an excellent reputation for his coaching and organisational skills.

In 1981, the Fulham manager Malcolm Macdonald invited Harford to join the coaching staff at Craven Cottage. The Fulham team played excellent attacking football and gained promotion into the old second division. The Macdonald-Harford pairing looked to be a match made in heaven but in 1984, Macdonald's private life was beginning to make more news in the press than his team were doing on the pitch and he was sacked in the spring of that year.

Harford had made such a big impression as first team coach that it was no surprise when he was appointed manager following Macdonald's departure. Ironically, his impressive start consisting of five wins in six games ultimately worked against him. It was impossible for Fulham to maintain such good form because events off the pitch were beginning to have a disastrous effect throughout the club.

They were beset by severe financial problems and Harford was utterly helpless as his best players – notably former Hammer and Republic of Ireland international Ray Houghton – were sold in a desperate, but vain, attempt to balance the books.

In his role as Fulham youth coach, Jack watches as Terry Gale signs on in July 1987.

The flow of promising youngsters progressing through the ranks at Craven Cottage had also virtually dried up.

For many years, Fulham had been described as a 'Cinderella' club. It may have been a description that irritated their loyal fans but it was almost a term of endearment. They did not seem to be afflicted by the tribal hatred that surrounds the likes of Manchester United, Chelsea, Liverpool, Arsenal, Tottenham and, indeed, West Ham. The word 'hatred' is not used lightly in this context because in the warped minds of many football fans, they do literally hate the opposition, often with a vengeance.

However, few fans seem to have hated dear old Fulham who play their games in the apparent peace and tranquillity of their Craven Cottage ground that stands on the banks of the River Thames. The actual 'Cottage' itself – a listed building just like the Stevenage Road Stand – overlooks the pitch from above the players' tunnel. It is the quaintest of grounds and, perhaps, exemplifies everything about the club.

They have never won a major trophy, although their most famous player was Johnny Haynes who played 594 league games for them and captained England with considerable distinction. Fulham also supplied a member of England's World Cup-winning team in right-back George Cohen. Apart from that, Fulham have achieved little of note with the exception of a fleeting taste of glory in 1975.

By this time, Bobby Moore – who was coming to the end of his illustrious playing career – had joined them from West Ham and, along with former England colleague Alan Mullery, he inspired Fulham to reach their only FA Cup Final appearance at Wembley. By the greatest irony, their opponents were West Ham but it was not a fairytale ending, since Hammers ran out 2-0 winners.

Thereafter, Fulham went into years of decline and by the time that Harford became their manager in 1984, they were in real trouble both on and off the field. They displayed the classic symptoms of 'how not to run a football club.' Many of their supporters had deserted the club after years of torpid non-achievement and nobody could blame them. The average attendance for league games at Craven Cottage had plummeted to around 4,000 – well below their break-even figure.

Fulham were in a perilous financial state and things weren't much better on the playing field. It was against this background that Harford offered Jack Burkett the chance to join Fulham's coaching staff prior to the 1985-86 season.

Unfortunately, Harford's days were numbered at Craven Cottage. Jack shakes his head as he recalls that agonising initial season with Fulham: "We suffered 26 defeats in 42 league games and finished bottom of the table. We were not even close to averting relegation and finished 13 points from safety. Ray was sacked at the end of the season, although I was told that I might be retained on the coaching staff assuming that the new manager agreed. As things turned out, that is exactly what happened.

"It was a really traumatic time at Fulham because the chairman, Ernie Clay, also left around the same time as Ray. He did a business deal and sold the club and ground to David Bulstrode. Ernie left with a few million quid in his pocket so he was happy at the outcome. The new chairman, Bulstrode, was a property man with Marler Estates and it quickly became apparent that he wanted to merge Fulham with Queens Park Rangers. The name 'Fulham Park Rangers' was suggested and the plan was for the new club to play their matches at Rangers' Loftus Road stadium.

"Once Marler Estates had obtained planning permission, it was proposed that they would build flats on the Craven Cottage ground. It was a real nightmare but these business tycoons completely misjudged the reaction of Fulham's fans. They were up in arms about it and gathered a lot of support from many people in the professional game. Everyone who cared about football was concerned because they could see that if this sort of merger could happen to famous clubs like Fulham and Queens Park Rangers, then it could happen to virtually anybody.

"Despite all of these off-the-field activities, we had to get things ready for the start of the new season in the third division. In the summer of 1986, Ray Lewington was appointed player-manager as Harford's successor. He joined us from Sheffield United and it was a popular choice because he had previously played for Fulham and been a big crowd favourite.

"I got on well with Ray and he asked me to become assistant manager. We formed a good partnership and worked well together. The players gave us everything but the season began against a backdrop of protests from the Fulham fans regarding the merger. There were demonstrations during matches at Craven Cottage and there was one very emotional game when we drew 2-2 at home to Walsall and even *their* fans gave the demonstrations their full support. It was fantastic and very moving to see two sets of fans unite in such a way."

Fortunately, things were about to improve because Jimmy Hill, the former Fulham player, PFA chairman and TV pundit, had gathered a groundswell of opposition to the merger. He got a group of businessmen together who bought Fulham Football Club back off Marler Estates – but not Craven Cottage, which still belonged to the property company.

"Basically, Jimmy gained Fulham some breathing space because part of the deal was that Fulham could continue to play at Craven Cottage by paying a preferential rent to Marler Estates. He was a very astute businessman and he saved Fulham from extinction during that period, despite the fact that the club were completely broke.

"By this time, things were so bad financially that we existed on a day to day basis. The club didn't even have the money to buy soap, shampoo or toilet paper for the players and they used to bring their own toiletries into training. And just like Southend United, the club didn't have a permanent training ground and often made use of local parks. We used Richmond Park and Wimbledon Common, which were hardly suitable for a Football League club.

"After training sessions, Ray Lewington and myself often scoured the local areas for private grounds that we could use but these invariably came at a cost and Fulham didn't have any money. In the end, we got permission for the players to train at a sports ground at Ewell in Surrey which belonged to the London Fire Brigade. We did a 'deal' by giving them free tickets for matches and, in return, they allowed us to use their facilities. At least, it gave the club a permanent training base and it made a big difference to our preparation for matches."

While things had partially settled down off the field, the Lewington-Burkett managerial partnership endured a real baptism of fire on the pitch in the early weeks of the 1986-87 season. In the second round of the League Cup, Fulham were drawn to play Liverpool over two legs.

"It was great a draw for the fans because the second leg was due to be played at Craven Cottage but Liverpool were in their prime," says Jack. "The previous season they had won the League and FA Cup double and they had all the 'big guns' out against us – Bruce Grobbelaar, Mark Lawrenson, Alan Hansen, Kenny Dalglish, Ian Rush, John Wark and Steve McMahon. It was a massacre. We were 4-0 down at half-time and they scored another six in the second-half. We lost 10-0 and it could have been worse but McMahon missed a penalty and Rush hit the post twice.

"Our goalkeeper, John Vaughan, who we had signed as a youngster from West Ham, played an absolute blinder. He was a good keeper and ended up being voted the supporters' Player-of-the-Season.

"We feared another slaughter in the second leg a couple of weeks later at Craven Cottage. Before the game, we realised that there was no soap in the dressing rooms because the club just couldn't afford it. Ray Lewington gave someone £20 out of his own pocket to go to the local supermarket just before the kick-off and buy some soap and shampoo!

"There was no hot water for the baths or showers after the game, so both sets of players had to make do with cold water. I don't know what the likes of Dalglish and Rush must have thought of the situation. They beat us 3-2 on the night but I don't suppose that they enjoyed their visit to Craven Cottage.

"Ray and I desperately needed to improve the side and we did some good business in the transfer market. We sold Dean Coney and Paul Parker to Queens Park Rangers for a combined fee of £500,000 which raised some much needed cash. Paul later proved his potential by moving to Manchester United and playing in the 1990 World Cup finals for England.

"Leroy Rosenior made the move in the opposite direction by joining us from Queens Park Rangers for £50,000. He did a great job for Fulham and was such a prolific goal scorer that West Ham's manager, John Lyall, signed him for a large £275,000 fee towards the end of the 1987-88 season. It was an offer that we couldn't refuse. Leroy's goals saved West Ham in their battle against relegation from the first division that season. I know John always rated Leroy very highly.

"We brought in the experienced Clive Walker from Chelsea and he gave us some flair down the left flank. We also signed Iain Dowie on loan from Luton Town for a few games but he only managed one goal for us and got sent off at Chester, so we released him after the loan period had expired. It was early in his career and he was a bit raw but it didn't surprise me that he went on to have a good career including two spells with West Ham and becoming a regular in the Northern Ireland side. He had an excellent attitude and was a good influence in the dressing room."

Despite the appalling lack of funds, Lewington and Burkett were gradually improving things and at the end of the 1988-89 season, they steered their team to the third division play-offs. In that era, the play-offs were not held at Wembley as they are today but, instead, were played over two legs. Their opponents were Bristol Rovers, who won the first leg by 1-0 at Eastville, and Fulham were confident of overcoming the one-goal deficit in the return at Craven Cottage four days later. Unfortunately, it turned out to be an unmitigated disaster. Rovers won 4-0 on the night and thus gained promotion to the second division by 5-0 on aggregate. Jack's curt comment says it all: "It was one of the worst nights of my career."

The hours that Burkett was working at Fulham were beginning to take their toll. "Sometimes, I was working a 17-hour day," he recalls. "I would leave my home near Southend at 6.30am for the two-hour drive around the M25 to Fulham's training ground in West London. I would take the morning session with the players and grab a sandwich for lunch. In those days, there were usually a few mid-week reserve matches played in and around the London area and I would go off to watch one of those games. It was a good way of taking a look at any players who may have been available on a free transfer and who could do a job for us.

"I would then drive up to the Midlands or north of England in the evening to watch a league match, involving one of our future opponents. I usually left about 10 minutes before the end of the game, so that I would be home by midnight. It got to the stage where, once again, I was seeing very little of my family."

Driving 30,000 miles a year around the motorways of Britain is stressful enough for any individual but when that is coupled with trying to keep a bankrupt organisation afloat, particularly in the high-profile world of professional football, it is inevitable that the stress levels are increased by several notches. On one such occasion in September 1989, Burkett endured another 17-hour day which culminated in an evening visit to the Midlands, this time to watch Walsall who were Fulham's opponents the following week.

"I left the ground just before 9.00pm," says Jack. "I was suffering from a lot of headaches at the time and I was driving down the M6, just south of Birmingham, when I started to feel disorientated. I thought I saw a lorry ahead of me when, in fact, there was no vehicle at all. Fortunately, I saw the signs for the Corley Services and pulled into the car park. I don't remember anything else until there was a knock on the window and a policeman was standing there.

"I was aware of the first cracks of daylight because dawn was just breaking. I had been in my car all night. I had completely blacked out when I pulled into the service area almost nine hours earlier.

"Ann wasn't aware that anything was wrong because she had gone to bed the

Fulham 1985-86: Jack is far right of picture, with manager Ray Harford in the centre of the front row. Two players with West Ham connections, Ray Houghton (far left in the front row) and Leroy Rosenior (two places along from Jack) are also in the line-up.

previous night and fallen asleep thinking that I would be home in the early hours. It was only when she woke up around 6.30am that she realised I was missing. There were obviously no mobile phones in those days, so she had no way of contacting me. She telephoned the police and, eventually, they were able to confirm what had happened."

Hospital tests showed that Burkett was suffering from severe stress and exhaustion and the doctor left him under no illusions about the possible consequences if he continued working at such a pressurised level. "He told me that I would be dead within a few months unless I eased back on my workload," recalls Jack. "It was a real wake-up call. I took a few days off and when I went back to Craven Cottage, I talked things over with Ray Lewington. It was eventually agreed that I would take up a role as Youth Development Officer, with former Fulham player Terry Bullivant taking over from me as Ray's assistant. In view of what had happened on the motorway, I wasn't entirely unhappy with the decision.

"My new job was invigorating because it consisted of a number of different roles. I would take the youngsters for training in the mornings and have responsibilities for looking after their welfare off the pitch as well. I would meet with their parents on a regular basis to give them updates on how the boys were progressing and any potential problems that lay ahead. I also had to help those who were released by the club if they weren't considered good enough to make the grade. It was a question of either finding them a lower league club or, alternatively, a job outside of football.

"I slotted into the job extremely easily and felt that I had a great deal of empathy with the youngsters, probably because of my own experiences in the game. I didn't entirely lose contact with first team matters because I would often go and watch games for Ray Lewington and report back on future opponents. It was a good period for me and it restored my enthusiasm for the game."

24

Premier League stars in the making

JACK may have been enjoying his new role at Fulham, but another job was on the horizon and it would give him the opportunity to become a mentor to a number of young players who would later become some of the biggest stars in the Premier League. It occurred in December 1990 when he received a phone call from a friend called Pat Lally, who worked at the offices of the Professional Footballers' Association in Manchester.

Jack takes up the story: "Pat said that he had heard I was doing a good job with the Fulham youngsters and asked if I fancied taking over the role of Regional Youth Co-ordinator at the PFA. Basically, it was ensuring that young players between the ages of 16 and 18-years-old were being suitably looked after by their clubs.

"Pat explained that there would be 32 clubs, mainly in the south of England including London and East Anglia, that would come under my jurisdiction if I accepted the role. They included teams throughout all divisions of the Football League such as West Ham, Arsenal, Spurs, Chelsea, Ipswich Town, Brentford, Leyton Orient, Swindon Town, Wycombe Wanderers, Reading, Portsmouth and Bournemouth. In essence, it mirrored the job I had been doing for Fulham but on a much larger scale. It also meant that I would be able to work from home apart from having to attend monthly meetings in Manchester.

"I talked it over with Ann and she was all for it. Likewise, I told Ray Lewington who said that it was too good an opportunity to turn down. I decided to take the job and while I had a lot of regrets about leaving Fulham, I went ahead and handed in my notice. I started my new job with the PFA the following month.

"Although I didn't realise it at the time, I would be employed in that role for the next 14 years and it gave me a huge amount of satisfaction."

Ann was delighted at Jack's new opportunity. She says: "It was a bit of a relief because of what had happened on the motorway when Jack blacked out. He always had a soft spot for Fulham but, at times, it had been incredibly stressful even though his role at the club had changed. I was glad that he was out of it.

"The new job with the PFA was great because it meant that he was working from home. He was very organised and set up an office in our spare room. Sometimes, Jack would stay overnight somewhere and be away for a couple of days during which time he would visit three or four clubs in that area and meet their young

players. For example, if he stayed on the south coast, then he would visit Southampton, Portsmouth, Brighton and Bournemouth. He would prepare his reports when he got home. The job was made for him because I believe that he developed a great affinity with the boys."

Jack was joining an organisation whose aim has always been to protect and improve the conditions and status of its members – the players themselves. This includes youngsters who are still trying to make their way in the game as well as the most seasoned internationals. The PFA helps with many different aspects – representing players at disciplinary hearings, or disputes with their clubs over fines or other disciplinary matters, negotiating contracts, enforcement of contracts, being trustees of contributory and non-contributory pension funds and providing insurance against death or disability.

It also provides for its members a full financial planning service which includes advice on mortgages, savings and other forms of investments. The PFA are represented on the ultimate appeals body for disciplinary measures and are directly involved with matters relating to on-field disciplinary offences.

When Jack began working for the PFA in the early 90s, young players still had to carry out various menial jobs at their respective clubs, like cleaning boots as well as the showers and toilets, in the same way that he had done at the beginning of his career. However, by this time, youngsters were also required to attend college on a one-day-a-week basis and the clubs were duty-bound to release them. It meant they could take an education course of their choice which would benefit them if they failed to make the grade as a professional footballer. It was all part of the PFA's ongoing education system.

Jack explains: "The youngsters were known as YTS boys and part of my role was to meet them on a regular basis. I had to ensure that they were attending college on their assigned days and not encountering any off-the-field problems. If there was a problem, then it was my job to rectify it – not only on behalf of the PFA, but also in conjunction with the club itself.

"I was responsible for around 600 YTS boys at the 32 clubs in my region, so it was inevitable that problems did arise from time to time. I usually saw each boy about once a month, so, again, it meant that I was spending many hours on the motorways. But I never felt the job contained the same pressures as when I was with Fulham.

"One of the most common misdemeanours I encountered as I did my 'rounds' of the various clubs was fare-dodging on buses or trains, particularly amongst some of the youngsters based in the London area. It is a relatively minor offence committed by numerous people in all walks of life but the PFA were able to offer legal representation to the young players if they had to go to court. It wasn't a question of trying to get them off the hook, but it was done to ensure that they didn't make the same mistakes again.

"Unfortunately, there were other more serious situations that occurred. There was one youngster who resented having to go to college and his attitude left much to be desired. His constant disruptive behaviour during his one-day-a-week attendance at

Jack doing good work for the PFA in 1997.

college caused a real problem. It got all the young players a bad name and the college threatened to completely ban anyone connected with football clubs from their premises. It was very unfair but it was a situation that had to be sorted out.

"In the end, I was able to smooth things over and the college rescinded their threat. Also, the behaviour and attitude of the lad himself improved considerably after that. He eventually made the grade in the professional game and became an international player. It gave me a lot of satisfaction to see him wearing the white shirt of England.

"On another occasion, a youngster turned up at his club's training ground with a brand new sports car. He had only just passed his driving test and, at that time, YTS boys certainly didn't earn the sort of money needed to buy a car like that.

"He was quizzed about where he had got it from and he explained that someone had given it to him as a present. The PFA were notified and we carried out some checks. It transpired that his girlfriend was working as a prostitute and she had got involved in the drugs scene. The young lad had been coerced into picking up packages on a regular basis from Felixstowe docks, which he had to deliver to a third party. He had been given the car as a 'reward.'

"Eventually, the police got involved but the lad maintained his innocence throughout, saying that he was unaware of what was contained in the packages. It wasn't difficult to hazard a guess at the contents but the police were unable to trace the third party or the packages and the case was eventually dropped. In the end, the youngster was released by his club because he wasn't considered good enough to make the grade. It was a great pity because he was one of the very few who chose to decline any help from the PFA in finding a job outside the game.

"Generally speaking, most YTS boys were decent and law-abiding. Admittedly, some clubs were better than others at keeping their young players in check and West Ham, in particular, came into that category. The exemplary conduct of their young

Catching up on his old club, Jack before giving an interview to Hammers News in 2003.

players was a great credit to Tony Carr, the club's Youth Academy Director. At the time, the likes of Rio Ferdinand, Michael Carrick, Glen Johnson, Joe Cole and Frank Lampard were youngsters starting out in the game and I was involved with all of them in my role with the PFA.

"Rio came from Peckham, a tough area in South London, and he was very street-wise for a young lad. Also, he was extremely bright academically and he chose a sports and leisure course during his one-day-a-week at Kingsway College in London.

"Michael Carrick was very unassuming and I always think that his manner reflects the way in which he plays the game – quietly, efficiently and without fuss. Michael took the same course as Rio and they both did well at college.

"Glen Johnson was a bit different because he really hated college – he just wanted to be on the training ground all the time – but he still attended because he knew it was part of the process. It epitomised the discipline that is ingrained in all the youngsters at West Ham.

"Joe Cole was another who didn't like attending college. He would be the first to admit that he wasn't very academically minded but it wasn't a problem because it was obvious that he was going to make a huge impact as a player. Even so, he still had to undertake educational training, just like all the others, but he didn't have a great deal of enthusiasm for any of the courses.

"I had a long chat with Joe and, apart from football, it was clear that golf was his greatest passion. I 'cheated' a bit and got him a placement on a green-keeping course. I worked on the basis that if it involved golf, then it would retain his interest and that is exactly what happened.

"Frank Lampard was brilliant at everything as a youngster, both on and off the field. He had attended a private school as a boy and he was very assured. He was a very bright and articulate lad and took a sports science course at college. Obviously, the fact that his father was one of West Ham's greatest players helped a lot because 'young' Frank was brought up in a football environment and he was totally dedicated to the game.

"Another young player who impressed me enormously with his attitude was John Terry. When I used to go to the Chelsea training ground and meet with their youngsters, it was always noticeable that John was a natural leader. If any of their boys moaned about going to college or started messing around, John would grab hold of them and say: 'Listen to what Jack is saying. You've got to do what he says. He's trying to help you.'

"In many ways, he almost did my job for me. John always led by example and that is reflected by the fact that he eventually became captain of England.

"In later years, Rio Ferdinand's brother, Anton, was another youngster with whom I had a lot of contact. It was difficult for him because he was always in the shadow of Rio, but he coped well with it. Anton wasn't as academic as his brother, but he had a fantastic singing voice and I arranged for him to attend a music college in London. Anton told me that, apart from wanting to make the grade as a professional footballer, his greatest ambition was to open up his own music studio.

"Norwich City was one of the clubs in my region and, in 1996, one of their coaching staff told me that an outstanding 16-year-old goalkeeper was about to join them. There was a strong feeling at Carrow Road that the boy was so special that he would play for England one day. His name was Rob Green and I got to know him well.

"Rob was incredibly dedicated and he was always asking questions about the pit-falls of being a professional footballer. Quite often, he would write down my answers for future reference. It seemed as though he was going to leave nothing to chance. He attended college and was another who chose the sports and leisure course.

"Once again, a major component of my job was helping youngsters who had been released by their clubs because they were considered not good enough to make the grade. A high percentage of young players come into that category and, probably, only about one in a hundred make the big-time. It can be a devastating experience and the PFA always try to help them take up new careers, which can be extremely wide and varied.

"As an example, one young lad went on to carve out a highly successful career for himself in London's financial sector. Another joined the Royal Marines, while another became a chef at a top restaurant in London – all thanks to the insight and endeavours of the PFA.

"I enjoyed the role immensely and developed a good working relationship with all the clubs in my area. It was stimulating, invigorating and satisfying and while I know it's a cliché, it gave me the opportunity to put something back into the game. The problem was that the focus of the job began to change towards the end of the 90s. There were a number of contributing factors.

"Firstly, the YTS scheme had always been part government-funded and New Labour had come to power with a landslide election victory in 1997. Their newly-implemented health and safety measures had started to take effect in all walks of life and football did not escape unscathed. The government were uncomfortable with YTS boys at clubs having to do menial tasks like cleaning boots, cleaning out the showers and toilets and all the other mundane jobs that had been part of the process for decades.

"Secondly, a tragic accident occurred around this time which was probably the catalyst for many of the changes that were subsequently implemented. It happened at a lower league club who did not come under my jurisdiction, since they were in another area of the country. It transpired that the club's first team players had a training session on the pitch at their home ground and one of the players had inadvertently kicked a football onto the roof of their main stand. It became lodged in guttering and, with some justification, the players and training staff decided to leave it there.

"Unfortunately, early the following morning, the YTS boys arrived at the ground to get everything laid out for the day's training session and one of the lads decided that he would go and retrieve the ball. He hadn't been instructed to do so by anyone at the club but, nevertheless, he felt that it was part of his job. He climbed on the roof but some of the guttering gave way and he plunged to his death.

"To make matters worse, three other YTS boys witnessed the tragedy and they were badly traumatised.

"Soon afterwards, the role of YTS boys at football clubs was scrapped and the 'Academy' system was introduced. It meant that young players no longer had to carry out the various menial tasks at their respective clubs. All that they were required to do was concentrate on their football and look after their own environment.

"Despite the tragedy that occurred, I think that it was a big mistake and it was noticeable that a number of Premier League stars, like Frank Lampard and Ryan Giggs, were recently critical of the Academy system. They recalled their days when they had to clean the boots of first-team players and expressed the view that it was all part of their football education. Once that has gone, then a young player can lose his edge.

"I also believe that statistics tend to support this theory. At the start of the 2008-09 season, only eight English players had progressed through the ranks of the Big Four – Manchester United, Chelsea, Arsenal and Liverpool – into their first teams. More interestingly, only two of them had made their debuts after 1999, which was the year that the present Academy system was introduced.

"Carrying out their 'duties' used to bring young players down to earth but now that

In September 2003 Jack and several former team-mates and other ex-Hammers attended a mini reunion when Brian Dear held his 60th birthday bash at Southend Golf Club. Jack is pictured (above) with his old mate Ron Boyce and (below) with Ken Tucker.

has been taken completely away.

"In time, I began to notice a distinct difference in the attitude of many of the young Academy players. Some were becoming lazy and big-headed and gave the impression that they had made it in the game when, in fact, they were only just starting out. West Ham were the exception to the rule.

"It is amazing to think that under the old YTS scheme, they produced the likes of Rio Ferdinand, Frank Lampard, Michael Carrick, Joe Cole and Glen Johnson. Yet, since the introduction of the Academy set-up, they have still managed to produce players of the calibre of Anton Ferdinand, Mark Noble, Kyel Reid, James Tomkins, Jack Collison, Freddie Sears, Junior Stanislas, Josh Payne and Zavon Hines.

"Their conveyor belt for producing young players, irrespective of the system and constraints in place, is quite phenomenal, but West Ham have always made sure that their youngsters keep their feet on the ground. In many ways, that is the secret of their success.

"As a result of the health and safety measures plus the new Academy system, my job was changing because the amount of paperwork had increased dramatically. I had always been very thorough in my record-keeping in terms of my meetings with the young players and it was something that I had always prided myself on but completing forms and formal paperwork was beginning to constitute the biggest part of the job.

"I carried on working until early 2005 but I was becoming seriously disillusioned. I wanted to be visiting the training grounds around the country meeting the youngsters, talking to them and helping them – not moving pieces of paper around the desk in my office at home."

At the time, Jack had been working for the PFA for 14 years which was the longest period he had spent in any one job throughout his entire working life. However, he was also 62-years-old and like most people of a similar age, he was becoming a trifle weary after a lifetime of working hard to make a good living for himself and his family. Not surprisingly, the thought of retirement was becoming a recurring theme in his mind.

As things turned out and within a few short months, he did indeed take the decision to retire. But in many ways, the decision was forced upon him by a devastating turn of events.

25

A Defining moment

THE world of professional football is often perceived as being glamorous and exciting. In fact, it can be a harsh and dreadfully cruel profession and often reflects the vagaries of life itself. There are good times and bad. Occasionally, some of those experiences in life are defining moments because it becomes instantly apparent that things will never be the same again – for better or worse.

It may be one of those intensely intimate moments which bring unbridled happiness and joy. Perhaps it is when you meet the person with whom you will happily spend the rest of your life. It may be the moment when a son or daughter is born or, in later years, when you cradle a grandchild in your arms for the first time.

Such moments should be cherished in the mind forever. They are life-changing, albeit for the very best reasons.

Conversely, that life-changing moment may bring great sadness when a parent or loved one passes away. It is inevitable that the searing pain of bereavement will touch us all at some point in our lives and it leaves a gaping wound that can never be fully healed.

In his own life-time, Jack Burkett has experienced all of those moments, together with the emotions that they generate, both good and bad. However, he was about to encounter a completely new emotion when he was given some news that would have a devastating impact upon his life and change it forever.

He says: "It was the moment when I was told by a specialist in Essex that I had a virulent form of skin cancer – a full malignant melanoma. I accepted then, just as I do now, that millions of people around the world have been given similar news. They have all gone on to fight their own brave and individual battles against the frightening disease but now, it was happening to me and it was the moment when time, literally, stood still.

"We all think that we are immortal and, until then, I was no exception. Suddenly, my own perceived immortality had been taken away from me. It was when I realised that I was going to have to fight for every minute of every single day. Life would never be the same again. I thought about my wonderful family – my wife Ann, my children Darrell, Dean and Elizabeth and, also, my lovely grandchildren. It was a defining moment in my life."

It all began in mid-March, 2005 and it was like any other Saturday in the Burkett household. Jack and Ann were both still working full-time, Monday to Friday – Jack with the PFA and Ann with a locally based printing company. Now it was the weekend and jobs around the house had to be done, including a trip to the supermarket plus a visit from members of their family.

It was another opportunity to see some of their adored grandchildren. It was a scene being re-enacted in millions of homes throughout Britain, except that this would prove to be a weekend with a difference.

During the morning, Jack felt an irritation on his back. It became worse as the day progressed and continued to be a problem on the Sunday. He says: "I asked Ann to look at it and she said that it resembled an insect bite. On the Monday when I went to work, it was beginning to get very sore and I made an appointment to see my GP that evening.

"He said that there was nothing to worry about – but I wasn't convinced. It was purely instinct and because I was in a private health scheme, I asked to be referred to a consultant for a second opinion. If I had not made the decision to ignore the diagnosis of my GP, I would not be alive today.

"Within 48 hours, I had an appointment at the hospital and Ann went with me. The consultant examined me and did a biopsy. She told us to go and have a cup of tea in the cafeteria and come back in half-an-hour, by which time she would have the results. When we returned, she told me that I had skin cancer and that she wanted me to go into hospital for an operation. She said that it was matter of urgency and stressed the seriousness of the situation.

"I was shocked and for a moment, I thought that I was going to pass out. It didn't seem possible because five days earlier, I didn't have a care in the world and felt 100 per cent fit and well. Suddenly, I was now faced with a life-threatening illness.

"The consultant explained that the tests showed there were five more lesions on my body as well as the one on my back. Five of them – including the one that had been irritating – were malignant while the sixth was benign, but they all needed to be surgically removed. The big danger was that if the skin cancer entered the glands, it could spread to other parts of the body and prove fatal.

"It transpired that I also needed chemotherapy treatment. She stressed that the cancer would be with me for the rest of my life. It was not possible to cure it.

"We went home that night and didn't sleep at all. I felt very frightened and we talked things over incessantly. Ann was very strong and kept saying that we would get through it together. It was the longest night of my life. The following day, I contacted the hospital and they arranged for my operation to be carried out six days later."

Jack had been desperately unlucky, although it is a fact that years spent in the sun take their toll on the skin in the form of moles, age spots and occasionally, skin cancer such as melanomas. Anybody can get a melanoma but people are more at risk if they have fair skin, red-hair, lots of freckles and burn easily, or if they are sun-worshippers.

Jack didn't have red-hair or freckles but he had fair skin and had spent years

Ann and Jack at home in Leigh-on-sea, Essex in the summer of 2006.

training bare-chested with West Ham during pre-season at Chadwell Heath, plus summer tours to America and Africa as well as working in the Middle-East – some of the hottest places in the world.

Scientists have pinpointed a gene that triggers the most deadly form of skin cancer. It is estimated that 70 per cent of cases of malignant melanomas could be sparked by a genetic mutation caused by ageing and over-exposure to the sun. It can be a silent killer, unless it is caught early enough and, fortunately, that was the situation so far as Jack was concerned.

The operation was carried out in early April, 2005 but the nightmare was only just beginning. Jack explains: "After I returned home, my chemotherapy treatment consisted of applying cream to my face, arms and body. The effect of the cream made me feel generally unwell. Within a couple of days, all the skin began to peel away. It looked as if I had been in a fire. I also lost some of my hair, which is another side-effect of chemotherapy.

"I tried to be positive during this period but I got to know a middle-aged couple at the hospital whose 22-year-old daughter had just died from the same form of skin cancer as me. She was a very beautiful girl who modelled swim-wear. Obviously, she was required to look good in the photographs and it was necessary for her to have a sun-tan all the year round. If she wasn't sunbathing on an exotic beach, then she would be under a sun-lamp. Unfortunately, her skin cancer spread to the glands and into her lungs. She died shortly afterwards. It shook me rigid."

Ann's recollections about those desperately worrying days are remarkably clear and concise. As a devout Roman Catholic, she had uttered many fervent prayers over the years but there were never prayers like the ones she offered to God in the spring of 2005.

She recalls: "Jack says that I was strong and, outwardly, I suppose I was. I certainly tried to give that impression to Jack and all the family. Inwardly, it was a different matter – but my faith was crucial to me. I prayed incessantly and it helped me more than I can ever explain. It was as simple as that."

As the days turned into weeks and the weeks turned into months, Jack began to come to terms with his diagnosis. He was required to return to the hospital every three months, so that further examinations could be carried out – each time searching for new lesions that developed on his skin. As the lesions appeared, so they were surgically removed, irrespective of whether they were malignant or benign and further chemotherapy treatment ensued.

Jack says: "At the time of the original diagnosis and treatment, I took three weeks off work before returning to my job with the PFA. But my heart wasn't in it any more. I had become disillusioned with the job before discovering that I had cancer, so in a sense, my decision to retire was made easier.

"The PFA were very understanding and they gave me a good send-off when I officially retired later that summer. I had enjoyed my time working with them but now there were more important things to consider. I wanted to give myself every opportunity to fight the cancer because it had completely changed my outlook on life.

"Since my diagnosis, I have to put a sun-cream factor 50 on my face whenever I go outside, even if it is a cloudy day. The rays from the sun can penetrate the clouds and cloudy days can be as lethal as when the sun is shining.

"I always have to wear a hat with a wide brim and I wear specially made clothing which deflects the sun's rays. I can never again expose my face, body, arms or legs to the sun – but it is a small price to pay.

"It is strange because throughout my life, I have always regarded the sun as a good friend – my best mate – but now it is my greatest enemy. I constantly have to be wary of it and never drop my guard.

"During the period that this book was being written, I 'celebrated' four years of life since the day when the specialist first gave me that dreadful news. I continue to visit the hospital every three months and will do so for the rest of my life. I will deal with the cancer as and when it reappears including the chemotherapy treatment. I will fight the disease to the bitter end.

"My ambition is to live until I am 90-years-old. I may not make it but I will have a damn good try because I owe it to my wonderful family."

26

West Ham re-United

ON May 20, 2005, a gala dinner was held at the imposing Britannia International Hotel in London's Docklands. It had been arranged by *EX*, the West Ham retro magazine, to commemorate the 40th anniversary of the club's cup-winning achievements in the mid-60s.

The quarterly produced *EX* is the only retro magazine dedicated to one English football club and the celebratory dinner was the brainchild of the magazine's publisher/editor Tony McDonald. The hosts for the evening were Martin Peters and the more recent Hammers' legend, Tony Cottee.

Every surviving member of both the 1964 FA Cup and 1965 European Cup Winners' Cup teams, together with their wives and partners, had been invited to attend the event. The players travelled from far and wide – John Sissons flew from his home in Cape Town, South Africa, while Jim Standen jetted in from California, USA and Joe Kirkup from the South of France.

Some 200 supporters were also in attendance and it was impossible not to be moved by the sheer joy that the evening generated for the former Hammers' heroes and their families. For one memorable night, 40 years after what was for most of them the finest achievement of their careers, they were once again feted stars, this time on the grandest of scales. The fans were honoured to be in the presence of their heroes but, typically, such was the genuine warmth, humility and gratitude of these former players that it was they who admitted to feeling the most honoured of all.

Jack describes it as being one of the greatest nights of his life. He recalls: "The mere fact that Ann and I had been invited was a huge thrill and the invitation to attend could not have come at a better time. It was only a couple of months after I had been diagnosed with cancer and, because of the on-going treatment, I was feeling very unwell.

"But I will never forget that night as long as I live. When Ann and I walked into the hotel, it was like putting the clock back 40 years seeing all my former team-mates again. It was quite emotional.

"In the intervening years, three of the lads – Bobby Moore, Alan Sealey and Budgie Byrne – had tragically passed away. Bobby died from bowel cancer in 1993 while Alan died following a liver complaint in 1996. Budgie suffered a heart attack and died in South Africa in 1999.

They came from far and wide ... together again at the 2005 Cup winners' reunion dinner. Back row, left to right: Ken Brown, Joe Kirkup, Alan Dickie, Jim Standen, John Bond, Jack Burkett, Martin Peters. Front: Eddie Bovington, Peter Brabrook, Brian Dear, Ron Boyce, John Sissons.

"Bobby and Alan had both remarried since their days at West Ham and it was great to meet Alan's widow, Barbara, and his son, Anthony. Unfortunately, neither Stephanie Moore nor Budgie's wife, Margaret, were able to make it. Also, we were all very upset because Ron Greenwood was unable to attend the dinner. He was too unwell to make the journey from his Brighton home. Sadly, Ron passed away in February 2006.

"The only surviving member of the team who was absent was Geoff Hurst, who had a business commitment. It was good that reserve goalkeeper Alan Dickie had been invited, as he had played in one of the early rounds of the European Cup Winners' Cup.

"If I am honest, I think we were all a bit taken aback by the reception that we received from the fans. It was very moving and fantastic that they remembered us with such affection."

At times during that memorable evening, Jack and his former team-mates appeared to be overwhelmed by the adulation that was rightly accorded to them. It was a just reward for 'Yesterdays' Heroes' because, for Hammers' fans of a certain age, the mid-60s was the most magical time of their football-supporting lives. The 15 West Ham players who took part in those two unforgettable Wembley finals against Preston North End and TSV Munich 1860 – together with manager Ron Greenwood – took the fans to levels of joy and jubilation that they had never experienced before or since.

The following year, in 1966, the magnificent efforts of Moore, Hurst and Peters meant that West Ham fans could also proudly boast that it was their team who had won the World Cup. In three consecutive years, three of football's greatest trophies had all been won at Wembley – the most famous stadium in the world. In terms of

Jack, John Bond and Martin Peters at the emotional 2005 Docklands gala dinner.

bragging rights, life did not get much better than that for the Upton Park faithful.

These days, when older West Ham fans close their eyes and cast their minds back through the mists of time, it is still possible to see those 15 heroes in action . . . the fair-haired Jack Burkett making a classic sliding tackle deep inside his own half . . . the ice-cool John Bond curling a pass down the right-flank with that cultured right-foot . . . Eddie Bovington making a thunderous tackle in midfield . . . the perpetual motion of Ron Boyce and his historic leap into the air as he scored the FA Cup-winning goal against Preston . . . Budgie Byrne controlling the ball on his chest and volleying it to a winger in one sublime movement . . . Ken Brown, always the last man out of the tunnel, sprinting across the Upton Park pitch to the strains of the inspiring *Post Horn Gallop* . . . the elusive Peter Brabrook turning an opposing full-back inside out with his trickery on the right-wing . . . the bustling Brian Dear shrugging off opponents with immense strength and power . . . the athletic Joe Kirkup making an overlap down the right flank . . . Martin Peters, all elegance and grace, moving stealthily into position . . . Geoff Hurst, cheeks characteristically puffed out, firing home another venomous shot into the opposition's net . . . Alan Sealey turning a somersault in celebration as his shot hit the back of the Munich net . . . .the lightning-quick John Sissons with his magical left-foot . . . .Jim Standen saving a shot with consummate ease just as if he were taking a catch in the slips for Worcestershire CCC . . . the majestic Bobby Moore chesting the ball down in his own penalty-area as the battle raged around him and stroking it away to a colleague as if it were nothing more than a training session.

They are just some of the memories that are forever etched in the minds of Hammers' loyal fans of a certain age.

These days, one of life's great pleasures is being in the company of the former West Ham players from that golden period. It is like returning to a bygone age –

when good, old fashioned virtues were scrupulously observed and money had not become the root of all football evil. Those players were just delighted to be paid for what they loved doing most of all. It was long before the game was tainted by greed and arrogance and the players of that era – even the greatest of them all – were always prepared to mix with the supporters who paid their wages.

These days, the mercenaries who adorn the Premier League are frequently seen kissing the badges on their shirts. It is supposedly an act of devotion to their clubs as they seek to ingratiate themselves with the fans. The 15 heroes who brought glory to West Ham in the mid-60s did not need to involve themselves in such pretentious nonsense. Most of them had come through the ranks together and they formed part of the very fabric of the club. The fans could easily identify with them and, unlike modern times, the players of yesteryear did not think that they were more important than the people who paid good money to watch them in action. In essence, it was a mutual appreciation society.

It is somewhat appropriate to conclude this book by repeating *verbatim* the words of Jack Burkett – an exceptionally modest man – which were contained in the introduction. It epitomises everything about the exemplary attitude that existed amongst the players from the mid-60s. Jack says: "It was a privilege to wear the claret and blue of West Ham. I loved the club and I loved the fans. During those years, I was proud to play for the most successful team in its history. Whatever happens in the future, it is something that nobody can ever take away from me."

The Burkett family in 2009. Back row, left to right: Son Dean, son Darrell, son-in-law Simon Ramsell, Jack. Middle row: daughter-in-law Caroline, daughter-in-law Jacqueline (with Tobias on her lap), daughter Elizabeth (holding Isla), Ann. Front: Jacob, Isabella, Siena, Owen.

Appendix 1
Statistics of the Hammers' heroes

THE following pages contain the statistics relating to the careers of the 15 West Ham players who participated in the 1964 FA Cup and 1965 European Cup Winners' Cup finals. All appearances relate to Football League matches only, unless otherwise stated.

James Alfred Standen (goalkeeper)
Born Edmonton, London – May 30, 1935
Appearances:
Arsenal – 35
Luton Town – 36
WHU – 179 + 57 cup appearances
Millwall – 8
Portsmouth – 13
Honours: FA Cup winner 1964, Charity Shield 1964, ECWC 1965, Football League Cup runner-up 1966 (+ County Cricket Championship medal with Worcestershire 1964)

John Bond (right-back)
Born Colchester, Essex – December 17, 1932
Appearances:
WHU – 381 (33 goals) + 47 cup appearances (2 goals)
Torquay United – 130 (12 goals)
Honours: Second Division Championship 1958, FA Cup winner 1964, Charity Shield 1964.

Joseph Robert Kirkup (right-back)
Born Hexham, Northumberland – December 17, 1939
Appearances:
WHU – 165 (6 goals) + 22 cup appearances
Chelsea – 53 (2 goals)
Southampton – 169 (3 goals)
Honours: ECWC 1965; (With Chelsea) FA Cup runner-up 1967 (unused substitute); England Youth international, 3 England Under-23 caps.

Jack William Burkett (left-back)
Born Bow, East London – August 21, 1942
Appearances:
WHU – 142 (4 goals) + 39 cup appearances
Charlton Athletic – 8
Honours: FA Cup winner 1964, Charity Shield 1964, ECWC 1965.

Edward Ernest Perrian Bovington (right-half)
Born Edmonton, London - April 23, 1941
Appearances:
WHU - 138 (1 Goal) + 45 cup appearances (1 goal)
Honours: FA Cup winner 1964, Charity Shield 1964, Football League Cup runner-up 1966.

Martin Stanford Peters (right-half) – MBE
Born Plaistow, London – November 8, 1943
Appearances:
WHU – 302 (81 goals) + 62 cup appearances (19 goals)
Tottenham Hotspur – 189 (46 goals)
Norwich City – 207 (44 goals)
Sheffield United – 24 (4 goals)
Honours: ECWC 1965, Football League Cup runner-up 1966, Hammer of the Year 1965; (With Spurs) Football League Cup winner 1970 and 1973, UEFA Cup winner 1972, UEFA Cup runner-up 1974; England Schools and England Youth international, 5 England Under-23 caps, 67 full England caps (20 goals), World Cup winner 1966.

Kenneth Brown (centre-half)
Born Forest Gate, London – February 16, 1934
Appearances:
WHU – 386 (4 goals) + 69 cup appearances
Torquay United – 42 (1 goal)
Honours: Second Division Championship 1958, FA Cup winner 1964, Charity Shield 1964, ECWC 1965, Football League Cup runner-up 1966, Hammer of the Year 1959; One full England cap.

WEST HAM IN THE SIXTIES

Robert Frederick Chelsea Moore (left-half) – OBE
Born Barking, London – April 12, 1941
Appearances:
WHU – 544 (24 goals) + 98 cup appearances
(3 goals)
Fulham – 124 (1 goal)
Honours: FA Cup winner 1964, Charity Shield
1964, ECWC 1965, Football
League Cup runner-up 1966, Hammer of the
Year 1961, 1963, 1968, 1970,
Footballer of the Year 1964; (With Fulham)
FA Cup runner-up 1975;
England Youth international, 8 England Under-23
caps, 108 full England caps
(2 goals), World Cup winner 1966,
Player of the World Cup 1966.

Peter Brabrook (outside-right)
Born Greenwich, London – November 8, 1937
Appearances:
Chelsea – 251 (47 goals)
WHU – 167 (33 goals) + 47 cup appearances
(10 goals)
Orient – 72 (6 goals)
Honours: FA Cup winner 1964, Charity Shield
1964, Football League Cup runner-up 1966;
(With Orient) Third Division
Championship 1970; England
Youth international, 9 England Under-23 caps,
3 full England caps.

Alan William Sealey (outside-right)
Born Canning Town, London – April 22, 1942
Appearances:
Leyton Orient – 4 (1 goal)
WHU 107 (22 goals) + 21 cup appearances
(4 goals)
Plymouth Argyle – 4
Honours: ECWC 1965.

Ronald William Boyce (inside-right)
Born East Ham, London – January 6, 1943
Appearances:
WHU – 282 (21 goals) + 57 cup appearances
(8 goals)
Honours: FA Cup winner 1964, Charity Shield
1964, ECWC 1965, Football
League Cup runner-up 1966; England Schools
and England Youth international.

John Joseph Byrne (centre-forward)
Born West Horsley, Surrey – May 13, 1939
Appearances:
Crystal Palace – 203 (85 goals)
WHU – 156 (79 goals) + 34 cup appearances
(28 goals)
Crystal Palace – 36 (5 goals)
Fulham – 19 (2 goals)
Honours: FA Cup winner 1964, Charity Shield
1964, Football League Cup runner-up 1966,
Hammer of the Year 1964; England Youth
international, 7 England Under- 23 caps,
11 full England caps (8 goals)

Sir Geoffrey Charles Hurst (inside-left) – MBE
Born Ashton-under-Lyne, Lancashire –
December 8, 1941
Appearances:
WHU – 411 (180 goals) + 91 cup appearances
(68 goals)
Stoke City – 108 (30 goals)
West Bromwich Albion – 10 (2 goals)
Honours: FA Cup winner 1964, Charity Shield
1964, ECWC 1965, Football
League Cup runner-up 1966, Hammer of the
Year 1966, 1967, 1969; England
Youth international, 4 England Under-23 caps,
49 full England caps (24 goals),
World Cup winner 1966.

Brian Charles Dear (inside-left)
Born West Ham, London – September 18, 1943
Appearances:
WHU (first spell) – 65 (33 goals) + 15 cup
appearances (6 goals)
Brighton & Hove Albion Albion - 7 (5 goals)
Fulham – 13 (7 goals)
Millwall – 6
WHU (second spell) – 4 + 1 cup appearance
Honours: ECWC 1965; England Schools
international.

John Leslie Sissons (outside-left)
Born Hayes, Middlesex – September 30, 1945
Appearances:
WHU – 213 (37 goals) + 52 cup appearances
(16 goals)
Sheffield Wednesday – 115 (14 goals)
Norwich City – 17 (2 goals)
Chelsea – 11
Honours: FA Cup winner 1964, Charity Shield
1964, ECWC 1965, Football League Cup runner-up
1966; England Schools and England Youth
international, 10 England Under-23 caps.

Back at the scene of their most glorious footballing triumphs . . . Peter Brabrook, Sir Geoff Hurst, Ken Brown, John Bond and Jack Burkett were among the VIP guests at Wembley Stadium in 2007 to witness the unveiling of the Bobby Moore Statue.

Appendix 2
West Ham in the 60s – season-by-season

THE following pages detail West Ham United's First Division league and cup record throughout the 60s. Home games are shown in bold type.

Football League Division One 1959-60

Date	Opps	Res	Scorers	Att
Aug-22	**(h) Leicester City**	**W 3-0**	**Smith, Keeble, Grice**	**28,000**
Aug-25	(a) Preston North End	D 1-1	Musgrove	29,433
Aug-29	(a) Burnley	W 3-1	Woosnam, Smillie, Grice	26,783
Aug-31	**(h) Preston North End**	**W 2-1**	**Smillie, Keeble**	**32,000**
Sep-05	**(h) Leeds United**	**L 1-2**	**Keeble**	**28,000**
Sep-09	(a) Tottenham Hotspur	D 2-2	Keeble, Musgrove	58,909
Sep-12	(a) Bolton Wanderers	L 1-5	Keeble	24,191
Sep-14	**(h) Tottenham Hotspur**	**L 1-2**	**Bond**	**37,500**
Sep-19	(a) Chelsea	W 4-2	Dick 2, Musgrove, Woosnam	54,349
Sep-26	**(h) West Bromwich Albion**	**W 4-1**	**Musgrove 2, Woosnam, Grice**	**30,570**
Oct-03	(a) Newcastle United	D 0-0		41,890
Oct-10	**(h) Luton Town**	**W 3-1**	**Woodley 2, Keeble**	**23,500**
Oct-17	(a) Everton	W 1-0	Musgrove	30, 563
Oct-24	**(h) Blackpool**	**W 1-0**	**Musgrove**	**32,500**
Oct-31	(a) Fulham	L 0-1		44, 695
Nov-07	**(h) Manchester City**	**W 4-1**	**Cantwell, Obeney, Musgrove, OG**	**25,500**
Nov-14	(a) Arsenal	W 3-1	Dick, Obeney, Musgrove	49,760
Nov-21	**(h) Wolverhampton W.**	**W 3-2**	**Dick 3**	**38,000**
Nov-28	(a) Sheffield Wednesday	L 0-7		38,367
Dec-05	**(h) Nottingham Forest**	**W 4-1**	**Woosnam 2, Obeney 2**	**26,000**
Dec-12	(a) Blackburn Rovers	L 2-6	Woosnam, Dick	22,400
Dec-19	(a) Leicester City	L 1-2	Obeney	20,000
Dec-26	(a) Birmingham City	L 0-2		29,745
Dec-28	**(h) Birmingham City**	**W 3-1**	**Musgrove 2, Brett**	**26,000**
Jan-02	**(h) Burnley**	**L 2-5**	**Woosnam, Cantwell**	**26,000**
Jan-16	(a) Leeds United	L 0-3		15,000
Jan-23	**(h) Bolton Wanderers**	**L 1-2**	**Dick**	**21,600**
Feb-06	**(h) Chelsea**	**W 4-2**	**Bond 3, Dick**	**29,500**
Feb-20	**(h) Newcastle United**	**L 3-5**	**Woosnam 2, Dick**	**25,000**
Feb-27	(a) Nottingham Forest	L 1-3	Musgrove	26,317
Mar-05	**(h) Everton**	**D 2-2**	**Bond, Dick**	**25,000**
Mar-09	(a) West Bromwich Albion	L 2-3	Grice, Bond	11,980
Mar-12	(a) Blackpool	L 2-3	Bond, Brett	14,515
Mar-19	**(h) Blackburn Rovers**	**W 2-1**	**Woosnam, Musgrove**	**26,000**
Mar-30	(a) Manchester City	L 1-3	Musgrove	29,572
Apr-02	**(h) Arsenal**	**D 0-0**		**29,000**
Apr-11	(a) Wolverhampton W.	L 0-5		48,086
Apr-15	**(h) Manchester United**	**W 2-1**	**Musgrove, Grice**	**35,000**
Apr-16	**(h) Fulham**	**L 1-2**	**Smillie, Keeble**	**24,085**
Apr-18	(a) Manchester United	L 3-5	Dunmore, Cantwell, Scott	34,676
Apr-23	(a) Luton Town	L 1-3	Dunmore	11,404
Apr-30	**(h) Sheffield Wednesday**	**D 1-1**	**Woosnam**	**22,000**

P	W	D	L	F	A	W	D	L	F	A	Pts	Pos
42	12	3	6	47	33	4	3	14	28	58	38	14th

F A Cup

Date	Opps	Res	Scorers	Att
Jan-09 3r	**(h) Huddersfield Town**	**D 1-1**	**Dick**	**40,526**
Jan-13 3rr	(h) Huddersfield Town	L 1-5	Musgrove	22,605

Football League Division One 1960-61

Date	Opps	Res	Scorers	Att
Aug-20	(a) Wolverhampton Wanderers	L 2-4	Dick, Woosnam	37,266
Aug-22	**(h) Aston Villa**	**W 5-2**	**Woosnam, Bond, Dick, Dunmore, Musgrove**	**28,959**
Aug-27	**(h) Bolton Wanderers**	**W 2-1**	**Musgrove, Dick**	**24, 283**
Aug-29	(a) Aston Villa	L 1-2	Dunmore	30,000
Sep-03	(a) Sheffield Wednesday	L 0-1		28,359
Sep-05	**(h) Manchester United**	**W 2-1**	**Brett, Musgrove**	**30,000**
Sep-10	(a) Chelsea	L 2-3	Dunmore, Grice	37, 873
Sep-14	(a) Manchester United	L 1-6	Brett	33, 695
Sep-17	**(h) Blackpool**	**D 3-3**	**Bond, Musgrove, Woodley**	**23,521**
Sep-24	(a) Everton	L 1-4	Beesley	46,291
Oct-01	**(h) Blackburn Rovers**	**W 3-2**	**Dick 2, Woosnam**	**17,519**
Oct-08	**(h) Birmingham City**	**W 4-3**	**Grice 2, Musgrove, Dunmore**	**16,000**
Oct-15	(a) West Bromwich Albion	L 0-1		21,300
Oct-22	**(h) Preston North End**	**W 5-2**	**Musgrove 3, Bond, Dick**	**16,287**
Oct-29	(a) Fulham	D 1-1	Dunmore	20,809
Nov-05	**(h) Arsenal**	**W 6-0**	**Dunmore 3, Dick, Woosnam, Malcolm**	**29,375**
Nov-12	(a) Manchester City	W 2-1	Dunmore, Grice	33,721
Nov-19	**(h) Nottingham Forest**	**L 2-4**	**Dunmore, OG**	**21,047**
Dec-03	**(h) Cardiff City**	**W 2-0**	**Musgrove, Dunmore**	**14,000**
Dec-10	(a) Newcastle United	D 5-5	Musgrove, Dick, Bond, Dunmore, OG	20,100
Dec-17	**(h) Wolverhampton Wanderers**	**W 5-0**	**Dunmore 2, Musgrove, Dick, Moore**	**22,336**
Dec-24	(a) Tottenham Hotspur	L 0-2		54,930
Dec-26	**(h) Tottenham Hotspur**	**L 0-3**		**34,481**
Dec-31	(a) Bolton Wanderers	L 1-3	Musgrove	15,931
Jan-14	**(h) Sheffield Wednesday**	**D 1-1**	**Dick**	**20,620**
Jan-21	**(h) Chelsea**	**W 3-1**	**Obeney, Woosnam, Dick**	**21,829**
Feb-04	(a) Blackpool	L 0-3		9,947
Feb-11	**(h) Everton**	**W 4-0**	**Obeney 2, Dick, Musgrove**	**22,322**
Feb-25	(a) Birmingham City	L 2-4	Musgrove, Scott	16,850
Mar-04	**(h) West Bromwich Albion**	**L 1-2**	**Dick**	**21,607**
Mar-11	(a) Preston North End	L 0-4		12,084
Mar-18	**(h) Fulham**	**L 1-2**	**Obeney**	**18,742**
Mar-20	(a) Blackburn Rovers	L 1-4	OG	14,000
Mar-25	(a) Arsenal	D 0-0		27,663
Mar-31	**(h) Leicester City**	**W 1-0**	**Dick**	**22,010**
Apr-01	**(h) Newcastle United**	**D 1-1**	**Musgrove**	**17,103**
Apr-03	(a) Leicester City	L 1-5	Kirkup	23,776
Apr-08	(a) Nottingham Forest	D 1-1	Dick	26,081
Apr-15	**(h) Manchester City**	**D 1-1**	**Sealey**	**17,982**
Apr-18	(a) Burnley	D 2-2	Musgrove 2	12,409
Apr-22	(a) Cardiff City	D 1-1	Dick	10,000
Apr-29	**(h) Burnley**	**L 1-2**	**Woosnam**	**18,761**

P	W	D	L	F	A	W	D	L	F	A	Pts	Pos
42	12	4	5	53	31	1	6	14	24	57	36	16th

F A Cup

Date	Opps	Res	Scorers	Att
Jan-07 3r	**(h) Stoke City**	**D 2-2**	**Dunmore, Dick**	**21,545**
Jan-11 3rr	(a) Stoke City	L 0-1		28,914

League Cup

Date	Opps	Res	Scorers	Att
Sep-26 2r	**(h) Charlton Athletic**	**W 3-1**	**Dick, Musgrove, Moore**	**12,000**
Oct-24 3r	(a) Darlington	L 2-3	Dunmore, Dick	16,911

Football League Division One 1961-62

Date	Opps	Res	Scorers	Att
Aug-19	(h) Manchester United	D 1-1	Dick	32,628
Aug-23	(a) Tottenham Hotspur	D 2-2	Woosnam, Musgrove	50,214
Aug-26	(a) Wolverhampton Wanderers	L 2-3	Musgrove, Sealey	25,471
Aug-28	(h) Tottenham Hotspur	W 2-1	Scott, Sealey	36,348
Sep-02	(h) Nottingham Forest	W 3-2	Scott, Sealey, Musgrove	23,000
Sep-04	(a) Blackpool	L 0-2		19,838
Sep-09	(a) Aston Villa	W 4-2	Dick 2, Scott, Sealey	32,000
Sep-16	(h) Chelsea	W 2-1	Dick, Musgrove	27,000
Sep-18	(h) Blackpool	D 2-2	Musgrove, Boyce	26,000
Sep-23	(a) Sheffield United	W 4-1	Dick 2, Musgrove, Sealey	21,034
Sep-30	(h) Leicester City	W 4-1	Dick 2, Sealey, Woosman	26,746
Oct-07	(a) Ipswich Town	L 2-4	Sealey, Musgrove	28,051
Oct-14	(h) Burnley	W 2-1	Crawford, Dick	32,234
Oct-21	(a) Fulham	L 0-2		32,275
Oct-28	(h) Sheffield Wednesday	L 2-3	Bond, Dick	26,463
Nov-04	(a) Manchester City	W 5-3	Dick 2, Sealey 2, Musgrove	18,839
Nov-11	(h) West Bromwich Albion	D 3-3	Musgrove, Sealey, Bond	18,000
Nov-18	(a) Birmingham City	L 0-4		20,645
Nov-25	(h) Everton	W 3-1	Dick 2, Crawford	27,100
Dec-02	(a) Arsenal	D 2-2	Tindall 2	47,206
Dec-09	(h) Bolton Wanderers	W 1-0	Woosnam	19,472
Dec-16	(a) Manchester United	W 2-1	Dick 2	29,472
Dec-18	(h) Wolverhampton Wanderers	W 4-2	Moore 2, Hurst, Musgrove	21,261
Dec-26	(h) Blackburn Rovers	L 2-3	Tindall, Dick	22,250
Jan-13	(a) Nottingham Forest	L 0-3		20,359
Jan-20	(h) Aston Villa	W 2-0	Woosnam, Dick	20,000
Feb-03	(a) Chelsea	W 1-0	Moore	34,258
Feb-10	(h) Sheffield United	L 1-2	Woosnam	21,829
Feb-17	(a) Leicester City	D 2-2	Woosnam, Dick	21,312
Feb-24	(h) Ipswich Town	D 2-2	Dick, Kirkup	27,760
Mar-03	(a) Burnley	L 0-6		24,279
Mar-17	(a) Sheffield Wednesday	D 0-0		31,403
Mar-24	(h) Manchester City	L 0-4		25,808
Mar-28	(a) Blackburn Rovers	L 0-1		8,800
Mar-31	(a) West Bromwich Albion	W 1-0	Musgrove	18,000
Apr-06	(h) Birmingham City	D 2-2	Musgrove 2	22,548
Apr-14	(a) Everton	L 0-3		45,171
Apr-20	(h) Cardiff City	W 4-1	Sealey, Crawford, Byrne, OG	25,459
Apr-21	(h) Arsenal	D 3-3	Scott, Dick, Lansdowne	31,912
Apr-23	(a) Cardiff City	L 0-3		11,200
Apr-28	(a) Bolton Wanderers	L 0-1		17,333
Apr-30	(h) Fulham	W 4-2	Dick 2, Crawford 2	22,000

P	W	D	L	F	A	W	D	L	F	A	Pts	Pos
42	11	6	4	49	37	6	4	11	27	45	44	8th

F A Cup

Jan-06	(a) Plymouth Argyle	L 0-3		26,915

League Cup

Sep-11	(h) Plymouth Argyle	W 3-2	Crawford 2, Woosman	12,170
Oct-09	(h) Aston Villa	L 1-3	Musgrove	17,775

Football League Division One 1962-63

Date	Opps	Res	Scorers	Att
Aug-18	(a) Aston Villa	L 1-3	Byrne	37,000
Aug-20	**(h) Wolverhampton Wanderers**	**L 1-4**	**Musgrove**	**30,020**
Aug-25	**(h) Tottenham Hotspur**	**L 1-6**	**Woosnam**	**30,000**
Aug-29	(a) Wolverhampton Wanderers	D 0-0		32,000
Sep-01	(a) Leyton Orient	L 0-2		23,918
Sep-03	**(h) Liverpool**	**W 1-0**	**Scott**	**22,262**
Sep-08	(a) Manchester City	W 6-1	Musgrove 2, Scott, Byrne, Peters, Hurst	25,000
Sep-12	(a) Liverpool	L 1-2	Byrne	39,261
Sep-14	**(h) Blackpool**	**D 2-2**	**Musgrove, Scott**	**24,000**
Sep-22	(a) Blackburn Rovers	W 4-0	Hurst, Musgrove, Byrne, Peters	15,400
Sep-29	**(h) Sheffield United**	**D 1-1**	**Scott**	**22,707**
Oct-06	**(h) Birmingham City**	**W 5-0**	**Byrne 2, Hurst, Musgrove, Brown**	**21,039**
Oct-13	(a) Arsenal	D 1-1	Scott	49,000
Oct-22	**(h) Burnley**	**D 1-1**	**Hurst**	**34,612**
Oct-27	(a) Manchester United	L 1-3	Musgrove	29,204
Nov-03	**(h) Bolton**	**L 1-2**	**Moore**	**19,866**
Nov-10	(a) Leicester City	L 0-2		21,064
Nov-17	**(h) Fulham**	**D 2-2**	**Hurst, Peters**	**17,668**
Nov-24	(a) Sheffield Wednesday	W 3-1	Brabrook, Peters, Scott	23,764
Dec-01	**(h) West Bromwich Albion**	**D 2-2**	**Moore, Hurst**	**20,680**
Dec-08	(a) Everton	D 1-1	Brabrook	38,701
Dec-15	**(h) Aston Villa**	**D 1-1**	**Peters**	**21,532**
Dec-22	(a) Tottenham Hotspur	D 4-4	Peters, Kirkup, Boyce, Scott	44,106
Dec-29	(a) Nottingham Forest	W 4-3	Brabrook, Byrne, OG	18,587
Feb-16	(a) Sheffield United	W 2-0	Boyce, Sealey	18,176
Mar-02	**(h) Arsenal**	**L 0-4**		**31,967**
Mar-09	(a) Burnley	D 1-1	Byrne	17,287
Mar-18	**(h) Manchester United**	**W 3-1**	**Brown, Sealey, OG**	**28,950**
Mar-23	(a) Bolton Wanderers	L 0-3		19,071
Mar-30	**(h) Sheffield Wednesday**	**W 2-0**	**Hurst, Byrne**	**22,408**
Apr-06	(a) Fulham	L 0-2		26,861
Apr-12	**(h) Ipswich Town**	**L 1-3**	**Scott**	**23,170**
Apr-13	**(h) Leicester City**	**W 2-0**	**Sealey 2**	**25,689**
Apr-15	(a) Ipswich Town	W 3-2	Brabrook, Peters, Hurst	21,971
Apr-20	(a) West Bromwich Albion	L 0-1		11,600
Apr-22	**(h) Nottingham Forest**	**W 4-1**	**Hurst 2, Peters, Moore**	**18,179**
Apr-27	**(h) Everton**	**L 1-2**	**OG**	**28,461**
May-01	(a) Birmingham City	L 2-3	Scott, Hurst	14,392
May-04	**(h) Blackburn Rovers**	**L 0-1**		**18,898**
May-11	**(h) Leyton Orient**	**W 2-0**	**Brabrook, Scott**	**16,745**
May-13	(a) Blackpool	D 0-0		12,434
May-18	**(h) Manchester City**	**W 6-1**	**Hurst 2, Sealey, Boyce, Brabrook**	**16,600**

P	W	D	L	F	A	W	D	L	F	A	Pts	Pos
42	8	6	7	39	34	6	6	9	34	35	40	12th

FA Cup

Feb-04 3r	**(h) Fulham**	**D 0-0**		**21,000**
Feb-20 3rr	(a) Fulham	W 2-1	Boyce, Byrne	20,000
Mar-04 4r	**(h) Swansea Town**	**W 1-0**	**Boyce**	**25,924**
Mar-16 5r	**(h) Everton**	**W 1-0**	**Byrne**	**31,770**
Mar-30 6r	(a) Liverpool	L 0-1		49,036

League Cup

Sep-26 2r	**(h) Plymouth Argyle**	**W 6-0**	**Byrne 3, Peters, Hurst, Musgrove**	**9,714**
Oct-16 3r	(a) Rotherham United	L 1-3	Hurst	11,581

Football League Division One 1963-64

Date	Opps	Res	Scorers	Att
Aug-24	(a) Chelsea	D 0-0		46,298
Aug-26	(h) Blackpool	W 3-1	Peters, Boyce, Brabrook	25,533
Aug-30	(h) Ipswich Town	D 2-2	Byrne, Boyce	27,599
Sep-02	(a) Blackpool	W 1-0	Byrne	18,407
Sep-07	(h) Sheffield United	L 2-3	Byrne, Boyce	23,837
Sep-09	(h) Nottingham Forest	L 0-2		26,200
Sep-14	(a) Liverpool	W 2-1	Peters, Hurst	45,495
Sep-17	(a) Nottingham Forest	L 1-3	Byrne	25,369
Sep-21	(h) Aston Villa	L 0-1		20,346
Sep-28	(a) Tottenham Hotspur	L 0-3		50,886
Oct-05	(h) Wolverhampton Wanderers	D 1-1	Byrne	21,409
Oct-07	(h) Burnley	D 1-1	Sealey	21,372
Oct-12	(a) Sheffield Wednesday	L 0-3		23,503
Oct-19	(h) Everton	W 4-2	Brabrook 2, Boyce, Hurst	25,163
Oct-26	(a) Manchester United	W 1-0	Britt	42,120
Nov-02	(h) West Bromwich Albion	W 4-2	Hurst 2, Brabrook, OG	22,888
Nov-09	(a) Arsenal	D 3-3	Byrne 2, Peters	52,742
Nov-16	(h) Leicester City	D 2-2	Britt, Hurst	23,073
Nov-23	(a) Bolton Wanderers	D 1-1	Hurst	10,864
Nov-30	(h) Fulham	D 1-1	Moore	23,715
Dec-07	(a) Birmingham City	L 1-2	Britt	15,357
Dec-14	(h) Chelsea	D 2-2	Byrne 2	21,950
Dec-20	(a) Ipswich Town	L 2-3	Byrne, Brabrook	11,765
Dec-26	(h) Blackburn Rovers	L 2-8	Byrne 2	20,500
Dec-28	(a) Blackburn Rovers	W 3-1	Byrne 2, Hurst	28,990
Jan-11	(a) Sheffield United	L 1-2	Sissons	18,733
Jan-18	(h) Liverpool	W 1-0	Byrne	25,546
Feb-01	(a) Aston Villa	D 2-2	Hurst 2	16,850
Feb-08	(h) Tottenham Hotspur	W 4-0	Hurst, Sissons, Boyce, Byrne	36,934
Feb-17	(a) Wolverhampton Wanderers	W 2-0	Hurst, Byrne	14,000
Feb-22	(h) Sheffield Wednesday	W 4-3	Byrne 3, Hurst	24,578
Mar-03	(a) Burnley	L 1-3	Byrne	14,328
Mar-07	(h) Manchester United	L 0-2		27,177
Mar-18	(a) Leicester City	D 2-2	Hugo, Burkett	11,980
Mar-21	(h) Arsenal	D 1-1	Hurst	28,170
Mar-27	(h) Stoke City	W 4-1	Moore, Byrne, Boyce, Brabrook	29,484
Mar-28	(a) West Bromwich Albion	W 1-0	Hugo	16,000
Mar-31	(a) Stoke City	L 0-3		24,900
Apr-04	(h) Bolton Wanderers	L 2-3	Sealey, Byrne	19,398
Apr-11	(a) Fulham	L 0-2		22,020
Apr-17	(h) Birmingham City	W 5-0	Brabrook 2, Hurst, Sissons, Byrne	22,106
Apr-25	(a) Everton	L 0-2		33,090

P	W	D	L	F	A	W	D	L	F	A	Pts	Pos
42	8	7	6	45	38	6	5	10	24	36	40	14th

F A Cup

Jan-04 3r	(h) Charlton Athletic	W 3-0	Hurst, Brabrook, Sissons	34,155
Jan-25 4r	(a) Leyton Orient	D 1-1	Brabrook	34,345
Jan-29 4rr	(h) Leyton Orient	W 3-0	Hurst 2, Byrne	35,383
Feb-15 5r	(a) Swindon Town	W 3-1	Hurst 2, Byrne	28,582
Feb-29 6r	(h) Burnley	W 3-2	Byrne 2, Sissons	36,651
Mar-14 sf	(n*) Manchester United	W 3-1	Boyce 2, Hurst	65,000
May-02 f	(n**) Preston North End	W 3-2	Sissons, Hurst, Boyce	100,000
	*Hillsborough, **Wembley			

League Cup

Sep-25 2r	(h) Leyton Orient	w 2-1	Scott, Byrne	11,800
Oct-16 3r	(a) Aston Villa	W 2-0	Bond, Britt	11,194
Nov-19 4r	(a) Swindon Town	D 3-3	Hurst, Brabrook, Boyce	12,050
Nov-25 4rr	(h) Swindon Town	W 4-1	Hurst, Brabrook, Byrne, Scott	15,778
Dec-16 5r	(h) Workington Town	W 6-0	Byrne 3, Boyce, Hurst, Scott	10,160
Feb-05 sf	(a) Leicester City	L 3-4	Hurst 2, Sealey	14, 087
Mar-23 sf	(h) Leicester City	L 0-2		27,393

Football League Division One 1964-65

Date	Opps	Res	Scorers	Att
Aug-22	(a) Fulham	W 2-1	Byrne, Sissons	31,200
Aug-24	**(h) Manchester United**	**W 3-1**	**Byrne, Hurst, Sissons**	**37,070**
Aug-28	**(h) Nottingham Forest**	**L 2-3**	**Byrne, Sissons**	**26,760**
Sep-02	(a) Manchester United	L 1-3	OG	45,123
Sep-05	(a) Stoke City	L 1-3	Byrne	26,420
Sep-07	**(h) Wolverhampton Wanderers**	**W 5-0**	**Hurst 2, Byrne, Sissons, Moore**	**26,879**
Sep-12	**(h) Tottenham Hotspur**	**W 3-2**	**Byrne 3**	**36,730**
Sep-14	(a) Wolverhampton Wanderers	L 3-4	Brabrook, Byrne, OG	16,000
Sep-19	(a) Burnley	L 2-3	Byrne, Boyce	13,541
Sep-26	**(h) Sheffield United**	**W 3-1**	**Byrne 2, Sissons**	**22,526**
Oct-03	(a) Everton	D 1-1	Byrne	45,430
Oct-10	**(h) Aston Villa**	**W 3-0**	**Byrne, Boyce, Peters**	**20,600**
Oct-17	(a) Liverpool	D 2-2	Hurst 2	36,029
Oct-24	**(h) Sheffield Wednesday**	**L 1-2**	**Brabrook**	**22,800**
Oct-31	(a) Blackpool	W 2-1	Hurst, Brabrook	14,383
Nov-07	**(h) Blackburn Rovers**	**D 1-1**	**Sissons**	**22,725**
Nov-14	(a) Arsenal	W 3-0	Byrne, Peters, Hurst	36,026
Nov-21	**(h) Leeds United**	**W 3-1**	**Kirkup, Byrne, Peters**	**28,150**
Nov-28	(a) Chelsea	W 3-0	Sealey, Peters, Hurst	44,204
Dec-05	**(h) Leicester City**	**D 0-0**		**20,515**
Dec-12	**(h) Fulham**	**W 2-0**	**Byrne 2**	**21,985**
Dec-19	(a) Nottingham Forest	L 2-3	Byrne, Hurst	20,009
Dec-26	(a) Birmingham City	L 1-2	Hurst	23,324
Dec-28	**(h) Birmingham City**	**W 2-1**	**Byrne, Kirkup**	**23,800**
Jan-02	**(h) Stoke City**	**L 0-1**		**23,913**
Jan-16	(a) Tottenham Hotspur	L 2-3	Byrne, Sissons	50,000
Jan-23	**(h) Burnley**	**W 3-2**	**Boyce, Bond, Byrne**	**25,490**
Feb-06	(a) Sheffield United	L 1-2	Sealey	16,265
Feb-13	**(h) Everton**	**L 0-1**		**25,163**
Feb-20	(a) Sunderland	L 2-3	Byrne, Hurst	32,885
Feb-27	**(h) Liverpool**	**W 2-1**	**Presland, Hurst**	**25,750**
Mar-06	(a) Sheffield Wednesday	L 0-2		14,931
Mar-13	**(h) Sunderland**	**L 2-3**	**Dear 2**	**23,360**
Mar-20	(a) Blackburn Rovers	L 0-4		8,990
Mar-27	**(h) Arsenal**	**W 2-1**	**Hurst, Byrne**	**24,000**
Mar-31	(a) Aston Villa	W 3-2	Hurst, Byrne, Dear	19,900
Apr-03	(a) Leeds United	L 1-2	Dear	41,918
Apr-12	**(h) Chelsea**	**W 3-2**	**Hurst 2, Sissons**	**33,288**
Apr-16	**(h) West Bromwich Albion**	**W 6-1**	**Dear 5, Peters**	**27,706**
Apr-17	(a) Leicester City	L 0-1		15,880
Apr-19	(a) West Bromwich Albion	L 2-4	Hurst, Boyce	14,000
Apr-23	**(h) Blackpool**	**W 2-1**	**Brown, Dear**	**22,762**

P	W	D	L	F	A	W	D	L	F	A	Pts	Pos
42	14	2	5	48	25	5	2	14	34	46	42	9th

FA Cup

Date	Opps	Res	Scorers	Att
Jan-09 3r	**(h) Birmingham City**	**W 4-2**	**Hurst 2, Byrne, Sissons**	**31,056**
Jan-30 4r	**(h) Chelsea**	**L 0-1**		**37,000**

League Cup

Date	Opps	Res	Scorers	Att
Sep-30 2r	(a) Sunderland	L 1-4	Brabrook	22,382

Football League Division One 1965-66

Date	Opps	Res	Scorers		Att
Aug-21	(a) West Bromwich Albion	L 0-3			19,900
Aug-23	**(h) Sunderland**	**D 1-1**	**Peters**		**34,700**
Aug-28	**(h) Leeds United**	**W 2-1**	**Peters, Hurst**		**27,900**
Sep-01	(a) Sunderland	L 1-2	Hurst		48,626
Sep-04	(a) Sheffield United	L 3-5	Byrne, Hurst, Kirkup		15,796
Sep-06	**(h) Liverpool**	**L 1-5**	**Peters**		**32,144**
Sep-11	**(h) Leicester City**	**L 2-5**	**Hurst 2**		**21,400**
Sep-15	(a) Liverpool	D 1-1	Hurst		44,397
Sep-18	(a) Blackburn Rovers	W 2-1	Peters 2		10,178
Sep-25	**(h) Blackpool**	**D 1-1**	**Hurst**		**21,000**
Oct-02	(a) Fulham	L 0-3			22,310
Oct-09	(a) Nottingham Forest	L 0-3			19,262
Oct-16	**(h) Sheffield Wednesday**	**W 4-2**	**Britt 2, Sissons, Peters**		**20,690**
Oct-23	(a) Northampton Town	L 1-2	Brown		15,367
Oct-30	**(h) Stoke City**	**D 0-0**			**21,545**
Nov-06	(a) Burnley	L 1-3	Britt		16,802
Nov-13	**(h) Chelsea**	**W 2-1**	**Brabrook, Peters**		**31,540**
Nov-20	(a) Arsenal	L 2-3	Hurst, Peters		35,855
Nov-27	**(h) Everton**	**W 3-0**	**Sissons 2, Brabrook**		**21,920**
Dec-04	(a) Manchester United	D 0-0			32,924
Dec-11	**(h) Newcastle United**	**W 4-3**	**Hurst 3, Brabrook**		**23,758**
Dec-18	(a) Sheffield Wednesday	D 0-0			12,996
Jan-01	**(h) Nottingham Forest**	**L 0-3**			**25,131**
Jan-08	(a) Newcastle United	L 1-2	Byrne		31,600
Jan-11	(a) Everton	D 2-2	Hurst, Peters		29,915
Jan-15	**(h) Northampton Town**	**D 1-1**	**Hurst**		**21,000**
Jan-29	**(h) West Bromwich Albion**	**W 4-0**	**Hurst 2, Sissons, Peters**		**25,500**
Feb-05	(a) Leeds United	L 0-5			33,312
Feb-07	(a) Aston Villa	W 2-1	Hurst, Sissons		13,440
Feb-19	**(h) Sheffield United**	**W 4-0**	**Brabrook, Hurst, Peters, OG**		**21,220**
Mar-05	**(h) Aston Villa**	**W 4-2**	**Burkett, Byrne, Brabrook, Hurst**		**22,058**
Mar-12	**(h) Blackburn Rovers**	**W 4-1**	**Dear, Brabrook, Hurst, Burkett**		**18,566**
Mar-19	(a) Blackpool	L 1-2	Boyce		10,559
Mar-26	**(h) Fulham**	**L 1-3**	**Hurst**		**18,977**
Apr-02	**(h) Burnley**	**D 1-1**	**Brabrook**		**17,635**
Apr-08	(a) Tottenham Hotspur	W 4-1	Redknapp, Hurst, Byrne, Boyce		50,188
Apr-09	(a) Chelsea	L 2-6	Bennett, OG		35,958
Apr-16	**(h) Arsenal**	**W 2-1**	**Byrne, Brabrook**		**26,022**
Apr-25	**(h) Tottenham Hotspur**	**W 2-0**	**Byrne 2**		**32,231**
Apr-30	**(h) Manchester United**	**W 3-2**	**Hurst 2, Byrne**		**36,416**
May-07	(a) Stoke City	L 0-1			15,670
May-09	(a) Leicester City	L 1-2	Byrne		16,066

P	W	D	L	F	A	W	D	L	F	A	Pts	Pos
42	12	5	4	46	33	3	4	14	24	50	39	12th

F A Cup

Date	Opps	Res	Scorers	Att
Jan-22	(a) Oldham Athletic	D 2-2	Burnett, Hurst	25,035
Jan-24	**(h) Oldham Athletic**	**W 2-1**	**Hurst, Brabrook**	**35,330**
Feb-12	**(h) Blackburn Rovers**	**D 3-3**	**Bloomfield, Hurst, Sissons**	**32,350**
Feb-16	(a) Blackburn Rovers	L 1-4	Hurst	25,547

League Cup

Date	Opps	Res	Scorers	Att
Sep-21 2r	(a) Bristol Rovers	D 3-3	Hurst 2, Byrne	18,354
Sep-29 2rr	**(h) Bristol Rovers**	**W 3-2**	**Byrne 2, Hurst**	**13,160**
Oct-13 3r	**(h) Mansfield Town**	**W 4-0**	**Hurst 2, Brabrook, Burnett**	**11,590**
Nov-03 4r	(a) Rotherham United	W 2-1	Hurst, Moore	13,902
Nov-17 5r	(a) Grimsby Town	D 2-2	Hurst, Charles	16,281
Dec-15 5rr	**(h) Grimsby Town**	**W 1-0**	**Hurst**	**17,500**
Dec-20 sf	**(h) Cardiff City**	**W 5-2**	**Hurst, Bovington, Brabrook, Byrne, Sissons**	**19,980**
Feb-02 sf	(a) Cardiff City	W 5-1	Hurst 2, Peters 2, Burnett	14,315
Mar-09 f	**(h) West Bromwich Albion**	**W 2-1**	**Moore, Byrne**	**28,323**
Mar-23 f	(a) West Bromwich Albion	L 1-4	Peters	31,925

Football League Division One 1966-67

Date	Opps	Res	Scorers		Att
Aug-20	(h) Chelsea	L 1-2	Boyce		36,126
Aug-23	(a) Arsenal	L 1-2	Byrne		40,533
Aug-27	(a) Leicester City	L 4-5	Brabrook 2, Hurst 2		26,850
Aug-29	(h) Arsenal	D 2-2	Moore, Brabrook		34,964
Sep-03	(h) Liverpool	D 1-1	Hurst		33,000
Sep-07	(a) Manchester City	W 4-1	Hurst 2, Boyce, Sissons		31,989
Sep-10	(h) Stoke City	D 1-1	Hurst		33,292
Sep-17	(a) Sheffield Wednesday	W 2-0	Boyce, Byrne		29,171
Sep-24	(h) Southampton	D 2-2	Hurst, Peters		32,301
Oct-01	(a) Sunderland	W 4-2	Byrne 2, Hurst, Peters		29,277
Oct-08	(h) Everton	L 2-3	Peters, Hurst		32,784
Oct-15	(a) Fulham	L 2-4	Byrne, Hurst		34,826
Oct-26	(h) Nottingham Forest	W 3-1	Hurst 2, Bovington		23,000
Oct-29	(a) Sheffield United	L 1-3	Peters		20,579
Nov-05	(h) Fulham	W 6-1	Hurst 4, Peters 2		22,260
Nov-12	(a) Tottenham Hotspur	W 4-3	Byrne, Brabrook, Sissons, Hurst		29,227
Nov-19	(h) Newcastle United	W 3-0	Peters, Byrne, Hurst		31,285
Nov-26	(a) Leeds United	L 1-2	Hurst		37,382
Dec-03	(h) West Bromwich Albion	W 3-0	Redknapp, Dear, Peters		22,961
Dec-10	(a) Burnley	L 2-4	Hurst 2		19,509
Dec-17	(a) Chelsea	D 5-5	Sissons 2, Brabrook, Peters, Byrne		47,805
Dec-26	(a) Blackpool	W 4-1	Hurst, Dear, Byrne, Sissons		26,901
Dec-27	(h) Blackpool	W 4-0	Byrne, Hurst, Moore, Peters		29,300
Dec-31	(h) Leicester City	L 0-1			34,168
Jan-07	(a) Liverpool	L 0-2			48,518
Jan-14	(a) Stoke City	D 1-1	Hurst		27,274
Jan-21	(h) Sheffield Wednesday	W 3-0	Dear, Hurst, Sissons		29,220
Feb-04	(a) Southampton	L 2-6	Hurst, Burkett		30,123
Feb-11	(h) Sunderland	D 2-2	Byrne, Hurst		27,965
Feb-25	(a) Everton	L 0-4			42,504
Mar-18	(a) Nottingham Forest	L 0-1			31,426
Mar-24	(h) Aston Villa	W 2-1	Boyce, Peters		28,716
Mar-25	(h) Burnley	W 3-2	Peters 2, Sissons		24,428
Mar-28	(a) Aston Villa	W 2-0	Hurst 2		22,033
Apr-01	(a) Manchester United	L 0-3			61,380
Apr-04	(h) Sheffield United	L 0-2			22,006
Apr-22	(h) Leeds United	L 0-1			25,429
Apr-26	(a) Newcastle United	L 0-1			38,870
Apr-28	(a) West Bromwich Albion	L 1-3	Bennett		23,219
May-06	(h) Manchester United	L 1-6	Charles		38,424
May-09	(h) Tottenham Hotspur	L 0-2			35,750
May-13	(h) Manchester City	D 1-1	Peters		17,186

P	W	D	L	F	A	W	D	L	F	A	Pts	Pos
42	8	6	7	40	31	6	2	13	40	53	36	16th

FA Cup

Jan-28 3r	(h) Swindon Town	D 3-3	Hurst 3		37,400
Jan-31 3rr	(a) Swindon Town	L 1-3	Sissons		25,789

League Cup

Sep-14 2r	(h) Tottenham Hotspur	W 1-0	Hurst		34,000
Oct-05 3r	(a) Arsenal	W 3-1	Hurst 2, Peters		33,647
Nov-07 4r	(h) Leeds United	W 7-0	Sissons 3, Hurst 3, Peters		27,474
Dec-07 5r	(a) Blackpool	W 3-1	Hurst 2, Byrne		15,831
Jan-18 sf	(a) West Bromwich Albion	L 0-4			29,796
Feb-08 sf	(h) West Bromwich Albion	D 2-2	Byrne, Hurst		35,790

Football League Division One 1967-68

Date	Opps	Res	Scorers		Att
Aug-19	**(h) Sheffield Wednesday**	**L 2-3**	**Hurst, Peters**		**29,603**
Aug-21	**(h) Burnley**	**W 4-2**	**Hurst 2, Peters, Redknapp**		**30,420**
Aug-26	(a) Tottenham Hotspur	L 1-5	Sissons		55,831
Aug-29	(a) Burnley	D 3-3	Hurst, Moore, Peters		16,620
Sep-02	**(h) Manchester United**	**L 1-3**	**Peters**		**36,562**
Sep-05	(a) Everton	L 0-2			46,762
Sep-09	(a) Sunderland	W 5-1	Hurst 2, Redknapp. Moore, Peters		39,772
Sep-16	**(h) Wolverhampton Wanderers**	**L 1-2**	**Hurst**		**30,780**
Sep-23	(a) Liverpool	W 3-0	Hurst, Moore, Sissons		29,234
Sep-30	**(h) Leeds United**	**D 0-0**			**29,740**
Oct-07	**(h) Stoke City**	**L 3-4**	**Hurst 2, Peters**		**24,471**
Oct-14	(a) Liverpool	L 1-3	Peters		46,951
Oct-23	**(h) Southampton**	**L 0-1**			**32,550**
Oct-28	(a) Chelsea	W 3-1	Dear, Hurst, Peters		40,303
Nov-11	(a) Newcastle United	L 0-1			32,850
Nov-18	**(h) Manchester City**	**L 2-3**	**Hurst, Peters**		**25,425**
Nov-25	(a) Arsenal	D 0-0			42,029
Dec-02	**(h) Sheffield United**	**W 3-0**	**Sissons 2, Brabrook**		**22,510**
Dec-08	(a) Coventry City	D 1-1	Hurst		28,393
Dec-11	**(h) West Bromwich Albion**	**L 2-3**	**Brabrook, Hurst**		**18,340**
Dec-16	(a) Sheffield Wednesday	L 1-4	Dear		24,003
Dec-23	**(h) Tottenham Hotspur**	**W 2-1**	**Bonds, Dear**		**32,116**
Dec-26	**(h) Leicester City**	**W 4-2**	**Dear 3, Brooking**		**26,520**
Dec-30	(a) Leicester City	W 4-2	Dear 2, Brooking, Sissons		24,589
Jan-06	(a) Manchester United	L 1-3	Brooking		58,498
Jan-20	(a) Wolverhampton Wanderers	W 2-1	Dear, Hurst		32,273
Feb-03	**(h) Fulham**	**W 7-2**	**Brooking 2, Hurst 2, Dear, Moore, Peters**		**31,248**
Feb-10	(a) Leeds United	L 1-2	Dear		41,814
Feb-26	(a) Stoke City	L 0-2			16,092
Mar-16	(a) Southampton	D 0-0			27,734
Mar-23	**(h) Chelsea**	**L 0-1**			**36,301**
Mar-29	**(h) Arsenal**	**D 1-1**	**Brooking**		**33,942**
Apr-06	**(h) Newcastle United**	**W 5-0**	**Brooking 3, Sissons 2**		**27,780**
Apr-12	**(h) Nottingham Forest**	**W 3-0**	**Dear 2, Sissons**		**36,589**
Apr-13	(a) Manchester City	L 0-3			38,754
Apr-16	(a) Nottingham Forest	D 1-1	Peters		22,198
Apr-20	**(h) Liverpool**	**W 1-0**	**Peters**		**33,060**
Apr-24	**(h) Sunderland**	**D 1-1**	**Dear**		**29,153**
Apr-27	(a) Sheffield United	W 2-1	Hurst 2		19,530
May-01	(a) West Bromwich Albion	L 1-3	Peters		25,009
May-04	**(h) Coventry City**	**D 0-0**			**30,180**
May-11	**(h) Everton**	**D 1-1**	**Peters**		**28,880**

P	W	D	L	F	A	W	D	L	F	A	Pts	Pos
42	8	5	8	43	30	6	5	10	30	39	38	12th

FA Cup

Jan-27 3r	(a) Burnley	W 3-1	Peters 2, Dear		23,452
Feb-17 4r	(a) Stoke City	W 3-0	Sissons 2, Hurst		36,704
Mar-09 5r	**(h) Sheffield United**	**L 1-2**	**Dear**		**38,400**

League Cup

Sep-13 2r	(a) Walsall	W 5-1	Peters 2, Brabrook, Hurst, OG		17,752
Oct-11 3r	**(h) Bolton Wanderers**	**W 4-1**	**Hurst 4**		**20,510**
Nov-01 4r	(a) Huddersfield Town	L 0-2			17,729

Football League Division One 1968-69

Date	Opps	Res	Scorers	Att
Aug-10	(a) Newcastle United	D 1-1	Dear	36,830
Aug-14	(a) Stoke City	W 2-0	Peters, Sissons	22,131
Aug-17	**(h) Nottingham Forest**	**W 1-0**	**Hurst**	**31,114**
Aug-19	**(h) Everton**	**L 1-4**	**Peters**	**34,895**
Aug-24	(a) Coventry City	W 2-1	Peters, Brooking	33,716
Aug-26	**(h) Burnley**	**W 5-0**	**Hurst 2, Brooking, Peters**	**28,430**
Aug-31	**(h) West Bromwich Albion**	**W 4-0**	**Peters 3, Redknapp**	**29,908**
Sep-07	(a) Manchester United	D 1-1	Hurst	63,274
Sep-14	**(h) Tottenham Hotspur**	**D 2-2**	**Peters, Hurst**	**35,802**
Sep-21	(a) Chelsea	D 1-1	Peters	58,062
Sep-28	**(h) Sheffield Wednesday**	**D 1-1**	**Hurst**	**31,182**
Oct-05	**(h) Southampton**	**D 0-0**		**29,558**
Oct-08	(a) Burnley	L 1-3	Brooking	13,869
Oct-12	(a) Leeds United	L 0-2		40,786
Oct-19	**(h) Sunderland**	**W 8-0**	**Hurst 6, Moore, Brooking**	**24,718**
Oct-26	(a) Arsenal	D 0-0		59,533
Nov-02	**(h) Queen's Park Rangers**	**W 4-3**	**Moore, Peters, Hurst, Redknapp**	**36,008**
Nov-09	(a) Wolverhampton Wanderers	L 0-2		29,704
Nov-16	**(h) Leicester City**	**W 4-0**	**Dear 2, Peters, OG**	**26,328**
Nov-23	(a) Ipswich Town	D 2-2	Hurst 2	28,964
Nov-30	**(h) Manchester City**	**W 2-1**	**Hurst, Peters**	**33,082**
Dec-07	(a) Liverpool	L 0-2		48,632
Dec-14	**(h) Leeds United**	**D 1-1**	**Peters**	**24,718**
Dec-21	(a) Sunderland	L 1-2	Hurst	23,094
Dec-26	(a) Southampton	D 2-2	Hurst 2	27,465
Jan-11	(a) Queen's Park Rangers	D 1-1	Dear	28,645
Feb-01	(a) Leicester City	D 1-1	Dear	31,002
Feb-22	**(h) Liverpool**	**D 1-1**	**Sissons**	**36,498**
Mar-01	**(h) Newcastle United**	**W 3-1**	**Brooking, Peters, Hurst**	**26,336**
Mar-08	(a) Nottingham Forest	W 1-0	Hurst	24,303
Mar-14	**(h) Coventry City**	**W 5-2**	**Hurst 2, Sissons, Peters, Bond**	**29,053**
Mar-21	**(h) Ipswich Town**	**L 1-3**	**Hurst**	**32,574**
Mar-24	**(h) Wolverhampton Wanderers**	**W 3-1**	**Peters 2, Brooking**	**25,221**
Mar-29	**(h) Manchester United**	**D 0-0**		**41,546**
Apr-01	(a) Everton	L 0-1		37,212
Apr-05	(a) Sheffield Wednesday	D 1-1	Hurst	24,268
Apr-08	**(h) Stoke City**	**D 0-0**		**26,577**
Apr-12	**(h) Chelsea**	**D 0-0**		**32,332**
Apr-14	(a) West Bromwich Albion	L 1-3	Peters	20,092
Apr-19	(a) Tottenham Hotspur	L 0-1		50,970
Apr-21	**(h) Arsenal**	**L 1-2**	**Sissons**	**34,941**
Apr-30	(a) Manchester City	D 1-1	Peters	31,846

P	W	D	L	F	A	W	D	L	F	A	Pts	Pos
42	10	8	3	47	22	3	10	8	19	28	44	8th

FA Cup

Jan-04 3r	**(h) Bristol City**	**W 3-2**	**Peters 2, Hurst**	**32,526**
Jan-25 4r	(a) Huddersfield Town	W 2-0	Peters, Hurst	30,992
Feb-26 5r	(a) Mansfield Town	L 0-3		21,117

League Cup

Sep-04 2r	**(h) Bolton Wanderers**	**W 7-2**	**Hurst 3, Peters, Sissons, Brooking, Redknapp**	**24,937**
Sep-25 3r	**(h) Coventry City**	**D 0-0**		**27,594**
Oct-01 3rr	(a) Coventry City	L 2-3	Hurst, Peters	25,988

Football League Division One 1969-70

Date	Opps	Res	Scorers	Att
Aug-09	**(h) Newcastle United**	**W 1-0**	**Hurst**	**33,323**
Aug-11	**(h) Chelsea**	**W 2-0**	**Hurst, Peters**	**39,003**
Aug-16	(a) Stoke City	L 1-2	Lindsay	23,361
Aug-20	(a) Chelsea	D 0-0		43,347
Aug-23	**(h) West Bromwich Albion**	**L 1-3**	**Peters**	**32,867**
Aug-25	**(h) Arsenal**	**D 1-1**	**Cross**	**39,590**
Aug-30	(a) Nottingham Forest	L 0-1		29,097
Sep-06	**(h) Tottenham Hotspur**	**L 0-1**		**40,561**
Sep-13	(a) Everton	L 0-2		49,052
Sep-20	**(h) Sheffield Wednesday**	**W 3-0**	**Hurst, Redknapp, OG**	**23,487**
Sep-27	(a) Manchester United	L 2-5	Hurst 2	58,579
Oct-04	**(h) Burnley**	**W 3-1**	**Best 2, Brooking**	**26,445**
Oct-06	**(h) Stoke City**	**D 3-3**	**Best, Brooking, Sissons**	**26,860**
Oct-11	(a) Coventry City	D 2-2	Brooking, Sissons	34,277
Oct-18	(a) Wolverhampton Wanderers	L 0-1		28,762
Oct-25	**(h) Sunderland**	**D 1-1**	**Peters**	**29,171**
Nov-01	(a) Southampton	D 1-1	Brooking	26,894
Nov-08	**(h) Crystal Palace**	**W 2-1**	**Best, Hurst**	**31,515**
Nov-15	(a) Liverpool	L 0-2		39,668
Nov-22	**(h) Derby County**	**W 3-0**	**Hurst 2, Peters**	**32,485**
Nov-29	(a) Ipswich Town	L 0-1		17,456
Dec-06	**(h) Manchester City**	**L 0-4**		**27,491**
Dec-13	**(h) Everton**	**L 0-1**		**26,689**
Dec-17	(a) Leeds United	L 1-4	Hurst	30,659
Dec-20	(a) Tottenham Hotspur	W 2-0	Hurst, Peters	23,375
Dec-26	(a) West Bromwich Albion	L 1-3	Peters	32,867
Dec-27	**(h) Nottingham Forest**	**D 1-1**	**Bonds**	**31,829**
Jan-10	(a) Sheffield Wednesday	W 3-2	Peters 2, Hurst	28,135
Jan-17	**(h) Manchester United**	**D 0-0**		**41,643**
Jan-31	(a) Burnley	L 2-3	Eustace, Lindsay	14,454
Feb-11	**(h) Coventry City**	**L 1-2**	**Hurst**	**22,723**
Feb-21	(a) Sunderland	W 1-0	Hurst	16,900
Feb-28	**(h) Southampton**	**D 0-0**		**27,088**
Mar-02	(a) Newcastle United	L 1-4	Eustace	27,500
Mar-07	(a) Derby County	L 0-3		35,615
Mar-14	**(h) Ipswich Town**	**D 0-0**		**20,934**
Mar-21	(a) Manchester City	W 5-1	Hurst 2, Greaves 2, Boyce	28,353
Mar-24	(a) Crystal Palace	D 0-0		34,801
Mar-28	**(h) Liverpool**	**W 1-0**	**Holland**	**38,239**
Mar-31	**(h) Wolverhampton Wanderers**	**W 3-0**	**Greaves, Bond, Howe**	**26,386**
Apr-02	**(h) Leeds United**	**D 2-2**	**Best, Bonds**	**26,140**
Apr-04	(a) Arsenal	L 1-2	Greaves	36,218

P	W	D	L	F	A	W	D	L	F	A	Pts	Pos
42	8	8	5	28	21	4	4	13	23	39	36	17th

F A Cup

Jan-03 3r	(a) Middlesbrough	L 1-2	Stephenson	31,295

League Cup

Sep-03 2r	**(h) Halifax Town**	**W 4-2**	**Hurst 2, Best, Lampard**	**20,717**
Sep-23 3r	(a) Nottingham Forest	L 0-1		20,939

West Ham in Europe

European Cup Winners' Cup 1964-65

Date	Opps	Res	Scorers		Att
Round 1					
Sep-23	(a) La Gantoise (Belgium)	W 1-0	Boyce		18,000
Oct-07	**(h) La Gantoise**	**D 1-1**	**Byrne**		**24,000**
Round 2					
Nov-25	**(h) Sparta Prague (Czech)**	**W 2-0**	**Bond, Sealey**		**27,590**
Dec-09	(a) Sparta Prague	L 1-2	Sissons		45,000
Quarter-final					
Mar-16	(a) Lausanne (Switzerland)	W 2-1	Dear, Byrne		20,000
Mar-23	**(h) Lausanne**	**W 4-3**	**Dear 2, Peters, OG**		**31,780**
Semi-final					
Apr-07	**(h) Real Zaragoza (Spain)**	**W 2-1**	**Dear, Byrne**		**35,000**
Apr-28	(a) Real Zaragoza	D 1-1	Sissons		28,000
Final (at Wembley)					
May-19	(n) TSV Munich 1860 (Ger)	W 2-0	Sealey 2		100,000

European Cup Winners' Cup 1965-66

Date	Opps	Res	Scorers	Att
Round 2				
Nov-24	**(h) Olympiakos (Greece)**	**W 4-0**	**Hurst 2, Byrne, Brabrook**	**27,250**
Dec-01	(a) Olympiakos	D 2-2	Peters 2	40,000
Quarter-final				
Mar-02	**(h) FC Magdeburg (Ger)**	**W 1-0**	**Byrne**	**30,620**
Mar-16	(a) FC Magdeburg	D 1-1	Sissons	35,000
Semi-final				
Apr-05	**(h) Borussia Dortmund (Ger)**	**L 1-2**	**Peters**	**28,130**
Apr-13	(a) Borussia Dortmund	L 1-3	Byrne	35,000

Two-goal hero Alan Sealey, Ron Boyce, Martin Peters, Ken Brown and Jack Burkett after the ECWC final victory over TSV Munich 1860.

Terry Roper and Jack Burkett pictured at the West Ham reunion dinner held in London in May 2005.

About the author

Terry Roper was born in 1947 at Ilford in Essex. His family were fervent West Ham fans and he attended his first match at Upton Park when he was five-years-old. He has missed few games in the ensuing years.

As a schoolboy footballer, he represented Ilford and Essex and spent a season with West Ham as a junior player but, by his own admission, he was never good enough to make the professional grade. Upon leaving school, he worked in the City of London in the marine insurance industry where he remained throughout most of his working life before retiring in 2007.

In his spare time, Terry is a keen runner and has completed 20 marathons, with a personal best time of three hours and six minutes, plus numerous half -marathons.

He is a regular contributor to *EX* – the West Ham retro magazine. This is his second book about the club, since he co-wrote *West Ham In My Day – Volume Two*, together with Tony McDonald, in 2008.

Terry and his wife, Maria, have been married for 36 years and have two sons, Ian and Neil – both loyal Hammers – and a baby grandson, Reece.

Bibliography:
West Ham United Who's Who (1895-2005) – Tony Hogg (Profile Sports Media); At Home with the Hammers – Ted Fenton (Nicholas Kaye); Yours Sincerely – Ron Greenwood (Willow); West Ham United – The Making of a Football Club - Charles Korr (Duckworth); Colours of My Life – Malcolm Allison (Everest); PFA Premier & Football League Players' Records 1946-2005 – Barry Hugman (Queen Anne); West Ham United: The Managers – Tony McDonald (Football World); Fulham: The Complete Record – Dennis Turner (Breedon); West Ham United: A Complete Record – John Northcutt and Roy Shoesmith (Breedon); Wartime Britain 1939-1945 – Juliet Gardiner (Headline); West Ham United: The Elite Era: A Complete Record – John Helliar and Clive Leatherdale (Desert Island Books); Days of Iron – Brian Belton (Breedon); Just Like My Dreams – John Lyall (Viking); Bobby Moore: The Authorised Biography – Jeff Powell (Everest); Bobby Moore – Tina Moore (Collins Willow); Bobby Moore: My Soccer Story - Bobby Moore (Stanley Paul); The Ghost of '66 – Martin Peters (Orion); 1966 And All That – Geoff Hurst (Headline); The World Game – Geoff Hurst (Stanley Paul); The Life of Neil Armstrong – James Hansen (Pocket Books); The Essential History of the England Football Team – Andrew Mourant and Jack Rollin (Headline).

Other sources of reference: Southend Evening Echo; Ilford Recorder; EX Magazine; official website of St Patrick's Athletic FC; 1964 FA Cup final programme (Wembley Stadium Ltd); 1965 European Cup Winners' Cup final programme (Wembley Stadium Ltd); West Ham United match day programmes 1958-1968 (Helliar & Son Ltd).

Index

Rivers, Ann – see Burkett, Ann (wife)
Rivers, Mary (sister-in-law) 78
Rivers, Sarah (nee Molony) (mother in-law) 77, 80, 206
Robinson, Bill 25, 28, 37
Rogers, Don 184, 185
Rooney, Coleen 79
Roper, Ian 6, 268
Roper, Maria 6, 268
Roper, Neil 6, 268
Roper, Reece 268
Rosenior, Leroy 234, 236
Ross, George 127
Rowe, Arthur 22
Rowley, Arthur 212, 214, 215, 223, 225
Rush, Ian 234
Russell, Tom 28
Ryan, Meg 95

Santamaria 151
Santos, Nilton 40
Scott of the Antarctic 66
Scott, Tony 31, 35, 37, 41, 48, 50, 51, 53, 61, 68, 69, 75, 82, 86, 91
Sealey, Alan 51, 53, 64, 68, 72, 74, 75, 79, 80, 84, 86, 138-140, 151, 154-156, 158, 159, 161, 169, 171, 249-251, 254
Sealey, Anthony 250
Sealey, Barbara 250
Sealey, Janice 79, 80, 154
Sears, Freddie 244
Setters, Maurice 97
Sexton, Dave 27
Shankly, Bill 67, 162, 164, 174
Shilton, Peter 191
Shoesmith, Roy
Silvester, Peter 215
Simmons, Barry 186
Simone, Luigi 72
Sinatra, Frank 82
Singleton, Tony 121
Sissons, John 10, 62, 75, 83, 87, 88, 91-93, 99, 107, 108, 111, 112, 114, 119, 121, 129, 131, 135, 140, 148, 151, 155-157, 159, 161, 172, 178, 179, 185, 186, 194, 249-251, 254
Skeen, Ken 185
Smillie, Andy 31, 34, 37, 40, 41, 48
Smith, Bobby 89
Smith, Dave 223, 225
Smith, John 37
Spavin, Alan 107, 110
Standen, Elise 80, 109
Standen, Jim 10, 51, 63-66, 75, 80, 82, 86-89, 96, 98, 101, 107-113, 119, 121, 123, 125, 135, 137, 140, 148, 156, 157, 168, 178, 185, 187, 189, 214, 249-251, 253
Stanislas, Junior 244
Starkey, John 30
Stavin, Mary 167
Stein, Jock 174
Stephenson, Alan 193
Stepney, Alex 189
Stevens, Dennis 66
Stiles, Nobby 187
St John, Ian 67, 69
St Pier, Wally 24-26, 30, 31
Swan, Peter 45, 46

Tambling, Bobby 145
Taylor, Graham 226
Taylor, Tony 215
Tees, Matt 198
Terrell, Ernie 183
Terry, John 241
Tomkins, James 244
Tucker, Ken 243
Turner, Dennis
Turner, Jack 34

Vaughan, John 234
Venables, Terry 26, 43
Vowden, Geoff 217

Wagner, Manfred 156
Walker, Albert 30, 37, 154, 179, 181, 182
Walker, Albert Mrs 163
Walker, Anne 6
Walker, Clive 234
Wallace, William 'Braveheart' 54
Wark, John 234
Watson, Bill 34
Webb, David 23
Wharton, Terry 59, 60
Wiederkehr, Gustav 160
Wignall, Frank 197
Wilkinson, Jonny 158
Williams, Cleveland 183
Wilson, Davie 105, 108, 110, 127, 154
Wilson, Sir Harold 164
Windsor, Barbara 78
Wolstenholme, Kenneth 156
Woodfield, Dave 217
Woodley, Derek 24, 30, 31, 37, 39, 48, 50
Woosnam, Phil 49, 50, 61, 62
Worthington, Dave 215
Wragg, Doug 37
Wright, Billy 164
Wright, Charlie 199

Yeats, Ron 67, 136

Zsolt, Istvan 155, 160

Other Hammers books from *FootballWorld*

MARK WARD: *From Right-Wing to B-Wing*
. . . Premier League to Prison
By Mark Ward
Hardback, 256 pages
Published June 2009
RRP £18.00 Our price: £15.00

WEST HAM UNITED: THE MANAGERS
By Tony McDonald
Hardback, 400 pages
Published December 2007
RRP £20.00 Our price: £10.00

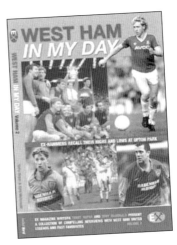

WEST HAM: IN MY DAY (Volume 1)
By Tony McDonald
Softback, 248 pages
Published August 2007
Our price: £12.00

WEST HAM: IN MY DAY (Volume 2)
By Terry Roper & Tony McDonald
Softback, 248 pages
Published November 2008
Our price: £12.00

To order, simply phone our Credit Card Hotline:
01708 744 333 or visit our website at **www.ex-hammers.com**